The *Campbell* Legacy

In 2004, a judgment from the highest court in the UK gave birth to a new era of privacy law. That case, brought by the supermodel Naomi Campbell against Mirror Group Newspapers, is today rightly regarded as a turning point for the protection of individuals' privacy. The case is seen as the turning point in the development of English privacy law, and has also had major implications for the law elsewhere, including in Australia, New Zealand, Ireland, and Canada. The manner in which the common law's privacy protections have developed since, and the direction in which they might develop still further, are the subject of this book. This collection, written by leading scholars in the privacy field from the UK and beyond, considers the legacy of Campbell's case. The contributors address the *Campbell* legacy from a range of legal perspectives and discuss broader themes of power, metaphor, consistency, and technological change.

This book was originally published as a special issue of the *Journal of Media Law.*

Thomas D. C. Bennett is a Lecturer in Law at Newcastle University, UK. He has written on the development of privacy torts in the UK and across the common law world.

Daithí Mac Síthigh is Professor of Law and Innovation at Queen's University Belfast, UK. His research interests are in law and technology.

The *Campbell* Legacy

Reflections on the Tort of Misuse of Private Information

Edited by
Thomas D. C. Bennett and Daithí Mac Síthigh

Routledge
Taylor & Francis Group
LONDON AND NEW YORK

First published 2018 by Routledge

2 Park Square, Milton Park, Abingdon, Oxfordshire OX14 4RN
52 Vanderbilt Avenue, New York, NY 10017

Routledge is an imprint of the Taylor & Francis Group, an informa business

First issued in paperback 2019

British Library Cataloguing in Publication Data
A catalogue record for this book is available from the British Library

ISBN 13: 978-1-138-05796-8 (hbk)
ISBN 13: 978-0-367-89037-7 (pbk)

Typeset in Times New Roman
by RefineCatch Limited, Bungay, Suffolk

Publisher's Note
The publisher accepts responsibility for any inconsistencies that may have arisen during the conversion of this book from journal articles to book chapters, namely the possible inclusion of journal terminology.

Contents

Citation Information

The chapters in this book were originally published in the *Journal of Media Law*, volume 7, issue 2 (2015). When citing this material, please use the original page numbering for each article, as follows:

Chapter 1
Liability for listening: why phone hacking is an actionable breach of privacy
N.A. Moreham
Journal of Media Law, volume 7, issue 2 (2015), pp. 155–169

Chapter 2
A landmark at a turning point: Campbell *and the use of privacy law to constrain media power*
Jacob Rowbottom
Journal of Media Law, volume 7, issue 2 (2015), pp. 170–195

Chapter 3
A just balance or just imbalance? The role of metaphor in misuse of private information
Rebecca Moosavian
Journal of Media Law, volume 7, issue 2 (2015), pp. 196–224

Chapter 4
Protecting private information of public interest: Campbell*'s great promise, unfulfilled*
Paul Wragg
Journal of Media Law, volume 7, issue 2 (2015), pp. 225–250

Chapter 5
Privacy, third parties and judicial method: Wainwright*'s legacy of uncertainty*
Thomas D. C. Bennett
Journal of Media Law, volume 7, issue 2 (2015), pp. 251–277

Chapter 6

The harms of privacy
Eric Descheemaeker
Journal of Media Law, volume 7, issue 2 (2015), pp. 278–306

Notes on Contributors

Thomas D. C. Bennett is a Lecturer in Law at Newcastle University, UK.

Eric Descheemaeker is Professor of Law at the University of Melbourne, Australia.

Daithí Mac Síthigh is Professor of Law and Innovation at Queen's University Belfast, UK.

Rebecca Moosavian is a Senior Lecturer at Northumbria University School of Law, UK.

N.A. Moreham is an Associate Professor of Law, Victoria University of Wellington, Australia.

Matthew Nicklin QC is joint Head of Chambers at 5RB, Gray's Inn, London, UK.

Jacob Rowbottom is a Fellow of University College, Oxford and Associate Professor at the Faculty of Law, University of Oxford, UK.

Paul Wragg is an Associate Professor of Law at the University of Leeds, UK.

Foreword

When I graduated in 1992, there was no such thing as "media law". The only real hint at its existence was the subject of defamation in the university tort curriculum, but – as in most textbooks – this was relegated to the final chapter or an awkward footnote (and, even then, with an unspoken assumption that it would not be assessed in the exam). In those days, defamation seemed to comprise the entirety of media law. That is not wholly accurate – breach of copyright, passing off, breach of confidence, malicious falsehood all loomed then – but being sued for defamation was the threat that publishers feared the most. Back in 1992 I don't think a single law school offered a media law course. Today, no self-respecting faculty is without one.

It is tempting to attribute the explosion of media law, and – in particular – the rise to prominence of a burgeoning privacy jurisprudence, to the incorporation of the European Convention of Human Rights into English law with the enacting of the Human Rights Act 1998. Certainly, this was a very significant event. But, as Sir Michael Tugendhat has explored in his new book, *Liberty Intact*, the notion of respect for privacy was already embedded in the common law, albeit not articulated in a unified concept.[1] As a result, its emergence in its present form is the fruit of a somewhat laboured and often murky process – aspects of which are explored in each of the essays in this collection.

Perhaps unhelpfully for the later development of a functioning law of privacy, the House of Lords in *Wainwright v Home Office* (a case that had begun in the lower courts in 1997) baldly declared that the English common law did not recognise a tort of invasion of privacy.[2] This followed an earlier example of judicial hand-wringing over the same issue in *Kaye v Robertson*.[3] One can wonder about the correctness of those decisions, particularly given that the European Court of Human Rights later found that the failure to afford a domestic remedy to the claimants in *Wainwright* for the unlawful strip search to which they were subjected amounted to a violation of Article 8 of the Convention.[4]

---

[1] Michael Tugendhat, *Liberty Intact: Human Rights in English Law* (OUP 2017) ch 10
[2] [2003] UKHL 53, [2004] 2 AC 406
[3] (1991) FSR 62
[4] *Wainwright v UK* (2007) 44 EHRR 40

This supposed judicial impotence was, however, overtaken by the arrival of the Human Rights Act 1998. The refusal by successive governments, prior to the passing of the Act, to introduce specific legislation for a statutory privacy law left English law ill-equipped to deal with the privacy claims that quickly resulted. The coming into force of the Act in 2000 entailed the wholesale incorporation of Article 8 into domestic law (without further ado) and rendering the common law compatible with the articles of the European Convention on Human Rights required some fast work by the courts. The courts undertook this task by attempting to modify the equitable action for breach of confidence to fashion a remedy for some breaches of privacy.

In *Campbell v MGN*, Lord Nicholls coined the term "misuse of private information" to describe what he labelled a new tort.[5] One fears that he had to choose this nomenclature rather than the more straightforward "breach of privacy" in deference to the *Wainwright* decision (to which Lord Nicholls had not been party). But the attempt to accommodate privacy interests in the conventional breach of confidence doctrine was never destined to have a happy ending. Lord Phillips MR confessed in *Douglas v Hello!* that a degree of shoe-horning was required to squeeze privacy claims into the confidence doctrine.[6] Fundamentally, as Lord Nicholls had noted, confidentiality and privacy are different interests.

The shoe-horning project – which threatened not only to radically alter the conventional cause of action of breach of confidence but also to hamper the development of the new privacy tort – was quickly abandoned. By 2007 Lord Nicholls in *Douglas v Hello!* felt able to say, just three years after *Campbell*, that the two causes of action had seemingly become distinct from one another.[7]

In the ten years since, the courts have refined and developed the new privacy law with remarkable speed, and some aspects of it have been given welcome clarification. For instance, its emergence from the doctrine of confidence gave rise to the question as to how the doctrine ought to be classified; was it tortious or equitable (or something else entirely)? In *Douglas*, the Court of Appeal expressed the view (reluctantly and *obiter*) that, given its parentage, "misuse of private information" was not a tort but was equitable.[8] However, a retreat from this received orthodoxy, which began in *Vestergaard Frandsen A/S v Bestnet Europe Ltd*,[9] was completed in *Vidal-Hall v Google Inc*.[10] In that case, Tugendhat J determined that breach of privacy was a tort (in the context of whether a claim could be served out of the jurisdiction). His decision was upheld by the Court of Appeal, which affirmed that breach of confidence and misuse of private information were

---

[5] [2004] UKHL 22, [2004] 2 AC 457, [14]
[6] [2005] EWCA Civ 595, [2006] QB 125, [53]
[7] [2007] UKHL 21, [2008] 1 AC 1, [255] (Lord Nicholls)
[8] [2006] QB 125, [96], relying upon *Kitetechnology BV v Unicor GmbH Plastmaschinen* [1995] FSR 765, 777-8.
[9] [2009] EWHC 1456 (Ch), [2010] FSR 2, [19]
[10] [2014] EWHC 13 (QB), [2014] EMLR 14, [70]

separate causes of action.[11] The *Campbell* cause of action now stood on its own two feet. In less than 15 years, then, something quite remarkable has occurred: an entirely new tort has come into being.

Despite this, much else about the doctrine of misuse of private information is yet to be resolved, and the essays published in this collection highlight remaining areas of uncertainty. The development of the common law by judges on an "incremental" basis has certain inherent weaknesses. Courts can only resolve the issues that arise in an individual case. Courts are not laboratories in which different theories can be tested; they exist to resolve disputes between parties. In an adversarial court system such as ours, that has a further weakness. Parties may make concessions or not argue points (for entirely understandable reasons) that might have been helpful to test developing principles.

Another significant challenge is the vastness of the landscape that privacy rights occupy. Breach of privacy by publication is only one part of this. And even in that part, cases like *Douglas* are actually very poor examples. Certainly, no scientist would have chosen *Douglas* as an early subject for a laboratory test of the new law. It is an example at one end of the spectrum of privacy rights that borders intellectual property rights. Some people (mostly celebrities) can, if they choose, commoditise and exploit their personal privacy. The Douglases did just this. But most people either cannot do so or would not want to. At the other end of the spectrum there is the more familiar intrusion into privacy that is totally unwanted.[12] The value of the privacy right cannot, in these more obviously intrusive cases, be measured in money.

A further problem is that the development of privacy law is particularly vulnerable to a "remedy-based" approach. Put very simply, cases involving breach of privacy by publication of private information are resolved by the – now familiar – "ultimate balancing test" that seeks to balance the privacy and free speech rights of the parties.[13] This balancing act is frequently undertaken by the court in a hurry, often on the eve of the threatened publication (when the claimant seeks interim injunctive relief). Any investigation into the facts is, at this stage, necessarily limited and risks being superficial. A legitimate complaint made in Thomas Bennett's essay is that assumptions are made as to an evidential position that are never in the end tested. On this imperfect foundation, very significant decisions as to the shape of the tort have been – and continue to be – made.

At the injunction stage, the issues are not only tricky to evidence appropriately but also stark in terms of their consequences. If the court does not grant an injunction restraining publication, the claimant's action will effectively be over. In the overwhelming majority of cases, damages are simply not an adequate remedy for the breach of privacy and the claimant will simply give up. (The notable exception being Max Mosley's action against News Group Newspapers Ltd.[14])

---

[11] [2015] EWCA Civ 311, [2016] QB 1003
[12] Eg *Mosley v News Group Newspapers Ltd* [2008] EWHC 1777 (QB), [2008] EMLR 20
[13] *Re S (A Child)* [2004] UKHL 47, [2005] 1 AC 593, [17]
[14] [2008] EWHC 1777 (QB), [2008] EMLR 20

Publishers complain that the reverse is also true. For if an injunction is granted, the ability to defend most privacy claims ends there. For example, even the most high-profile and hard-fought privacy case in recent years, *PJS v News Group Newspapers Ltd*, has been settled. There will now be no trial. The significant legal principles that emerge from the Supreme Court's judgment in it come from a case that has been all the way to the top of our legal system solely on the basis of an interim injunction; none of the findings of fact that would be made in a trial have had the opportunity to see the light of day.

That is not to say that some important principles have not been established in *PJS*; there is still value in the judgment. The Supreme Court endorsed the approach the lower courts had adopted in a number of cases that loss of the confidential nature of the information (eg by publication on the internet) is not necessarily deleterious to the privacy claim.[15] Relevant to Bennett's paper is the Supreme Court's emphatic endorsement of "third party interests" in the assessment of the nature and weight of the Article 8 rights in the balance, but the criticisms of this approach that he has identified remain valid.[16]

Something that is missing from the recent privacy case law is any real exploration or explanation of how the balance between the two rights (to privacy and freedom of expression) is actually to be carried out. This is something that Paul Wragg dwells on in his essay. For the question remains: how is the value of each competing right in a case to be assessed? The relatively straightforward job of setting out the nature of the task was done by the House of Lords in *Re S*; no presumptive priority was to be given to either right and an "intense focus" must be placed on the respective rights in play.[17] However, since then, the law has developed little by way of further guidance as to how this "intense focus" is actually to be carried out and what, precisely, is to be measured; only some broad principles have emerged. Information about health and sexual activities, for example, are likely (rightly) to be regarded as giving rise to weighty Article 8 (privacy) considerations. On the other side, there is a notional hierarchy of the value of speech ranging from political speech at the top, to purely commercial speech at the bottom.[18] Exposing hypocrisy or preventing the public from being misled are often regarded as weighty factors on the Article 10 (free speech) side. Conventional kiss 'n' tell stories frequently add into the mix issues involving the privacy and/or free speech rights of the person wanting to reveal the information, complicating the balancing task further.

Despite being a major, high-profile piece of litigation, little attention was actually paid to the balancing act in *PJS*. The focus of the judgment was, instead, on whether there was anything left to protect by injunction given the publication of

[15] [2016] UKSC 26, [2016] AC 1081
[16] Ibid, [72]-[73]
[17] [2004] UKHL 47, [2005] 1 AC 593, [17]
[18] [2016] UKSC 26, [2016] AC 1081, [24]

the claimant's private information that had already taken place in the UK, abroad and on the internet. That omission is no fault of the Supreme Court. It is a result of the adversarial process. For by the time the case reached the Supreme Court, the newspaper was not arguing any countervailing public interest or Article 10 right to resist the injunction. Insofar as a view was expressed, the majority of the Supreme Court observed (*obiter*):

> [I]t may be that the mere reporting of sexual encounters of someone like the claimant, however well known to the public, with a view to criticising them does not even fall within the concept of freedom of expression under article 10. But, accepting that article 10 is not only engaged but capable in principle of protecting any form of expression, these cases clearly demonstrate that this type of expression is at the bottom end of the spectrum.[19]

Setting to nought the value in Article 10 terms of revelations of sexual (mis)conduct of a public figure is a striking proposition (even if advanced tentatively). Given that there are countless decisions both of the European Court of Human Rights and of the Supreme Court itself holding there to be an intrinsic value of freedom of expression in a democratic society (embracing not only the right to publish but also the right to *receive* information), this sort of judicial ruminating carries dangers. Principally, it risks exposing courts to the charge that they are simply making a subjective value judgment as to whether the information should be published, turning the court from judicial assessor into editor. Barring instances like falsely shouting "fire" in a theatre, all speech has value. The difficulty is assessing its value when balancing it against competing rights. Not appearing to slip into the role of editor or censor is made harder by the absence of properly calibrated tools for carrying out the balance. The problem is all the more acute if the interim injunction stage effectively determines the outcome of the whole case.

I pay tribute to the scholarship that has gone into these papers. It has been a pleasure to read them and an honour to have been asked to write this foreword.

Matthew Nicklin QC
5RB
Gray's Inn
London

[19] Ibid

Introduction: The *Campbell* Legacy

Thomas D. C. Bennett and Daithí Mac Síthigh

The case of *Campbell v Mirror Group Newspapers Ltd* was decided by the House of Lords in 2004. Largely as a result of that case's introduction of novel nomenclature into the English legal lexicon – in the form of the recognition of a cause of action for 'misuse of private information' – the case quickly came to be seen as seminal for privacy rights. In the thirteen years that have now passed since the House handed down its judgments, the English law of privacy has developed considerably. This rapid period of development has thrown up a number of matters of acute controversy and it is to the study of this controversial legacy of the *Campbell* case, within and beyond England and Wales, that this collection of essays is devoted.

Prior to the *Campbell* case, privacy rights attracted only sporadic protection under the English common law. The equitable doctrine of confidence, once primarily used to protect trade secrets, had been mobilised by enterprising lawyers in the latter years of the twentieth century to protect individuals against the dissemination of their private information.[1] But as Lord Nicholls noted in *Campbell*, this state of affairs was 'not altogether comfortable'.[2] In preference to continuing down the confidence path, he preferred to speak of the law as guarding against the 'misuse of private information' ('MPI').

The emergence of MPI from the doctrine of confidence has neither been an easy nor a particularly clear-cut one. For whilst Lord Nicholls labelled it a 'tort' in *Campbell*, it was far from clear whether the other judges on the panel regarded the action as lying within the domain of equity or that of tort. In the years that immediately followed *Campbell*, this confusion persisted; counsel regularly pleaded claims in both MPI *and* breach of confidence to be doubly sure of grounding them in the appropriate legal mechanism. Courts, likewise, used the terms interchangeably for a considerable period. It was only when the High Court was forced, in *Vidal-Hall v Google Inc*, to rule on the categorisation of the MPI cause of action (for procedural reasons relating to out-of-jurisdiction service) that the judiciary finally rendered an answer. MPI is to be regarded as a tort; breach of confidence remains a parallel action in equity.

[1] Megan Richardson, Michael Bryan, Martin Vranken and Katy Barnett, *Breach of Confidence: Social Origins and Modern Developments* (Edward Elgar Publishing Ltd 2012).
[2] [2004] UKHL 22, [2004] 2 AC 457, [14]

The fact that the lack of clarity afflicting the infancy of MPI goes so far as to call into question the very *nature* of that doctrine serves to emphasise just how controversial this area of English law has proven to be. This collection of essays highlights several discrete areas of controversy and explores the legacy that the *Campbell* case has left through detailed analysis and discussion of those controversies. There are several themes that pervade the essays in this book. Concerns about doctrinal coherence, for example, bulk large in the contributions made by Bennett and Descheemaeker, whilst the lack of clarity in judicial statements on the task of 'balancing' privacy interests against free speech are raised by both Moosavian and Wragg. Moreham and Rowbottom dwell on the rapidity of the doctrinal development in this field and the extent to which intrusive acts beyond the mere publication of private information now fall under the ambit of this tort. And, in their own ways, each author is concerned with the extent to which *Campbell*'s legacy has been to promote justice. Moreham finds the development of MPI into the realms of intrusion to be normatively appealing, whilst Rowbottom wonders whether the tort is likely to remain a useful mechanism for securing justice in the years to come. Moosavian and Wragg locate justice in the ability of courts' decisions to provide certainty for prospective litigants, whilst Bennett cautions that judges' claims to be able to promote justice by limiting the scope of judicial activism appear rather empty in the light of some unexpected doctrinal developments. At the heart of Descheemaeker's essay is the notion that justice requires some coherence of principle underpinning the tort – something he finds sorely lacking in MPI.

Nicole Moreham's essay focuses on her long-standing concern with the lack of protection in English law for intrusion-type privacy violations – an area which brings together concerns around privacy, technology, and the nature of intrusion, and has been the subject of significant developments in other jurisdictions. English law, whilst it has found ways to protect individuals from the publication of private facts (through both equitable confidence and MPI), has traditionally been 'unable, perhaps unwilling' to guard against physical or sensory intrusions into an individual's personal space or affairs.[3] Moreham scrutinises the recent judgment of the High Court in *Gulati v Mirror Group Newspapers Ltd*, which concerned a number of high-profile claims against a newspaper group for 'phone hacking'.[4] The practice of phone and voicemail hacking is found, in the judgment of Mann J, to constitute a misuse of private information. For Moreham, this has considerable significance because it indicates a willingness on the part of the Court to move MPI law beyond its traditionally narrow focus on remedying unauthorised publications of private information. By awarding damages for the activities of hacking and listening to voicemails, even where none of the information gleaned was published, the Court has moved towards recognising intrusive

[3] *Wainwright v Home Office* [2003] UKHL 53, [2004] 2 AC 406, [18]
[4] [2015] EWHC 1482 (Ch), [2016] FSR 12

conduct itself as tortious. Seen in this way, Moreham argues that the intrusion lacuna in English law may be closer to being resolved than at any point previously.

Jacob Rowbottom, in his essay, explores the shaping influence that concerns about abuses of power by mass media entities has had on the *Campbell* doctrine. By placing *Campbell* in its historical context (and, in particular, in the context of parliamentary and governmental discussions about legislative responses to invasions of privacy perpetrated by the media), he locates evidence that the MPI tort was developed by courts with a focus on responding to media abuses bulking large in their minds. This, he argues, helps to explain why the courts have accorded expansive, generous interpretations to the concept of private information. It also provides an explanation for the courts' recent flirtation with attaching liability to intrusive acts such as wrongfully *acquiring* (as distinguished from *disseminating*) information. This structural focus on media power, Rowbottom cautions, may reduce MPI's effectiveness as a means of response to the invasions of privacy that may today be perpetrated by private citizens with the aid of rapidly developing technology. This leads him to question whether tort liability is likely to remain a suitable vehicle for counteracting privacy violations in future.

The decision in *Campbell* is replete with provocative and complex terms such as 'balance'. Rebecca Moosavian's essay engages with what she sees as the poorly-understood significance of metaphors within legal discourses. Moosavian employs deconstructionist analytical techniques to the MPI doctrine in a bid to uncover the deeper metaphorical significances in play. She traces the use of the 'balance' metaphor in *Campbell* and subsequent cases (with particular regard to Articles 8 and 10 of the European Convention on Human Rights), arguing that the frequent judicial use of this metaphor serves to promote the wider acceptance of decisions. The 'balance' metaphor is able to achieve this, on her analysis, by alluding to ideals of justice and giving the appearance that certain and calculable measures of each of the conflicting interests in play (principally privacy and free speech) are amenable to relatively straightforward assessment.

Like Moosavian, Paul Wragg's primary concern is with the courts' treatment of the 'balancing' stage of MPI methodology. On his analysis, a close reading of post-*Campbell* privacy cases reveals that, for all the judicial talk of 'balancing' privacy and free speech interests, something very different is going on in reality. For Wragg demonstrates that courts are routinely finding no public interest whatsoever in the information complained-of in successful MPI claims. Conversely, *any* amount of public interest in the information complained-of seems always to trump a claimant's privacy. This leads him to argue that the courts, rather than 'balancing' these competing interests, are in fact adopting a binary approach that he identifies as 'zoning'. Having flagged up this problem, Wragg proposes a reformulation of the *Campbell* tort to involve a four-part test, in a bid to enable courts to render more principled decisions in this field.

Thomas Bennett focuses on the difficulties that the courts have faced in dealing with privacy claims in circumstances where the publication of private information relating to one person will have an adverse impact on third parties (typically the claimant's relatives). Whilst the courts have shown an admirable desire to protect vulnerable third parties (often children) from the adverse effects of unfavourable publicity about a parent in these cases, an inability to locate a clear or coherent doctrinal basis for developing the law in this direction raises significant rule of law concerns. Bennett attributes the lack of clarity in these cases to the House of Lords' pre-*Campbell* decision in *Wainwright v Home Office*.[5] For *Wainwright*, he argues, in which the House rejected the opportunity to recognise a broad and general tort of invasion of privacy, is the authority that has forced the judicial development of privacy law to be shoe-horned – often uncomfortably – within the confines of an informational tort developed (rather murkily) out of the equitable doctrine of confidence. Thus whilst *Wainwright*'s rejection of a broad privacy tort was predicated on the House's keenness to curtail judicial activism and maintain legal certainty going forward, its legacy has been to set the scene for considerable doctrinal uncertainty and incoherence. For Bennett, then, *Campbell*'s legacy is rather overshadowed by that of the restrictive *Wainwright* ruling.

Eric Descheemaeker's essay, like several of the others, pursues themes relating to tort design and coherence. The occasioning of some harm to the claimant is a feature that lies at the heart of all English torts. Yet he finds it unclear from recent case law how the harm that underpins MPI is conceptualised by the courts. Descheemaeker outlines two models by which harm may be said to underpin torts. Under the 'bi-polar' model, which is the model that most torts adopt, harm is said to be consequent upon some tortious act; that harm must be proved (except in the case of torts actionable *per se*) if the claim is to succeed. By contrast, under the 'uni-polar' model, harm inheres within the wrongful act itself. Thus Descheemaeker argues it is unclear whether English courts perceive MPI as following a bi-polar or uni-polar model. This is a state of affairs he finds unsatisfactory, for the courts seem not to have appreciated the importance in coming to a clear conclusion on this issue. A uni-polar model that finds harm inherent in the privacy-breaching act – such as is suggested by the High Court in the *Gulati* phone hacking case – would have profound implications; not only would it impact upon the sorts of claimants able to bring suit for MPI, it also raises substantial questions over the extent to which MPI coheres with the prevailing bi-polar model in other tort doctrines.

The collection, then, provides a wide-ranging resource for those interested in the development of post-*Campbell* privacy law. The critiques made here have uniformly been made with a view to pinning down precise and detailed accounts of difficulties that have arisen – in just the way they might be expected to – in the years of this doctrine's infancy.

[5] n3, above

The essays in this collection were first presented as papers at *The Campbell Legacy*, a workshop held at Newcastle University on 17 April 2015, and were subsequently published in a special issue of the Journal of Media Law. Each of the writers has, at various points, expressed gratitude to the participants in that workshop, and the editors echo those thanks here. The workshop was made possible by sponsorship from Schillings LLP and the Journal of Media Law, and through funding provided by the Newcastle University Conference Support Scheme.

Liability for listening: why phone hacking is an actionable breach of privacy

N.A. Moreham

This article considers what the award of substantial damages for phone hacking in *Gulati v MGN Ltd* says about the nature of the English privacy action and where it might be heading. By accepting that the defendants were liable simply for listening to the claimants' messages, the judge in that case moved the privacy tort beyond its traditional focus on the disclosure of private information. The article considers possible juridical bases for that extension arguing that, while breach of confidence principles can justify the move, the case also reflects a growing judicial willingness to protect physical privacy interests i.e. freedom from being watched, listened to, or physically encroached upon against one's wishes.

Introduction

The fallout from the phone hacking scandal which has engulfed two of the United Kingdom's major newspaper companies is well known to anyone with an interest in media law. Condemnation for the hacking – specifically, unauthorised listening in on people's mobile telephone messages – has been universal. Journalists have been convicted and imprisoned, an inquiry into the culture, practice and ethics of the press has been completed, and compensation claims launched. But in spite of this attention, until the recent case of *Gulati v MGN Ltd*,[1] the matter has been largely kept out of the civil courts. Both News Group International and MGN Ltd swiftly admitted liability and dozens of claims have been settled out of court. As a result, many of the legal issues arising from the hacking – including the juridical basis for liability for listening to private conversations – have not been tested.[2]

[1] [2015] EWHC 1482 (Ch).

[2] See further NA Moreham, 'Beyond Information: Physical Privacy in English Law' (2014) 73 *Cambridge Law Journal* 350, 367. Andrew Scott also makes this argument in Parkes et al, *Gatley on Libel and Slander* (Sweet & Maxwell, rev 12th edn 2015) para 22.1 and in G Millar and A Scott, *Newsgathering: Law, Regulation and the Public Interest* (Oxford University Press, forthcoming 2016) ch 8.

The recent damages decision in *Gulati* therefore sheds important light on the legal implications of the phone hacking saga. This article will explore one aspect of that decision – the significance of Mann J's acceptance that phone hacking itself is an actionable wrong. It begins by explaining how Mann J's judgment in *Gulati* moves the privacy tort beyond its traditional focus on the disclosure of private information. It then explains how breach of confidence – particularly the Court of Appeal's decision in *Tchenguiz v Imerman*[3] – provides a possible juridical bases for that extension. The article goes on to argue, though, that Mann J's judgment does more than just extend breach of confidence principles into the privacy context. It also reflects a growing recognition that there is more to privacy than the dissemination, or indeed the acquisition, of private information; that privacy can also be breached by watching, listening to or physically encroaching on a person against his or her wishes. By recognising these physical privacy interests, the article argues, *Gulati* is ushering in both a conceptual sea-change in English law and, potentially, a new facet of the privacy tort.

Liability for listening: *Gulati v MGN Ltd*

In *Gulati*, eight claimants – all of them celebrity actors, sports people or those closely associated with such people – brought a claim to ascertain the damages payable for privacy breaches admitted by the defendant, proprietor of *The Mirror*, *The Sunday Mirror* and *The People*.[4] All of the claimants had had their mobile telephone messages repeatedly intercepted by journalists at the defendant's titles over a period of years.[5] Those on the 'back-pocket list' of *Sunday Mirror* journalist, Dan Evans, had had their messages accessed at least twice a day for four years. In addition, all were the subject of private investigators' inquiries. The nature of this activity has never been fully revealed but was likely to include the use of 'blagging' to obtain telephone numbers, call histories, credit card details, and some medical information.[6] With the exception of BBC

[3] *Tchenguiz v Imerman* [2010] EWCA Civ 908, [2011] 2 WLR 592.

[4] The cases were brought before the court as part of managed litigation with the intention that the case would provide guidance for the settlement of multitudes of other cases being brought against the defendants.

[5] The judge explains that many targets failed to use personal identification numbers (PINs) to protect their phone messages or never changed them from the default settings. Where there was a PIN, journalists would systematically try to guess them, often after engaging private investigators to ascertain significant dates such as relatives' birthdates. Journalists also used 'double-tapping' techniques which involved ringing a mobile with two phones simultaneously so that the second call would be diverted directly to voicemail. (On the Orange network, the hacker could simply call the message exchange.)

[6] *Gulati* (n 1) [12]. Mann J explained ([12]) that 'blagging' is 'the process of obtaining information from the person holding it by deception, including wrongfully claiming to be the person entitled to it or otherwise convincing the holder to part with it by some form of pretence'. As with phone hacking, it is unclear on what basis the defendants conceded liability

executive, Alan Yentob, in all cases the phone hacking yielded information which formed the basis of articles about the claimants' private lives. The claims in *Gulati* were therefore said to fall into three main categories: wrongfully listening to private or confidential information left for or by the claimant; wrongfully obtaining private information via private investigators; and the publication of stories based on that information.[7] The defendant admitted that all three categories of activity took place and that damages were payable as a result.[8]

Mann J clearly thought that these concessions were rightly made, including acceptance of liability for listening to the claimants' private messages. He said when setting out his approach to the compensation exercise:

> I accept that there are three areas of wrongful behaviour which need to be looked at separately. First there is the general hacking activity. Each of the individuals had their voicemails (and some of those whom they rang) hacked frequently (in their own cases daily), with most hacks not resulting directly in an article. Their private information was thus acquired and their right to privacy infringed, irrespective of whether an article was published. That fact makes it appropriate to take the activity separately and assess its effect (in terms of compensation) separately from damage arising from publication. It is something in respect of which the claimants are entitled to be compensated and if it is not treated separately from the effect of the articles its real impact may be lost, or perhaps even exaggerated. The only sensible approach is to take it separately from the effect of the articles. It amounts to a separate category of wrong which has to be separately reflected in order to ensure that the objective of the damages award achieves its aim.[9]

This was reflected in the damages awards made. Where the hacking resulted in an article, compensation for the hacking and any private investigator activity was built into damages for the publication.[10] An additional sum was also awarded for phone hacking which did not result in articles. Thus, in addition to the sums awarded for publication of articles resulting from hacking, actor Shane Roche was awarded £40,000 for 'the invasions by hacking generally for 6 years, during which all sorts of private matters will have been heard'.[11] Mann J makes specific reference to evidence that journalists had listened to a number of emotional voicemails relating to the difficult birth of his child and sister-in-law's death

for the private investigators' activities (although passing on information obtained by blagging is likely to be a breach of confidence). Since the precise nature of the private investigators' activities is unclear, they will not be discussed in detail in this article.

[7] *ibid* [13].

[8] *ibid* [13]. The only matters really in contention were the scale of the hacking and private investigator activity and the damages payable as a result (*ibid* [13]) and whether some of the articles were the result of phone hacking (*ibid* [2]).

[9] *ibid* [155].

[10] See, eg, *Gulati* (n 1) [287], [288], [361], and [432]. Mann J's starting point was £10,000 for each year of serious hacking [230].

[11] *ibid* [534].

even though no articles resulted from it.[12] Alan Yentob, who never had an article published about him, was awarded £85,000 for regular phone hacking over a period of roughly seven years.[13]

In the course of making these awards, Mann J took account of the impact of the hacking on the claimants' dignity, autonomy and emotional equilibrium.[14] He explained that victims felt 'violated' and 'sickened' by the hacking.[15] One said that the list of calls and private investigators' invoices made him think 'that the newspaper considered that he and [his former wife] were just pieces of news to be played with'.[16] Another likened the experience to having someone searching through his personal belongings.[17] The claimants also described the serious toll that the surveillance itself (as distinct from the articles which resulted from it) had on their emotional equilibrium and, in some cases, mental health. One described feeling 'persecuted' and 'hunted'.[18] Another explained how the sense that he was under surveillance exacerbated existing mental health problems.[19] Another's loss of trust in others was such that at the time of the hearing he still lived in a house surrounded by CCTV cameras.[20]

---

[12] *ibid* [534].

[13] *ibid* [243].

[14] See *ibid* [108]–[145].

[15] See e.g. the summary of the evidence of Alan Yentob (*ibid* [247]) and Lucy Taggart (*ibid* [407]) and Mann J's general summary (*ibid* [32(i)]). The word 'sick' or 'sickening' was also used by four other claimants to describe their response to the hackers' activities (see summary of the evidence of Lauren Alcorn (*ibid* [273]), Shane Roche (*ibid* [513]), Paul Gascoigne (*ibid* [571]), and Sadie Frost (*ibid* [661])). References to 'violation' are consistent with the widely held theoretical view that privacy is closely related to dignity: see eg S Benn, 'Privacy, Freedom, and Respect for Persons' in J Pennock and J Chapman (eds), *Privacy: NOMOS XIII* (Atherton, 1971).

[16] *Gulati* (n 1) [336] (Robert Ashworth).

[17] *ibid* [247] (Yentob).

[18] *ibid* [405] (Taggart).

[19] *ibid* [569] (Gasgoine). The claimants' responses are consistent with those of witnesses in other physical privacy cases. See, eg, *Wainwright v Home Office* [2003] UKHL 53, [2004] 2 AC 406 [4] (effects of an intrusive strip search); *AM v News Group Newspapers Ltd* [2012] EWHC 308 (QB) [4] and *AAA v Associated Newspapers Ltd* [2012] EWHC 2103 (QB) [15]–[16] and [31] (effects of media 'doorstepping') (although the reliability of some witnesses' recollection of events was doubted in the latter case, their evidence about the effect it had upon them was not called into question at [40]–[49]); and The Rt Hon Lord Justice Leveson, *An Inquiry into the Culture, Practices and Ethics of the Press*, House of Commons Paper No 780 (London 2012), 484 para 3.4. Further, the claimant in *C v Holland* [2012] NZHC 2155, [2012] 3 NZLR 672 (interviewed by this author and Dr Yvette Tinsley on 27 March 2014) suffered distress and anxiety that affected her ability to sleep and interact with others for months after the discovery of the filming.

[20] See e.g. *Gulati* (n 1) [362] (Ashworth). The fact that hacking was resulting in the publication of information that very few people knew, also led to suspicion, mistrust and in some cases, the breakdown of significant relationships.

Possible juridical bases for the defendant's liability

Misuse of private information

It is not surprising, in light of this evidence, that Mann J saw fit to compensate the claimants for the effects of the hacking itself. To borrow a phrase from the Ontarian Court of Appeal, the facts cry out for a remedy.[21] The move is not, however, supported by misuse of private information precedent.[22] Although it is called 'misuse of private information', at least before *Gulati*, the English privacy action had only ever been applied to one type of misuse, the *disclosure* of private information. This restriction of liability to this type of breach has been clear from the action's inception; all of the tests set out in the leading case of *Campbell v MGN Ltd* confined the action to this type of activity. Thus, although Lord Nicholls re-labelled the tort 'misuse of private information',[23] he later explained that, '[e]ssentially the touchstone of private life is whether in respect of the *disclosed facts* the person in question had a reasonable expectation of privacy'.[24] Baroness Hale agreed, stating that:

> the exercise of balancing Article 8 and Article 10 may begin when the person *publishing* the information knows or ought to know that there is a reasonable expectation that the information in question will be kept confidential.[25]

Lord Hope, likewise, said that in cases where the information is not 'obviously private':

> the broad test is whether *disclosure* of the information about the individual ('A') would give substantial offence to A, assuming that A was placed in similar circumstances and was a person of ordinary sensibilities.[26]

Subsequent articulations of the requirements of the action have been similarly limited. For example, although the first question in the 'new methodology' set out by the Court of Appeal in *McKennitt v Ash* was whether 'the information [is] private in the sense that it is in principle protected by Article 8?', Buxton LJ makes it clear that he is only talking about cases 'such as the present where the complaint is of the wrongful publication of private information'.[27] Publication is also assumed in the second question, which is 'whether the owner of the private information must yield to the right of freedom of expression conferred on the *publisher* by Article 10'.[28] Similar emphasis can be found in *Murray* where the Court

[21] *Jones v Tsige* 2012 ONCA 32 [69].
[22] The information was shared amongst the journalists themselves (see *Gulati* (n 1) [99](iii)) but Mann J did not emphasise the point.
[23] *Campbell v MGN Ltd* [2004] UKHL 22, [2004] 2 AC 457 [14]. The Court of Appeal confirmed that misuse of private information is a tort in of *Vidal-Hall v Google Inc* [2014] EWHC 13 (QB). The Supreme Court has declined leave to appeal on this issue.
[24] *Campbell* (n 23) [21] emphasis added.
[25] *ibid* [134].
[26] *ibid* [92].
[27] *McKennitt v Ash* [2006] EWCA Civ 1714 [11].

of Appeal stressed that 'the reasonable expectation was that of the person who is affected by the *publicity*'[29] and listed 'the circumstances in which and the purposes for which the information came into the hands of the *publisher*' as one of the factors to be taken into account when determining whether such an expectation had been established.[30]

It stands to reason, then, that although the misuse of private information tort has been applied to a range of private material – information about extra marital affairs, drug addiction treatment, the depiction of sexual activity, photographs of children – previous applications have invariably involved the disclosure of the private material in question. The label 'misuse of private information' is therefore something of a misnomer; the action is in fact about taking private information and publishing it to others.

Tchenguiz and breach of confidence

So *Gulati* does not fit into the standard misuse of private information rubric: absent publication, a hacking victim will be unable to satisfy the touchstone requirement that 'in respect of the *disclosed facts* the person in question had a reasonable expectation of privacy'.[31] But that is not to say that there is no authority supporting the defendant's concession that listening in on a private conversation is actionable. Breach of confidence must also be considered.

It is clear that the fact that those listening to the claimants' phone messages acquired significant private information about them was at least part of Mann J's concern in *Gulati*. He stressed that even where no article resulted from the hacking, the claimants' 'private information was acquired and their right to privacy infringed'.[32] Later, when explaining why the claimants should receive significant compensation for the hacking itself, he said:

> Each of the claimants (in differing degrees) had their private information rendered freely available, on a daily basis (if on any given day there was any private information in the voicemails) to journalists who used it as they thought fit. Even if not used it was known to them ... Their privacy was set at nought by the newspaper. I shall come to detail in due course, but in all cases, and again in differing degrees, the claimants' right to control their information was taken from them.[33]

---

[28] *ibid* [11].

[29] *Murray v Express Newspapers Plc* [2008] EWCA Civ 446, [2009] Ch 481 [35] citing *Campbell* (n 23) [99].

[30] *Murray* (n 29) [36].

[31] *Campbell* (n 23) [21] emphasis added. It is not clear from Mann J's judgment how the claim in *Gulati* was pleaded but his reference at (n1) [1] to 'confidential or private information' suggests that the claimants claimed in both breach of confidence and misuse of private information.

[32] *Gulati* (n 1) [155].

[33] *ibid* [169].

This is significant because the Court of Appeal case of *Tchenguiz v Imerman* provides authority for the proposition that *acquiring* private information about a person can be actionable in breach of confidence.[34] The Court in that case held that the defendants breached the claimant's confidence when, acting out of concern that he was failing to disclose assets in matrimonial proceedings with their sister, they accessed, copied and passed on to their sister's solicitor, documents which the claimant kept on a computer server in their shared office. The Court of Appeal held that obtaining the information, without more, was enough to breach the confidence of the defendant. Speaking for the Court, Lord Neuberger MR said:

> intentionally obtaining information [in respect of which the defendants must have appreciated that the claimant had an expectation of privacy] secretly and knowing that the claimant reasonably expects it to be private, *is itself* a breach of confidence. The notion that looking at documents which one knows to be confidential is itself capable of constituting an actionable wrong (albeit perhaps only in equity) is also consistent with the decision of the Strasbourg court that monitoring private telephone calls can infringe the Article 8 rights of the caller: see *Copland v United Kingdom* … In our view, it would be a breach of confidence for a defendant, without the authority of the claimant, to examine, or to make, retain, or supply copies to a third party of, a document whose contents are, and were (or ought to have been) appreciated by the defendant to be, confidential to the claimant.[35]

The claimant was therefore able to restrain the defendants from looking at the documents again even though there was no evidence that they intended to reveal the contents to any third party.[36] This is because 'given that the information is confidential, the defendant should not be seeing it' and 'whatever the defendant's intentions, there would be a risk of the information getting out'.[37]

Mann J makes no mention of *Tchenguiz* in *Gulati* but the case supports the defendant's concession that listening to a telephone message is itself actionable. If, as the Court of Appeal says in *Tchenguiz*, a person can be liable for acquiring private information by looking at or copying confidential documents, then why not also for acquiring private information by other means? More particularly, if it is breach of confidence to obtain private information by reading a document, can it not also be a breach of confidence to obtain private information by listening to a person's private telephone messages? The Court's reliance on the Strasbourg

---

[34] *Tchenguiz v Imerman* [2010] EWCA Civ 908, [2011] 2 WLR 592.

[35] *Tchenguiz* (*ibid*) [68]–[69] (emphasis added) citing *Copland v United Kingdom* (2007) 45 EHRR 37. 'Misuse' of information for the purpose of breach of confidence had traditionally involved something more than access to confidential information, such as disclosure to a third party or unauthorised exploitation of trade secrets: see T Aplin, L Bently, P Johnson and S Malynciz, *Gurry on Breach of Confidence: The Protection of Confidential Information* (Oxford University Press, 2nd edn 2012) paras 15.02 and 15.18–15.23.

[36] *Tchenguiz* (n 34) [72]. Cf *Jones v Tsige* (n 21) where unauthorised access to computer files was addressed under the tort of intrusion into solitude and seclusion. Little was made, in *Tchenguiz*, of the fact that the documents had been passed to the sister's solicitor.

[37] *ibid* [72].

telephone monitoring case of *Copland v United Kingdom* suggests that other forms of information-acquisition were contemplated in *Tchenguiz*, including those involving the monitoring of calls.[38] And the rationale for the decision in *Tchenguiz* – that a claimant has a right to 'choose whether, to whom and in what circumstances and on what terms to reveal the information' is the essence of the breach of confidence – is as pertinent to information gleaned by phone hacking as to information obtained on a computer.[39]

Importantly, the reasoning in *Tchenguiz* can also be translated readily into the privacy context. Speaking for the Court, Lord Neuberger MR held that, 'the law should be developed and applied consistently and coherently in both privacy and "old fashioned confidence" cases, even if they sometimes may have different features'.[40] He continued that in cases where Article 8 interests are being considered, 'whether the claimant had a "reasonable expectation of privacy" in respect of the information in issue, is … a good test to apply when considering whether a claim for confidence is well-founded'.[41] That test was then applied to determine whether there was a breach of confidence in that case.[42] This is important in the context of *Gulati*. Mann J's judgment was consistently couched in the language of privacy, not confidence. So if he was applying the principles in *Tchenguiz*, it seems it must have been in the context of the misuse of privacy action.

Beyond information

It will be suggested below that Mann J's judgment in *Gulati* does more than simply extend the privacy action to situations where private information is acquired but, for present purposes, it can be seen to have done two things. First, it implicitly applies the conclusion in *Tchenguiz* – that acquiring information about a person can breach his or her reasonable expectations of privacy – in the context of the privacy tort. Further, it suggests that it is not just reading private documents which gives rise to liability for information-acquisition; obtaining information by hearing a person will result in liability as well. (Liability would presumably also extend to visual observation: if a claimant can be liable for unauthorised acquisition of information from a computer or phone message, then why not also by obtaining information by spying on a person?)[43]

38 *ibid* [68]. Indeed, the monitoring in *Copland v United Kingdom* (n 35) was less intrusive than the hacking in *Gulati* since the defendants in the former merely monitored to whom the calls were made.

39 *Tchenguiz* (n 34) [69].

40 *ibid* [67]. The Court was explaining why it should draw on misuse of private information cases in the breach of confidence context but it is suggested that the converse also applies.

41 *ibid* [66].

42 *ibid* [77].

43 For example, the principles in *Tchenguiz* (n 34) and *Gulati* (n 1) could apply to the acquisition of information by an abortion campaigner operating a surveillance campaign at an abortion clinic.

These extensions to the misuse of private information tort are significant for their own sake but also because, by protecting the *content* of documents on a computer or a message left on a mobile phone, the law incidentally protects the privacy of the computer and the conversations *themselves*. The rule against the acquisition of private information therefore provides some protection against unjustified incursions into private activities, belongings or spaces themselves. This is to be welcomed. It is widely accepted that physical privacy – the right to be free from intrusion into private spaces or activities – is an important part of the privacy interest. Most people, it is suggested, would feel that their privacy had been breached if someone listened to their private conversations; watched them engaged in private activities; or obtained access to their private spaces or belongings.[44] Commentators therefore consistently argue that interferences with privacy include 'peeping, following, watching, and photographing individuals; intruding or entering "private" places; eavesdropping, wiretapping, reading of letters'.[45]

Courts are increasingly willing to recognise the importance of protecting against these physical privacy intrusions. For example, in the New Zealand case of *C v Holland*, a man who surreptitiously videoed his flatmate in the shower was found liable for a new tort of intrusion into seclusion.[46] The Ontarian Court of Appeal also held that it was an actionable intrusion for a bank clerk to look up the banking transactions of her partner's former wife repeatedly over a four-year period to see where and on what she was spending her money.[47] The well-established US tort of intrusion into solitude and seclusion similarly applies to defendants who bug their tenants; spy on people in bathrooms or changing rooms; or intercept people's telephone calls.[48] Closer to home, the UK legislature has consistently recognised the impact of non-disclosure based intrusions on individuals. For example, the Data Protection Act 1998 imposes obligations on those who make recordings on a digital camera, video or listening

[44]For a fuller discussion of theoretical justifications for protecting physical privacy, see Moreham, 'Beyond Information' (n 2) 352–55 and NA Moreham 'The Protection of Privacy in English Common Law: A Doctrinal and Theoretical Analysis' (2005) 121 *Law Quarterly Review* 628, 648–51.

[45]R Gavison, 'Privacy and the Limits of the Law' (1979) 89 *Yale Law Journal* 421, 436. See also K Hughes, 'A Behavioural Understanding of Privacy and its Implications for Privacy Law' (2012) 75 *Modern Law Review* 806, 810–11; D Solove, 'A Taxonomy of Privacy' (2006) 154 *University of Pennsylvania Law Review* 447, 552–57; and R Parker, 'A Definition of Privacy' (1974) 27 *Rutgers Law Review* 275, 275–88.

[46]*C v Holland* (n 19).

[47]*Jones v Tsige* (n 21). Privacy protection in Canadian provincial statutory torts also extends to physical privacy interests: see, eg, *Lee v Jacobson* (1992) 87 DLR (4th) 401, 31 ACWS (3d) 329 (BCSC); *Malcolm v Fleming* 2000 Carswell BC 1316 (SC); *Watts v Klaemt* 2007 BCSC 662, [2007] BCWLD 4106; and *LAM v JELI* 2008 BCSC 1147, 170 ACWS (3d) 674.

[48]See e.g. respectively, *Amati v City of Woodstock, Illinois* 829 F Supp 998 (ND Ill 1993); *Harkey v Abate* 346 NW 2d 74 (Mich App 1983); *Benitez v KFC National Management* 714 NE 2d 1002 (Ill App 2 Dist 1999); *Rhodes v Graham* 37 SW (2d) 46 (1931).

device even if no publication follows. Various criminal measures also protect against non-consensual filming of sexual activity or the naked body; against repeated acts of filming, following or spying and against telephone and computer hacking.[49] Judges developing the common law have also expressed support for increased protection for privacy rights.[50]

The physical privacy interests at stake in *Gulati*

Gulati should be seen as part of this trend towards greater protection for physical privacy interests. Although, as outlined above, the case can be explained in informational terms, physical privacy was in fact of central importance in *Gulati*. Protecting against intrusion into the conversations themselves was one of the principal bases for Mann J's damages awards. Thus, although Mann J sometimes emphasised the fact that private information was obtained by the hackers, he also stressed that when it comes to liability the nature of the information obtained is immaterial: '[e]ach claimant can justifiably say that their privacy was infringed when any voicemail was listened to, whatever its content'.[51] The claimants were therefore entitled to compensation for disclosure of information obtained by hacking 'even absent any real privacy level in the information itself';[52] or put another way, they were liable 'even if someone else, discovering the information from a different route, and publishing it, might not be liable'.[53] In other words, the information in the messages was private because of the way it was being communicated, i.e. via private phone message, not because of what the messages were about.[54]

---

[49]See, respectively, Sexual Offences Act 2003, s 67; Protection from Harassment Act 1997; Regulation of Investigatory Powers Act 2000; Computer Misuse Act 1990. However, gaps in legislative protection for physical privacy remain: see NA Moreham, 'Protection against Intrusion in English Legislation' in N Witzleb, D Lindsay, M Paterson and S Rodrick (eds), *Emerging Challenges in Privacy Law: Comparative Perspectives* (Cambridge University Press, 2014), 141–156.

[50]See eg, *Campbell* (n 23) [15] (Lord Nicholls) and *Mosley v News Group Newspapers Ltd* [2008] EWHC 1777 (QB), [2008] EMLR 20 [17].

[51]*Gulati* (n 1) [218].

[52]*ibid* [224].

[53]*ibid*. Jacob Rowbottom agrees with this analysis (see 'A Landmark at a Turning Point: *Campbell* and the Use of Privacy Law to Constrain Media Power', in this issue of the *Journal of Media Law*).

[54]The circumstances in which information is obtained are also important in the misuse of private information action. The fact that the infant claimant was expressly targeted by photographers acting surreptitiously bore on the Court of Appeal's decision in *Murray* (n 29) not to strike out his claim for a misuse of private information ([54]–[57]). In *Campbell* (n 23), Baroness Hale also took account of the fact that publication of a photograph of the claimant outside a Narcotics Anonymous meeting 'added to the potential harm, by making her think that she was being followed or betrayed, and deterring her from going back to the same place again' ([155]).

This is consistent with other indications in Mann J's judgment that compensation was at least in part for harm inherent in the hacking itself, for the interference with the right to be free from surveillance and scrutiny. He stressed that compensation for hacking which did not result in articles was designed:

> to reflect the fact that for a considerable period an individual's voicemail, and those of associates, were listened to and the private lives exposed there were studied by at least one journalist and probably more, on a frequent, sometimes daily, basis.[55]

Compensation was therefore as much about the claimants' 'horror' that 'journalists had been listening, on a regular and frequent basis, to all sorts of aspects of their private lives',[56] as it was about the acquisition of specific pieces of information. As Mann J noted, 'many aspects of their personal, medical and professional lives were, to a very significant degree, laid bare'.[57] As one witness put it, the hacking 'opened a window into … the darkest period of his life'.[58]

These statements seem to recognise that, as well as a right to keep private information to oneself, privacy includes the right to be free from unwarranted watching, listening and incursions into private space *per se*. It recognises that observation and intrusion cases are not just about what the observer might find out about you but also about the intrusion itself; the incursion into a realm of life that you were entitled to keep private. On this analysis, the compensation in *Gulati* was at least partly for the fact that the hacker had become a party to conversations that were meant for others; that he or she heard what the claimants said, how they said it and when. It is unsurprising that claimants in *Gulati* felt 'violated' by such intrusions; like unwanted watching and incursions into private space, they have a serious impact on one's right to choose to whom you reveal yourself and how.[59]

Thus, although there is superficial appeal in seeing *Gulati* simply as an application of the information-acquisition principles advanced in *Tchenguiz*, an action which focuses exclusively on 'information' fails to capture these sensory and physical aspects of the privacy interest. It is not intuitive to say that 'information' is obtained in surveillance cases; for example, by a person who secretly spies on a person in the shower, records a father playing with his children in their bedroom or

[55] *Gulati* (n 1) [230].
[56] *ibid* [32(i)].
[57] *ibid*.
[58] *ibid* [261]. See also [378] and [432]. As Mann J put it at the end of his judgment ([702]): 'People whose private voicemail messages were hacked so often and for so long, and had very significant parts of their private lives exposed, and then reported on, are entitled to significant compensation.'
[59] The authors of *Gurry on Breach of Confidence* observe that, 'if English courts seek to protect against "intrusions" into private life as well as disclosure of private information then the connection to breach of confidence will become increasingly tenuous, and the case for recognizing a separate tort of privacy much stronger' (Aplin (n 35) para 7.102).

listens in on an anodyne conversation. Instead, the objection is to the fact that the intruder is observing you when you do not wish to be observed; that someone is getting access to *you* against your wishes – they are *seeing* you, *hearing* you talk, insinuating themselves into a space or an activity which was never meant for their observation.[60] We use terms like intrusion, surveillance, peeping, spying and eavesdropping to describe these activities. These nuances are lost if we simply talk about the acquisition of information.

Further, even if some information is obtained in physical privacy cases, the significance of the information is unlikely to reflect the seriousness of the intrusion. As *Gulati* shows, the information obtained by phone hacking will often be anodyne and unimportant. Perhaps the hacker will hear a shopping list or a call to say that someone is on the way home. It is too easy on an information-based approach to dismiss these kinds of intrusions; to equate the seriousness of the intrusion with the intimacy of the information, or more importantly, a lack thereof.[61] Indeed in some cases the intruder will not get any meaningful information at all. What information does an ex-lover get if he installs a camera in the bathroom of the home he had shared with the claimant only days before? What say the phone hacker merely hears of holiday plans that are already widely known? If we focus simply on the acquisition of *information*, these intrusions can be trivialised. The sanctity of a realm in which people can reveal themselves (both physically and emotionally) without intrusion from outsider can, in turn, be overlooked.

A new facet to the privacy tort

It is suggested then that the awards in *Gulati* do not just extend breach of confidence principles into the privacy context. They also lend support to recognition of a new facet of the privacy tort: a tort of intrusion into physical privacy. Such a tort would protect against unjustified observation of or access to the physical body, private activities and private space. As in misuse of private information, 'private' here connotes places and activities in respect of which one has a

[60]For further discussion of the theoretical dimensions of physical privacy, see Moreham 'Beyond Information' (n 2) 352–55 and 'The Protection of Privacy in English Common Law' (n 44) 649–51; R Wacks, *Personal Information: Privacy and the Law* (Oxford University Press, 1989), 248; *Privacy and Media Freedom* (n 10) 120–22; 186–219; Parker, 'A Definition of Privacy' (n 45) 275–88.

[61]As discussed above, Mann J was right to recognise that '[e]ach claimant can justifiably say that their privacy was infringed when any voicemail was listened to, whatever its content' (*Gulati* (n 1) [218]) but not all judges have distinguished so clearly between the seriousness of the hacking and the intimacy of any information obtained. For example, in *Coogan v News Group Newspapers Ltd* [2012] EWCA Civ 48, [2012] 2 WLR 848 [53] the Court of Appeal held that '[w]here a person's voice messages are intercepted, particularly over a period, there will often be some messages which contain confidential information and some which do not'.

reasonable expectation of privacy. The 'archetypal case would involve observing or recording an intimate conversation, domestic life, or activities (such as sexual activity, medical procedures, changing, or using a bathroom) during which private body parts are exposed'. The tort would therefore create liability for watching a person in the shower, hacking his or her phone, installing a camera in a person's living room, or going through a person's wallet, handbag or car.[62] Importantly, liability should not depend on 'information' having been disseminated or obtained.[63]

This new facet of the English privacy tort aligns loosely with the intrusion tort which has been recognised in most US states since the 1960s and more recently adopted in New Zealand and Ontario. It is, however, more carefully circumscribed than the concept of highly offensive 'intrusion into solitude and seclusion' on which these torts are usually based.[64] It would not, for example, extend to wrongs such as nuisance phone calls and sexual harassment which have fallen within the US tort.[65] It also delineates more clearly between the physical and informational components of the privacy interest. On the formulation set out above, cases which involve the dissemination, and perhaps also the non-physical acquisition, of private information would be addressed by the misuse of private information tort.[66] Those involving intrusions into physical privacy – listening,

[62]*Wainwright* would not prevent courts from doing this. Although Lord Hoffmann was opposed to recognition of a broad-ranging right to privacy, he did contemplate the incremental development of privacy protection (see *Wainwright v Home Office* (n 19) [28]–[33]).

[63]It is suggested that a defence would also be needed to ensure that a physical privacy action did not interfere with legitimate attempts to expose harmful or wrongful behaviour or with the appropriate reporting of newsworthy events. For further discussion of the desirable scope of such a defence and the physical privacy tort generally, see Moreham, 'Beyond Information' (n 2) 375–77.

[64]See e.g. *C v Holland* (n 19) which requires a highly offensive, intentional and unauthorised intrusion into seclusion (which in turn means 'intimate personal activity, space or affairs … involving infringement of a reasonable expectation of privacy'): [94]. The formulation in the Restatement of the Law (Second) of Torts (1977) s 652B (which has been adopted by many US States and by the Ontarian Court of Appeal in *Jones v Tsige* (n 20)) imposes liability for highly offensive, intentional intrusions whether 'physically or otherwise, upon the solitude or seclusion of another or his private affairs or concerns'. It is suggested that requirement that the intrusion be 'highly offensive' is unnecessary and undesirable (see, NA Moreham 'Why is Privacy Important? Privacy, Dignity and the Development of the New Zealand Breach of Privacy Tort' in J Finn and S Todd (eds), *Law Liberty, Legislation* (LexisNexis, 2008) 231–247, 238–47).

[65]See e.g. regarding persistent phone calls *Housh v Peth* 133 NE 2d 340, 344 and *Household Credit Services Inc v Driscol* 989 SW 2d 72, 84–85 (Tex App–El Paso 1998) and commentary to Restatement of the Law (Second) of Torts (1977) s 652B. Regarding sexual harassment, see e.g. *Phillips v Smalley Maintenance Services* 435 So 2d 705, 711 (Ala 1983); *Sphere Drake Insurance Plc v Shoney's Inc* 923 F Supp 1481, 1490 (MD Ala 1996); and *Scott v Estes* 60 F Supp 2d 1260, 1275 (MD Ala 1999).

[66]'Non-physical' means not involving physical access (i.e. looking at, listening to or gaining physical proximity) to the claimant's physical body, private activities or private space.

watching, recording, incursions into personal space and belongings – would be dealt with by the physical privacy tort.

Thus formulated, a physical privacy action could exist comfortably alongside misuse of private information. As *Gulati* itself shows, a defendant who hacked someone's phone and uploaded a recording of the conversation to the Internet would be liable both for the hacking (under physical privacy) and the dissemination of the material (in misuse of private information). The claimant would be compensated accordingly: first, for any feelings of vulnerability, violation and mistrust engendered by the eavesdropping; and then for the embarrassment, violation and possible pecuniary damage caused by the disclosure.[67] But the categories need not be entirely watertight. Some activities – such as computer hacking – could potentially fit into either tort, depending perhaps on the circumstances of the case. Compensation could also retain elements of flexibility. Damages for the acquisition of private information could, for instance, be built into awards for eavesdropping or spying. Conversely, damages for disclosure of recordings (such as videos or photographs) could recognise the physical privacy elements at issue when someone views or listens to them. The important thing is that both elements of the privacy interest are recognised appropriately.

Conclusion

Gulati is under appeal. It is hoped that, like this author, the Court of Appeal see the case not just as an important step in the resolution of the phone hacking saga but also in the development of privacy law as a whole. At the very least, the case imports into the tort of privacy the rule that acquiring private information is actionable in itself. This is consistent with the Court of Appeal's exhortation in *Tchenguiz* that privacy and breach of confidence should develop consistently. But *Gulati* also does something more. It recognises that the right to privacy extends beyond information and includes protection from unwarranted prying, eavesdropping, surveillance and incursion into personal space themselves, i.e. physical privacy. On both a conceptual and doctrinal level, this takes the English law of privacy into new territory. It is hoped that the Court of Appeal will seize the opportunity to endorse this change.

Acknowledgements

This paper has been developed out of a keynote address delivered at 'The Campbell Legacy: A decade of misuse of private information', Newcastle Law School, April 2015. I would like to thank Drs Tom Bennett and Daithí Mac Síthigh and the Newcastle University Conference Fund for facilitating my attendance at that event. Thanks also to Dr Jake

[67] In *Gulati* (n 1), Mann J made separate awards for the publication of private facts and the hacking itself (see p 3 above). For a US example of this approach, see *Schulman v Group W Productions Ltd* 955 P 2d 469 (Cal 1998).

Rowbottom, University of Oxford, and Dr Eric Descheemaeker, University of Edinburgh, for very useful discussions about *Gulati*; to Duncan McLachlan for copy-editing assistance; and the anonymous reviewer for his or her very useful comments. The usual disclaimers apply.

Disclosure statement

No potential conflict of interest was reported by the author.

A landmark at a turning point: *Campbell* and the use of privacy law to constrain media power

Jacob Rowbottom

This article argues that the decision in *Campbell* can be seen as a response to long-term concerns about the abuse of media power. After outlining some of the key developments in debates about privacy law, the article considers the features that distinguish the media as powerful institutions. It will be argued that the focus on media power has shaped the doctrine of misuse of private information, for example in expanding the scope of the tort and focusing on the public interest as the main defence. The decision in *Campbell* arrived at a moment when the communications environment was about to change dramatically. Since *Campbell*, the use of social media and the opportunities to share user-generated content has given many people the capacity to bring private facts to a large audience. The article will consider whether the *Campbell* tort remains applicable in the case of non-powerful publishers and looks at the alternative ways to protect privacy.

Introduction

Debates about privacy laws in the UK often revolve around the media and the need to curb 'abuses' of press power.[1] For well over a decade before *Campbell v MGN*[2] was decided, the need for legislation to protect private information from the press had been the subject of discussion in Parliament, the media, academic articles, independent inquiries and judicial decisions. A few years before *Campbell* was decided, Fenwick and Phillipson called for greater judicial protection of privacy, arguing that the 'power of the media to invade privacy is at least equal to that of the state'.[3] More recently, Sir David Eady commented that there has

---

[1]The references to 'abuses' by thepress, which is also common in the privacy debate, implies the press holds some position or power that can be abused.

[2][2004] UKHL 22, [2004] 2 AC 457 ('*Campbell*')

[3]G Phillipson and H Fenwick, 'Breach of Confidence as a Privacy Remedy in the Human Rights Act Era' (2000) 63 *Modern Law Review* 660, 668.

been 'gradual recognition that individual privacy sometimes needs to be protected also from the fourth estate' and that 'the media can wield greater power than government in influencing public opinion'.[4] The point is not new. Warren and Brandeis' famous article on privacy was a reaction against the press 'overstepping in every direction the obvious bounds of propriety and of decency'.[5] The power of the media is seen to warrant the legal protection from certain types of intrusion.

Given this background, it was unsurprising that the opportunity to restate the law relating to private information came with an action by a supermodel against a tabloid newspaper. While the ramifications of *Campbell* continue to be debated, the decision can now be taken as creating a new tort of misuse of private information.[6] The House of Lords built on the law of confidence, but signalled a move away from a focus on the conscience of the defendant and placed an emphasis on 'human autonomy and dignity'.[7] The rights-based focus, it was said, had led to a 'shift in the centre of gravity' away from that found in the law of confidence.[8] In this article, I do not advance a view on the merits of that shift or assess the balance struck with press freedom in any cases. The goal here is to give an account of this shift in the context of long-standing concerns about media power.

While much attention has focused on media intrusions, privacy is not simply about the press. Threats can come from the state and other powerful actors. Privacy concerns engage a range of issues and activities, such as government surveillance, credit rating agencies, blacklisting political activities and the tracking of consumer habits. Nor is privacy law to be equated solely with the tort of misuse of private information. Legislation such as the Data Protection Act 1998 and the Protection from Harassment Act 1997 offers protection to certain privacy interests, as do other private law actions and public law controls. However, and as will be shown, the debate about the merits of a general privacy law or a publication of private facts tort has been framed largely in terms a perceived need to curb 'abuses' by the media.[9]

Campbell v MGN is a landmark in media law, but a landmark that was established at a turning point in the system of communications. At the time of the House of Lords' decision, a revolution in communications was about to take off in which individual media users had greater scope to collect information, share and publish

[4]D Eady, 'Privacy: A Judicial Perspective' in J Lewis and P Crick (eds), *Media Law and Ethics in the 21st Century* (Routledge, 2014) 3–34, 3.

[5]S Warren and L Brandeis, 'The Right to Privacy' (1890) 4 *Harvard Law Review* 193, 196. For discussion locating that article within a 'wave of privacy anxiety' focused on the press, see N Richards, *Intellectual Privacy* (OUP, 2015) 16–20

[6]See *Vidal-Hall v Google* [2015] EWCA Civ 311 [25] and [43].

[7]Lord Hoffmann in *Campbell* [50].

[8]*ibid* [51].

[9]The focus on the press has been dominant, but not exclusive. For example, privacy rights were discussed in non-media law cases such as *Malone v Metropolitan Police Commissioner* [1979] Ch 344, *R v Khan* [1997] AC 558, *Wainwright v Home Office* [2003] UKHL 53, [2004] 2 AC 406.

content. That gave users of the digital media greater opportunity to disseminate content that intrudes upon the private lives of others. The majority of these users do not, however, hold the type of communicative power associated with the mass media. Later sections of this article will consider whether the justifications for a privacy law formulated with reference to the media are transferable to other types of media. Decoupling arguments to protect privacy and arguments to control abuses of concentrated power raises a number of questions about the legal controls on publication. Should the scope of the tort, in the reasonable expectation test, be drawn differently? Does a different balance need to be struck between privacy and freedom of expression in the context of social media? Furthermore, tort liability may not be as effective against certain non-media defendants. Legal actions may be too expensive and lengthy for many claimants in non-media cases. Damages and injunctions may be less appropriate and harder to enforce in the context of user-generated content. In some cases, an intrusion may be the result of lots of comments from large numbers of social media users, rather than a specific tortfeasor. As soon as *Campbell* arrived to address a set of long-standing privacy issues, the world of media and communications became a lot more complicated.

In order to assess these changes and the impact on the rationale for a legal privacy right, the article will consider the features of the media that are thought to give it power and the ways this has shaped the application of the misuse of private information tort. The consequences of the change in communications will also be considered. However, before getting on to these issues, the article will first locate the decision in *Campbell* within a broader debate about media ethics. While the discussion could start at various points in time, the late 1980s provides a useful place to set the scene for *Campbell*. By this time, an aggressive and intrusive tabloid press had gained considerable notoriety, which gave fresh impetus to calls for reform.

The path to *Campbell*

The 1980s and 1990s were perceived as breaking new ground in terms of the intrusiveness of certain sections of the media. As is well known, some tabloid newspapers maintained very high circulations off the back of various 'kiss and tell' stories, scandals and articles about the personal lives of celebrities. Reporters engaged in various dubious practices, including snooping on celebrity patients while in hospital and publishing stolen material.[10] The newspaper coverage of the illness and death of Russell Harty in 1988 provides a notable example. Reporters camped outside the hospital where Harty was being treated, approached hospital staff to see if there was an Aids-related angle to the story, used long lens

[10]D Calcutt, *Report of the Committee on Privacy and Related Matters* (Cm 1102, 1990) (Calcutt Committee) para 1.5.

cameras from neighbouring buildings to photograph Harty in his hospital bed and even posed as hospital staff in order to get information about the celebrity.[11]

The concern about the press was such that during the 1980s several private members bills were introduced in the House of Commons to strengthen the protection of privacy. In December 1988, the Conservative MP John Browne introduced a bill to create tort liability where private information was used publicly without the subject's consent.[12] The Labour MP Tony Worthington introduced a bill to give individuals a legal to right of reply to factual inaccuracies about themselves in the media, which would be enforced by a government appointed Press Commission.[13] Both bills received the support of MPs from different political parties, and received a second reading.

At the report stage of the Worthington bill, Timothy Renton MP expressed the government's opposition to either Bill and announced the government's intention to launch an independent review of the 'general issue of privacy and related matters'.[14] Some saw the announcement as an attempt by the government, having been lobbied by the press, to deflate the momentum towards any legislative intervention.[15] The bills never made it into law, but a reviewing body, titled the Committee on Privacy and Related Matters (the 'Calcutt Committee') was established under the chairmanship of Sir David Calcutt to examine the activities of the press.[16]

As the Calcutt Committee investigated these issues, a now notorious episode of press intrusion paved the way for a significant legal ruling on privacy. While the actor Gordon Kaye was hospitalised following a serious injury, reporters for the *Sunday Sport* accessed Kaye's hospital room where he was recovering following a period in intensive care (despite the presence of notices on the door requiring visitors to first see the hospital staff). The reporters interviewed Kaye and took photographs of his scars, even though the actor was in no fit state to consent to an interview. Kaye applied for an injunction to restrain publication of the *Sunday Sport* article. While his claim for malicious falsehood succeeded, the Court of Appeal ruled that there was no general tort of privacy.[17] Despite that conclusion, the ruling did little to vindicate press freedom and dicta from the three judges gave the campaign for privacy laws some support. Glidewell LJ said that the facts of the case illustrated 'the desirability of Parliament considering whether and in what circumstances statutory provision can be made to protect the privacy of individuals'. Bingham LJ also noted 'the failure of both the common law of

---

[11] See M Wainwright, 'The haunting of Harty', *The Guardian*, 27 June 1988.
[12] Protection of Privacy HC Bill (1988–89).
[13] Right of Reply HC Bill, (1988–89).
[14] HC Deb 21 April 1989, vol 151, col 595.
[15] Mark Fisher MP, HC Deb 21 April 1989, vol 151, col 596.
[16] The remit as stated by Douglas Hurd MP, see Calcutt Committee (n 10) para 1.1.
[17] *Kaye v Robertson* [1991] FSR 62.

England and statute to protect in an effective way the personal privacy of individual citizens'. Leggatt LJ stated that the right to privacy 'has so long been disregarded here that it can be recognised now only by the legislature'. All three judges indicated what they thought ought to happen, but left it to Parliament to make that change.[18]

When the Calcutt Committee reported in 1990, the Committee discussed the Kaye episode. The Committee believed that the conduct of the *Sunday Sport* showed that assurances from the press that they had mended their ways were 'not enough to meet public demand for more effective redress'.[19] However, the Committee did not think a general privacy tort was yet appropriate, taking into account the potential impact on press freedom and the effectiveness of other remedies dealing with intrusive reporting.[20] A general tort protecting private information would also have implications for media sectors other than the press, which were outside the Committee's remit. The Committee recommended a number of reforms, including the establishment of a new self-regulatory body called the Press Complaints Commission (PCC) which was subsequently established in 1991. At the end of an 18-month trial period in January 1993, Calcutt reviewed the new self-regulatory system in a second report ('Calcutt 2') and found that the PCC did not follow the recommendations of his earlier report and that it should be replaced with a statutory tribunal.[21] While he did not recommend a privacy tort, he called on the government to consider the introduction of such a cause of action. Calcutt put the ball in Parliament's court.

Prior to the publication of Calcutt's second report, the National Heritage Select Committee launched its own investigation into privacy and media intrusion, and published its report in March 1993.[22] The Select Committee opposed Calcutt's proposal for statutory regulation of the press, but recommended the introduction of a civil remedy for invasions of privacy. While the government consulted on a new tort in July 1993, calls for statutory press regulation and a privacy tort were rejected in the government's final response to Calcutt 2 and the National Heritage Committee in July 1995.[23] The government rejected tort liability on the grounds that there was not a 'sufficient consensus on which to base statutory intervention in this area' and that 'the Government strongly prefer the principle of self-regulation'.[24] This conclusion can be seen partly to reflect the government's

---

[18]Compare *Wainwright v Home Office* [2003] UKHL 53, [2004] 2 AC 406 [27] for a different interpretation of this dicta.
[19]Calcutt Committee (n 10) para 13.21.
[20]*ibid* paras 12.1–12.29. For example the Committee warned that a privacy tort could have the 'effect of stifling reports about the failings of people in the public eye'.
[21]D Calcutt, *Review of Press Self-Regulation* (Cm 2135, 1993).
[22]National Heritage Select Committee, *Privacy and Media Intrusion* (HC 1992–93, 294-I).
[23]Secretary of State for National Heritage, *The Government's Response to the House of Commons National Heritage Select Committee: Privacy and Media Intrusion* (Cm 2918, 1995).

desire to avoid 'a major row with the press', which privacy legislation would likely have entailed.[25] The perceived political power of the press gave the industry lobbying leverage over the Major government, which was already receiving much negative media coverage.

The decision by the government not to act on either of the Calcutt and National Heritage Committee reports was seen by some as a failure by the political channels to plug the gap in protection demonstrated by the *Kaye* case. In the eyes of privacy advocates, Parliament had failed to address concerns about privacy, due to fears of provoking a potentially hostile press. Accordingly, privacy advocates thought that the courts had the legitimacy to correct the perceived political failure. In 1996, Lord Bingham – one of the judges in *Kaye* – wrote that there was a powerful case for a privacy law and that this would best be implemented through legislation. However, he concluded that:

> if, for whatever reason, legislation is not forthcoming, I think it almost inevitable that cases will arise in the courts in which the need to give relief is obvious and pressing; and when such cases do arise, I do not think the courts will be found wanting.[26]

Lacking a statutory cause of action, the courts continued to develop breach of confidence to protect certain privacy interests. For example, in *Barrymore v News Group Newspapers*, the court granted an injunction to restrain the further publication of personal details contained in private letters that the celebrity had sent to the defendant.[27] Outside the context of personal privacy, the law of confidence steadily expanded to capture reporters taking unauthorised photographs of artistic works, when security measures were in place.[28] Similarly, dicta in *Hellewell* indicated that the law of confidence can restrict people using longs lens cameras to take 'from a distance and with no authority a picture of another engaged in some private act'.[29] While these developments offered the potential widening of protection to some types of privacy, breach of confidence still had limits. Critics of the press continued to campaign for stronger controls.

The catalyst for further change came with the Human Rights Act 1998. The Act did not directly create a privacy law enforceable against the press – and the

---

[24]Virginia Bottomley MP, Secretary of State for National Heritage, HC Deb, 17 July 1995, vol 263, col 1325. See also the government response, *ibid* para 4.13.

[25]Lord Justice Leveson, *An Inquiry into the Culture, Practices and Ethics of the Press: Report* (HC 780, 2012), 1253.

[26]T Bingham, 'Should There Be a Law to Protect Rights of Personal Privacy?' (1996) 5 *European Human Rights Law Review* 455, 462. See also R Wacks, *Privacy and Press Freedom* (Blackstone, 1995) 173.

[27][1997] FSR 600

[28]*Creation Records v News Group Newspapers* [1997] EMLR 444; *Shelley Films v Rex Features* [1994] EMLR 134.

[29]*Hellewell v Chief Constable of Derbyshire* [1995] 1 WLR 804, 807

press representatives did what they could to foreclose such a result.[30] The Act, however, imposed a duty on the courts to 'act compatibly' with the European Convention when adjudicating disputes between private parties.[31] The 'right to respect' private and family life under Article 8 also entailed a number of positive obligations, including 'the adoption of measures designed to secure respect for private life even in the sphere of the relations of individuals between themselves'.[32] In 1998, the Commission had ruled that the absence of a remedy in UK law for certain press intrusions into private life 'could show a lack of respect for their private lives' and thereby fell short of the positive obligations.[33] Both the new duties on the domestic courts, along with the developing Article 8 jurisprudence gave the courts the tools to move away from the constraints of *Kaye v Robertson*.

In some early rulings under the HRA, these new tools were taken up. In *Douglas v Hello*, Sedley LJ commented that 'we have reached a point at which it can be said with confidence that the law recognises and will appropriately protect a right of personal privacy'.[34] Those words were taken by some commentators to herald a new protection for privacy. When *Douglas v Hello* returned to the Chancery Division in 2003, Lindsay J stated that when the domestic law is found to offer inadequate protection, 'if Parliament does not step in then the Courts will be obliged to'.[35] Lindsay J then offered a prediction:

> A glance at a crystal ball of, so to speak, only a low wattage suggests that if Parliament does not act soon the less satisfactory course, of the Courts creating the law bit by bit at the expense of litigants and with inevitable delays and uncertainty, will be thrust upon the judiciary.[36]

Once again, the perceived political deadlock was seen by some to legitimise the use of the HRA to provide a stronger remedy. However, the early decisions did not all point in one direction and *Theakston* and *A v B* seemed to reinforce the limited protection under breach of confidence.[37]

At the same time, the House of Commons Culture, Media and Sport Committee considered the issue of privacy and press intrusion once again in 2003. The contrast between the developing protection of privacy under Article 8 and the government's resolve not to legislate, led the Committee to comment that the issue has

[30]For background, see Leveson (n 25).
[31]*Campbell* [132].
[32]*X and Y v Netherlands* (1985) 8 EHRR 235, [23]. *Von Hannover v Germany (No 2)* (2012) 32 BHRC 527 [98].
[33]*Earl and Countess Spencer v UK* (1998) 25 EHRR CD105.
[34]*Douglas v Hello* [2001] QB 967 [110].
[35]*Douglas v Hello* [2003] EWHC 786 [229].
[36]*ibid.*
[37]*Theakston* v MGN Ltd [2002] EMLR 398; *A v B* [2003] QB 195.

'never been simultaneously colder and hotter'.[38] The Committee noted that the HRA had 'sown the seed of privacy law',[39] but concluded that a privacy statute should be considered as an alternative to the gradual protection of privacy on a case-by-case basis.[40] In its response in October 2003, the government rejected that invitation, finding the combination of media regulation (subject to some modifications) and existing legal controls provided the best approach to protecting privacy.[41]

After these early mixed signals, the House of Lords' decision in *Campbell* provided a restatement of the law that provided a foundation for the new tort. The decision was not an inevitable consequence of the Human Rights Act. While the court took an approach of 'indirect horizontal effect' to apply Article 8 in cases involving the press, what was required of the courts to act compatibly with ECHR rights when developing the common law was (and remains) unclear.[42] It is not clear why the technique of indirect horizontal effect has been so prominent in media privacy cases, but less so in relation to other areas of the common law and other rights. Aside from the domestic law, the positive obligations under Article 8 are also unclear in scope, fact sensitive and subject to a margin of appreciation.[43] While Article 8 and the HRA allowed for the interpretation taken in *Campbell*, it did not mandate the development of a new tort.

The decision in *Campbell* needs to be understood against the background of the ongoing debate about privacy. As the preceding discussion shows, the protection of private information secured in the *Campbell* reformulation was a live issue in the 1990s and early 2000s. The potential legal reform was considered judicially, by independent reviewers and in Parliament, and also generated considerable public debate. In the various debates, invasion of privacy was largely a byword for concerns about the excesses of the press. The move taken in *Campbell* had therefore been on the cards for some time and the HRA provided the courts with the necessary tools to take that step. While building on previous rulings, the court in *Campbell* utilised its powers to help break a political deadlock and remedy a perceived inadequacy in the law. While the court's reasoning was not specific to the press, it was the culmination of long-standing concerns about the power of the press.

---

[38]Culture, Media and Sport Committee, *Privacy and Media Intrusion* (HC 2002–03, 458-I) para 99.
[39]*ibid* para 107.
[40]*ibid* para 110.
[41]Department for Culture, Media and Sport, *Government's Response to the Fifth Report of the Culture Media and Sport Select Committee* (Cm 5985, 2003) paras 2.3–2.6
[42]For a more recent contribution, see G Phillipson and A Williams, 'Horizontal Effect and Constitutional Constraint' (2011) 74 *Modern Law Review* 878.
[43]See D Harris, M O'Boyle, E Bates, and C Buckley, *O'Boyle and Warbrick Law of the European Convention on Human Rights, Third Edition* (OUP, 2014) 533, 591.

The decision in *Campbell* may have been the culmination of a long process, but it has not ended the debate. Frequent controversies arise about whether the new tort offers adequate protection to privacy or whether it goes too far. When the tort was in its infancy, the Culture Media and Sport Select Committee in 2007 rejected calls for a statutory privacy law as an alternative to self-regulation, on the grounds that drafting such a law would pose too many challenges. The Committee also noted that 'a number of recent cases have established case law which extends individuals' rights of privacy'.[44] When the same Committee considered the matter again in 2010, the impact of *Campbell* was reflected in some witnesses' calls for privacy legislation as a way of reigning in the tort and protecting press freedom.[45] While noting the piecemeal development of the misuse tort, the Committee thought legislation was unnecessary and the tort's scope would be clarified over time.[46] In 2012, the Joint Committee on Privacy and Injunctions, put together following the 'super-injunction' controversy, saw no advantage in putting the tort on a statutory footing.[47] Finally, and most famously, the Leveson Report considered the matter of press regulation in wake of the phone hacking scandal.[48] The debate about privacy and the press continues, but since *Campbell* the terms of the debate have shifted. The question is no longer whether a tort should be introduced, but rather how well that tort is functioning and whether it should be replaced by statute.

Privacy rights and media power

The debate that preceded *Campbell* and much of the subsequent litigation may have focused on the media, but the cause of action established in *Campbell* is about protecting privacy from any actor. Arguments about general privacy rights and arguments about abuse of media power have a different focus. Privacy rights protect an area of a person's life from intrusion. The fact of the intrusion is key, rather than the identity of the defendant. The focus is on the individual affected. By contrast, when discussing abuse of media power, the focus is on the behaviour of media institutions, and the standards of conduct expected of those institutions. Privacy is just one type of abuse of power for which the media institutions should be held to account.

Despite differences in focus, arguments to protect privacy rights and control abuses of media power have generally been complementary. While privacy

---

[44]House of Commons, Culture, Media and Sport Committee, *Self-regulation of the Press* (HC 2006–07, 375) para 52.

[45]Culture, Media and Sport Committee, *Press Standards, Privacy and Libel* (HC 2009–10, 362-I) para 65.

[46]*ibid* [67].

[47]Joint Committee on Privacy and Injunctions, *Privacy and Injunctions* (HL 2010–12, 273, 1443).

[48]Leveson (n 25).

rights may be of general application, the biggest threat of unwanted publicity has traditionally been from the media. It is therefore natural to justify changes in the law with reference to the press. So while a privacy tort applies to anyone, it may be motivated by concerns about media intrusion. Furthermore, the scope of a legal right to privacy may be fashioned so that it primarily captures the worst abuses, which the media would most likely be responsible for (at least until the digital revolution in communications). Along these lines, Nissenbaum argues that the legal protection of 'informational norms' of privacy are warranted 'when the parties involved perpetrating the violations are overwhelmingly more powerful or wealthy and moved by pure self-interest'.[49] While the privacy interests might refer to an aspect of a person's life, the justification for legal protection may be centred on powerful institutions.

It might be thought that if the media poses a threat to a particular interest or right, then the obvious solution is to fashion some media-specific regulations, rather than develop private law. The discussion so far has shown that at various points prior to *Campbell*, press regulation and a statutory privacy law were discussed as alternatives to one another. Media regulation can protect legal interests, and is sometimes seen to be a low-cost alternative to the courts. The dilemma in this area is that a strong system of media regulation might undermine press freedom, while press self-regulation has so far been seen by many to provide inadequate protection to victims of intrusion. The use of private law offers a method of stronger remedies for a particular exercise of media power without regulating all aspects of press behaviour.

The use of private law to guard against abuses of media power is not limited to privacy and an analogous approach can be found with defamation law. While the protection of reputation has a long history, much of its recent rationale has focused on the media. As Kirby P stated in his dissent in *Ballina Shire Council v Ringland*:

> One role of the law of defamation is to correct and redress abuse of power by the media. As defamation proceedings in the courts demonstrate, the hurt to honour and reputation felt by most plaintiffs attaches to the publication of the matter complained of by various outlets of the media. They are very powerful. The law of defamation is one of the comparatively few checks upon their great power.[50]

In the European Court of Human Rights, Judge Loucaides, in a concurring opinion in *Lindon v France* spoke of the need for the media to 'remain legally accountable to the persons concerned for any false defamatory allegations', and that 'Like any power, the mass media cannot be accountable only to themselves'.[51] Writing extra-judicially, Sir David Eady defended the reverse burden of proof in

[49]H Nissenbaum, *Privacy in Context* (Stanford University Press, 2010) 237.
[50](1994) 33 NSWLR 680, 700.
[51]*Lindon v France* (2008) 46 EHRR 35.

defamation law by referring to the 'awesome power of the press' and queried whether an already powerful institution should benefit from an assumption that 'their allegations, however serious, are true?'[52] Paul Mitchell has also written that it was 'no coincidence' that the affirmation of a strict liability standard in defamation law in *Hulton v Jones* came at a time that saw the growth of mass circulation newspapers and a change in journalistic style that emphasises personal interest stories.[53] The strictness of defamation laws can be seen in part as a response to concerns about press power. The context of *Campbell* and the preceding debate suggest a similar response to media power, albeit a century later, took place in creating the new privacy tort.

What is media power

The discussion so far has assumed that the term 'media power' has a clear meaning. The term is intuitively appealing and seems to capture a sense of why press ethics are so important. As Onora O'Neill argues, the 'communication of the powerful can shape and influence, improve and damage others' lives' and therefore provides a rationale for controls on the media.[54] Yet as Freedman points out, the popular usage of the term 'media power' begs a range of questions – for example, 'what is the nature of this power', whom is it held by and over whom is the power exerted.[55] These questions are most commonly asked in relation to the political power of the press, to shape public opinion and influence government. The type of power considered here is more specific in looking at the capacity of the press to reveal private facts and shape a person's public identity. This type of power is connected with the political power of the press, as the power to expose and shame is one of the most potent tools held by the media to gain attention and shape opinion. Furthermore, the capacity to expose also gives the media leverage over officials and those in positions of power. A politician may think twice before taking on the media, for fear that it will trigger intensive scrutiny into aspects of his life. While linked to political power in the broad sense, the concern here is on a particular type of exercise of power over specific individuals.

At this stage, it may be objected that all privacy cases are to some degree about power. If person A shares an intimate secret with person B, then the latter enjoys some degree of power in relation to former. For example, the ex-boyfriend who

[52]D Eady, 'Defamation: Some Recent Developments and Non-Developments' in M Saville and R Susskind (eds), *Essays in Honour of Sir Brian Neil: the Quintessential Judge* (Lexis Nexis, 2003) 155.

[53]P Mitchell, 'Nineteenth Century Defamation: Was It A Law Of The Press' (2008) 75 *Amicus Curiae* 27, 31. However, Mitchell notes that the court took a more sympathetic approach to the press on other issues in defamation.

[54]O O'Neil, 'The Rights of Journalism and the Needs of Audiences' in J Lewis and P Crick (eds), *Media Law and Ethics in the 21st Century* (Routledge, 2014) 41.

[55]D Freedman, *The Contradictions of Media Power* (Bloomsbury, 2014) 2–3.

publishes revenge pornography exerts a type of power over his former girlfriend. Information confers some degree of power, which is what gives it such value as a building block for social relationships.[56] The information is shared on the understanding that the power will not be abused.[57] It is nonetheless assumed here that the media have traditionally held a distinctive type of power. To develop this point, I will take a simple account of media power, which refers to media institutions having unequal economic and organisational resources to investigate and communicate private information about others, while enjoying a degree of authority from a substantial audience. While the workings of media power are more complex, this simple account helps to explain why concerns about informational privacy have often focused on the media.

There are several factors that have traditionally given the media power in privacy cases. The first is that the institutional media normally has far greater opportunity to communicate to a mass audience than most other people. If the mass media publish details about your private life, such matters will become widely available to the world at large. What is more, the institutional media does not just make such information available, but commands attention. It is likely to be seen by a significant number of people. Eady J referred to this power in *CTB*, stating that it 'is fairly obvious that wall-to-wall excoriation in national newspapers, whether tabloid or "broadsheet", is likely to be significantly more intrusive and distressing for those concerned than the availability of information on the Internet'.[58] The power of the media means that it is in a greater position to inflict greater harm on privacy rights.

Furthermore, there is typically an inequality of communicative power between the person being reported on and the media institution. The relationship between the media and the subject of a disclosure can be contrasted with the relationship between two individuals. If person A discloses something embarrassing about person B among a circle of B's friend and acquaintances, the latter can contextualise the information through a reply. For example, the interpretation of the fact of B's arrest for a public order offence may change if B explains that it was on a political protest.[59] However, in the case of a media disclosure, the inequality in communicative power means that, most individuals lack the resources to make an effective reply that contextualises the media story. The ability to reply is important, but should not be overstated as a means to combat unwanted disclosures. For example, when revealing that someone has a terminal illness or circulating a nude photograph, the individual does not want to contextualise that information, but is likely to wish that it had never been released.

---

[56] C Fried 'Privacy' (1968) 77 *Yale Law Journal* 475.
[57] *ibid* 481.
[58] *CTB v News Group Newspapers* [2011] EWHC 1326 [24].
[59] The example is taken from Nissenbaum (n 49) 80.

Closely related to communicative power are concerns about the authority of the media. If the media publishes a story unambiguously declaring a person's sexual orientation or illness, the status of press means that the story is not treated as a mere rumour, but becomes almost a matter of public record. The concern with the press is that it is not simply another voice that interprets a person's actions, but it can more or less define a person in the public eye and it will be hard for the person to shake that definition off, given the authority, influence and circulation of the media. Just as we may object to government institutions labelling people in certain ways without chance for correction, we have similar concerns about the press acting in such a way. While nobody can be the sole author of their public profile and a sceptical approach to strong claims of informational autonomy should be taken, there is a strong argument that people should not be completely defined by the communication of a particular person or institution. People should have the right to negotiate their public profile, challenge claims made and contextualise information.

In response to this line of argument, the point is sometimes made that widespread dissemination should not be equated with maximal harm to privacy interests.[60] People may be most concerned when private information is repeated to a friend, relative or colleague. The loss of dignity, it is thought, can be most acute when facing the people immediately around us. For example, a person may be happy for the general public to know that he is having an extra-marital affair, but simply wants to keep it from his wife and immediate family. That much will, however, depend on the particular circumstances. Furthermore, the fact that greatest harm occurs from a particular disclosure does not mean the privacy interest is deserving of strong protection. While disclosing the fact of an affair to a person's partner may be regarded as most damaging, there is an argument that the partner has the strongest interest in receiving that information.[61] While disclosures to certain individuals may cause the greatest harm in some cases, the matter is complex and will depend on the nature of the issue and people involved. The position with the mass media is less complex and a general assumption can be made that publication to the world at large will in most cases harm the privacy interest. Publication in the media will more or less guarantee that the information reaches the people that the claimant wants to keep it from and that it will be received by people that lack a corresponding interest to know the information.

A further objection to using media power as a rationale for the legal protection of privacy is that the law is not concerned solely with the conduct of powerful actors. The media may only be able to get hold of information with the assistance

[60]See R Post , 'The Social Foundations of Privacy: Community and Self in the Common Law Tort' (1989) 77 *California Law Review* 957, 989–90

[61]Though Eady expressed skepticism as to whether the press can act as relationship counselor. *CTB v News Group Newspapers* [2011] EWHC 1326 [27].

of sources that lack institutional power. Lord Nicholls in *Campbell* noted that the primary source of the harm was the individual within *Narcotics Anonymous* that tipped off the *Daily Mirror*.[62] Such an analysis, however, seems to fit with traditional breach of confidence. In terms of misuse of private information, *Campbell* is primarily focused on the actions of the media. While the actions of the source may be reprehensible, it seems likely that the claimant's main concern was not the betrayal by the group member, but having the details splashed all over the tabloid newspapers. Widespread publicity may not be required in all misuse of private information cases, but the power to publicise is certain a relevant factor and will generally damage any privacy interests.

The inequality of power in media cases can also be distinguished from the reciprocity that may be found between individuals in the social setting. For example, person A and B will share information with each other about their own lives and trust the other not to disclose it. If A breaches that trust, then there is a danger that B will release private information about A. The breach may lead to the loss of that social relationship. This does not stop people disclosing private information, but there is a social cost that acts as a deterrent. In some cases, people will decide that the social cost is worth paying. For example, if a relationship has already ended, then one party may feel the social cost of disclosing the information is minimal. The reciprocal deterrent is also limited where the information exchanged is of a different nature. If person A holds a nude photograph of B, that is likely to confer greater power than B holding details of A's salary. The level of reciprocity may also be affected by the status of the parties. If person A is a celebrity, then disclosure will generate considerable interest, which is unlikely to be gained from disclosing something about the non-celebrity B. Despite these limits, social relations can impose a restraint on disclosure. By contrast, the media institution acquires its information through professional means or by paying others, rather than exchanging information about itself. Consequently, the media is not usually constrained by the reciprocal exchange of personal information that is the norm in social relationships. The media institution might have to consider costs of a different nature prior to publication. For example, it will have to calculate the risks of a celebrity not cooperating with the publication in future if they publish the private information. However, those costs are different from those in a social setting.

The process of media newsgathering also points to another dimension of media power that contrasts with the sharing of personal information in other contexts. The average individual will normally acquire private information about a relatively small number of people (through social sharing) or information of a limited type about a larger number of people (such as a doctor getting only medical information). By contrast, the possibilities for media investigation have few limits. The media have the means and networks (and in some cases legal

---

[62] *Campbell* [33].

privileges) to gather information about any person they take an interest in and attempt to look into any aspect of that person's life. The media can choose which stories to pursue and whose lives to investigate. The possibility of investigation gives the media power even where it does not publish an intrusive story about a particular person.

Consequences of the media focus

So far the discussion has shown that the introduction of the tort was justified in terms of abuses of media power. The mass media context is not, however, merely a matter of justification, but has arguably shaped the content of the tort. Here it will be argued that in claims against media defendants, the courts have taken a broad definition of private information and may even be extending the tort to cover media intrusions. Furthermore, the media context explains why misuse of private information cases have been preoccupied with press freedom, using a public interest test as the primary means to strike the balance. Finally, the rationale of constraining press power provides a possible reason why powerful claimants tend to receive little public sympathy in privacy claims.

Starting with the first stage of the *Campbell* test, the question is whether the claimant has a reasonable expectation of privacy. The courts have stated that the expectation does not *solely* depend on the nature of the information, but also the circumstances of the case. The relevant factors include the nature of the activity being disclosed, the location of activity, the nature and purpose of the intrusion, and how the defendant got hold of that information.[63] On this approach, the expectation not to be subject to media intrusion and have personal details disseminated in the media for profit will often apply to a wider range of information than is the case with other forms of attention. Having aspects of our personal life gossiped about among acquaintances might be expected, but publication in the media would breach the expectation of privacy. The courts have held that it is one thing for an ex-husband to complain among friends about his wife's adultery, but another to sell his story to a newspaper.[64]

The expansion of the range of protected information in media cases is illustrated by cases concerning photographs in public places. In *Campbell*, Baroness Hale stated that to fulfil the reasonable expectation test the 'activity photographed must be private' and that there is nothing private about how the claimant 'looks if and when she pops out to the shops for a bottle of milk'.[65] The court seemed to move beyond this approach in *Murray*, where the court was faced with a claim that a photograph of a family walking in the street violated a small child's expectation of privacy. The photographs did not capture an obviously private activity

[63] *Murray v Express Newspapers* [2008] EWCA Civ 446, [2009] Ch 481 [36].
[64] *ibid* [35].
[65] *Campbell* [154].

and were not embarrassing or humiliating. The Court of Appeal nonetheless found the child to have an arguable claim, stating that a reasonable expectation of privacy depends on circumstances of the case.[66] While partly influenced by the expanded protection of images by the Strasbourg Court,[67] the domestic judicial reasoning seems to be pre-occupied with the power of the media. In *Murray*, the Court of Appeal noted that widespread publicity in newspapers is intrusive and can adversely affect a person's private recreational activity. Sir Anthony Clarke MR stated 'the law should indeed protect children from intrusive media attention'.[68]

The approach of the courts, therefore, does not treat private information as a fixed category and much will depend on the context of the case. The approach taken in *Murray* provides flexibility, in which information might be private for some purposes but not for others. Such an approach is consistent with Nissenbaum's view that privacy is 'neither a right to secrecy nor a right to control but a right to appropriate flow of personal information', which depends on the particular context.[69] The mass media poses challenges to privacy in so far as it takes information that was previously limited to a specific context and releases it to the world at large. The context sensitive approach means that, while the tort is of general application, specific factors may operate to increase the level of control over media publications. While the flexibility of the approach is useful, it raises difficult questions as to what contextual factors shape the expectation of privacy and in what way. Furthermore, the expansion of the tort to control the publication of relatively innocuous images strains the elements of the cause of action that is supposed to protect *private* information.

Another area of expansion is the element of *misuse* of information in the tort. The requirement of 'misuse' of private information has typically referred to the disclosure or publication of information.[70] In some cases, the courts have hinted that the acquisition of information without publication would be actionable. In the non-media case of *Imerman*, Lord Neuberger stated 'it would be a breach of confidence for a defendant, without the authority of the claimant, to examine, or to make, retain, or supply copies to a third party' of a confidential document.[71] A similar extension of the conditions for the *Campbell* tort appears to have been assumed in the recent phone hacking decisions in *Gulati*, in which the defendants accepted liability for accessing private phone messages even where the information acquired was not used in a subsequent publication. For example,

---

[66]The approach was later confirmed in *Weller v Associated Newspapers* [2014] EWHC 2127.
[67]See *Reklos v Greece* [2009] EMLR 16.
[68]*Murray v Express Newspapers* [2008] EWCA Civ 446, [2009] Ch 481 [57].
[69]Nissenbaum (n 49) 127.
[70]R Wacks, *Privacy and Media Freedom* (OUP, 2013) 247, citing Hoffmann's reference to 'dissemination' in *Campbell*.
[71]*Tchenguiz v Imerman* [2010] EWCA Civ 908 [69]. Though compare *Abbey v Gilligan* [2012] EWHC 3217 [61–63].

Alan Yentob received damages for misuse following an interception of his messages, even though he was not the subject of any articles based on the information acquired.[72] Along these lines, the case proceeded on the basis that misappropriation, as well as disclosure, constitutes a misuse of private information.[73] Furthermore, in some places the court suggested that liability in the tort can arise when the defendant publishes information acquired through intrusive means, even when that information would not normally be considered private.[74] So, it seems, that a prima facie case for misuse of private information can be made even where the information is not private (as traditionally understood) or misused (in the sense of being disseminated). Instead, the reasoning in *Gulati* suggests the method of acquiring the information can violate the expectation.

The decision in *Gulati* was only to assess damages and the scope of the tort was not the issue before the court. If the change in the scope of the tort is confirmed then it will possibly be as big a step as that taken in *Campbell* (if not bigger).[75] What is important for the present discussion is that such a shift partly comes on the back of another media scandal, this time in relation to phone hacking. Of course, concerns about intrusion are not restricted to the media, but the objections to such intrusion seem particularly compelling when associated with a powerful actor. The high level of damages in *Gulati* reflected the tabloid newspaper's industrial scale hacking and interceptions. The persistent monitoring and intrusion into personal messages could, Mann J stated, contribute to a 'sense of persecution'.[76] That sense of persecution can come from the fact that a powerful actor is mobilising its resources against you and repeatedly picking on you. Such harms are amplified by the investigative powers of the media and its power to publicise what it discovers (even if that power is not exercised). If the tort is expanded in this way, it begs the question as to what type of intrusion provides the basis for tort liability. Phone hacking provides an easy case, as most people would see such a method as a gross intrusion whether by the media or anyone else. Would non-criminal methods such as photographing or recording be deemed an intrusive method of capturing information? The desire to constrain media power may, again, steer the courts towards a broader application.

The above discussion argues that the tort has expanded partly as a response to the power of the media to publicise and investigate.[77] The difficulty is that one of the things the media is expected to do is take information from various contexts

---

[72]*Gulati and Others v MGN* [2015] EWHC 1482 [15].
[73]*ibid* [143].
[74]*ibid* [224], [228]. However, compare *Abbey v Gilligan* [2012] EWHC 3217 [35], stressing the nature of the information as the key factor.
[75]For an argument for such a step, see N Moreham, 'Beyond Information: Physical Privacy in English Law' (2014) 73 *Cambridge Law Journal* 350, 375–7.
[76]*Gulati and Others v MGN* [2015] EWHC 1482 [229].
[77]I use the word 'partly' as *Imerman* was not a media case. However, the issue of media intrusion is likely spur on such a development.

and bring it to the world at large. At its best, the media is expected to shine a light on areas that are less visible to the public. Similarly, the media is expected to investigate certain areas, leaving no stone unturned. While the media holds a power that can be abused, that power is also necessary to perform its social function. For that reason, privacy controls can be on a collision course with media freedom. The presence of this tension explains the sharp focus on the public interest in deciding whether the publication of private facts is justified. When media institutions act as servants of the people in providing information and holding government to account, then their power is legitimated.[78] Asking whether the publication was in the public interest or not, is another way of asking whether the media was acting pursuant to its public function or abusing its power. The balancing stage of the *Campbell* test has therefore been seen as resolving a tension between privacy rights and expression rights. That approach has been forged largely with media defendants in mind. Some adjustment may be required when private individuals are defendants in privacy cases. While an individual speaker may assert a public interest in disclosure, there may be other justifications that warrant stronger weight, such as the individual's right to tell his life story. The sharp focus on an audience-centred account of the public interest highlights the concern with the institutional power of the press.

Finally, the concern with constraining media power maybe explains why people are hostile to the use of privacy laws by the famous, wealthy or powerful. For example, many seem to have little sympathy for Douglas, Zeta-Jones, Campbell and Ryan Giggs, but are more troubled when a non-celebrity is being ridiculed in the press. If we view privacy law solely as protecting rights, that reaction makes little sense. Both celebrity and private citizen enjoy the same rights. One response is to assume that the celebrity has to some degree waived their rights by stepping into the limelight. While there is force in that argument, another explanation is that the inequality of power is not as great in the case of the celebrity. Douglas, Zeta-Jones and Campbell were not defined in the public eye by the one disclosure. Their public profiles were well established. The celebrity might also have greater chance to respond to and contextualise any disclosures.[79] The private individual, by contrast, has little opportunity to reply, and the disclosure of private information may be the only piece of information about that person known to the world at large. Of course, there are some types of disclosure that might define and have a big impact on even the public figure.[80] Inequalities of power can still emerge, but the communicative power of the celebrity might explain why their complaints often win little public support.

---

[78] *Observer v UK* (1992) 14 EHRR 153 [59].

[79] See Richards (n 5) 56.

[80] Max Mosley is the obvious example of a person having an existing public profile redefined as a consequence of a media disclosure.

The shift in media communications

So far, I have argued that *Campbell* was decided against the backdrop of increasing concern about the power of the mass media. Yet the House of Lords' decision came at a moment in which power was seen to be shifting away from traditional media sources and towards the users of the new media, who could more easily produce, disseminate and share content. 2003 saw the launch of MySpace, which grew as a popular social network and was bought by News Corporation in 2005. Four months before *Campbell* was decided, the then Harvard student Mark Zuckerberg launched Facebook. Around this period, the term 'Web 2.0′ became popular and a spate of books and magazine articles championed the revolutionary potential of such technologies. For example, a month after *Campbell* was decided, Dan Gillmor, in *We the Media*, wrote about 'journalism's transformation from a twentieth century mass-media structure to something more grassroots and democratic'.[81] In 2006, *Time Magazine* named 'You' as the person of the year, as a result of the tools 'for bringing together the small contributions of millions of people and making them matter'.[82] The technologies continued to develop, with Twitter being launched in 2006 and many other communication tools, such as Snapchat and Instagram, have become hugely popular in more recent years.

These developments are often thought to challenge the traditional view of media power, transferring greater communicative power into the hands of other speakers. The most obvious change is in the power to disseminate. As has already been indicated, the power to communicate is now more widely distributed. People have the opportunity to make information available to a mass audience, and in some cases that information also gains mass attention.

The second type of change is in the way information is gathered. Much of what we do is recorded and potentially monitored. For example, the prevalence of digital cameras means that people can easily be photographed at any time, and the resulting image shared within seconds. Celebrities are more likely to be photographed in public places by people with a phone than by paparazzi. Such capabilities to gather information are only likely increase with the technology. While the issue of photographs taken in public places has been particularly difficult following *Campbell*, the new technology poses new scenarios, whereby devices used in public places can monitor and remotely gather considerable intimate data – such as a thermal image or a person's heart rate. With such technology a tabloid or gossip website could use such devices in a public place to surreptitiously determine whether a celebrity's new girlfriend really does raise his heart rate or temperature. This is just one example of the new types of intrusion and others include companies tracking the data of individuals' Internet browsing habits, search terms and so on. New technologies facilitate intrusive investigation not just by the media but

[81]D Gillmor, *We the Media* (O'Reilly, 2004) xxii.
[82]L Grossman, 'You – Yes, You – Are TIME's Person of the Year', *TIME*, 25 December 2006.

also by other actors. The types of intrusion seen in the phone hacking scandal are not confined to large well-resourced organisations, and can be committed by people that have the technical skills to hack into a person's email or social media accounts

The third change is in the aggregation of data. A single photograph of a person in a public place may raise minimal privacy issues. A sequence of photographs of that individual taken throughout the day, each taken by different users, could be aggregated to provide a picture of that person's various movements over a period of time. The problem is well known in the era of big data, that information not thought to be private when viewed in isolation can be far more intrusive when assembled with lots of other data. As stated, the more flexible interpretation on the reasonable expectation test provides some guard against this development. However, the application of the tort to such uses strains the cause of action said to be about private information. The difficulty seems to be that lots of information captured and shared every day, none of which is sensitive or private in itself, has the potential to become private once aggregated.

The discussion above notes just three developments, and there are many others. Privacy interests face threats from an increasing range of actors. However, the discussion of media power that preceded *Campbell* should not be dismissed as old fashioned. While the technology has had a revolutionary effect, concerns about mass media power remain important. Newspapers still have strong incentives to publish intrusive stories and inequalities in communicative power are likely to persist.[83] This does not mean that the same institutions will dominate. Power may shift from old to new media institutions. Nonetheless, at present the traditional media institutions continue to hold considerable power. Even those who largely celebrate the changes in communications as a democratising force still accept that the media continues to play a powerful role.[84]

The arguments about constraining media power and making it accountable retain their force, but the media is just one piece of the picture. Threats to privacy can come from a number of other sources. Much discussion now focuses on the threat posed by the major technology companies that collect data about users, such as Google, Facebook, Apple, Amazon, and so on. The concern with the threat to privacy from such powerful companies may be seen to follow on from the earlier concern with the mass media – the campaign for privacy has simply shifted from one set of powerful actors to another. As a result, the *Campbell* tort may be increasingly invoked where a technology

[83]J Rowbottom, 'Media Freedom and Political Debate in the Digital Era' (2006) 69 *Modern Law Review* 489.

[84]For example, M Naim, *The End of Power* (Basic Books, 2013) 215–16; H Jenkins, S Ford and J Green, *Spreadable Media* (NYU Press, 2013) 15, 259.

company shares collected data.[85] However, the tort may not be as well suited to tackling some of the distinctive privacy issues raised by such companies.[86] For example, Internet users may be concerned about a company holding data on search enquiries or purchasing habits for long periods, even where that information has not been acquired through intrusion or been disseminated. Instead, it seems likely that data protection laws will take on an increasingly important role in relation to such companies.

The specific privacy interest at stake in the *Campbell* tort, primarily protection from unwanted publicity, has also been affected by the changes in communications. Ordinary people have increasing power to gather information about people, disseminate that information and allow that information to be aggregated with similar information or posted on easily accessible sites. Anyone has the means to shame, humiliate and harass. In some instances, misuse of private information provides a remedy. For example, if person A posts medical information about person B on a social network, then there is a clear case of misuse of the information. In other cases, the *Campbell* framework might need some adjustment. For example, the discussion earlier argued that the concern with media intrusions has led the court to take a broad definition of private information and its misuse. This begs the question of whether a narrower approach to the reasonable expectation test should be applied in relation to non-media speakers. Is the comment on a social network akin to the person sharing information with friends and family or should it be seen as equivalent to a media publication? If the tort is expanded to include intrusion as well as dissemination, then should it apply to an individual taking a photograph in a street or accessing confidential documents that that have been posted on a leaker website. Changes may also be required at the second stage of the *Campbell* test; individual speakers are not bound to serve the public interest and greater emphasis may be placed on their expression rights.[87]

While challenging, these examples at least can be analysed in the *Campbell* framework as an identifiable speaker has posted arguably private information. More difficult examples arise where there is no clear agent responsible for the invasion of privacy. An obvious example arises where a person posts a message to small group of people and that message quickly gets recirculated and goes viral. In various examples, people have quickly become the objects of national or even worldwide ridicule. In such scenarios, there may be no institution with a concentration of power or even an individual acting to destroy someone's privacy. Instead, such publicity can come from a largely leaderless and undirected

[85]For example, *Vidal-Hall v Google* [2015] EWCA Civ 311.
[86]For discussion of the various privacy issues posed by technology companies, see P Bernal, *Internet Privacy Rights* (CUP, 2014).
[87]Along such lines, Laws LJ distinguishes the justifications for individual and media expression in *R (Miranda) v Secretary of State for the Home Department* [2014] EWHC 255.

form of power, where the harmful consequences come from the aggregate effect of lots of different users. In his recent book on shaming, Jon Ronson commented that he initially viewed such decentralised communications as a type of 'democratization of justice'.[88] However, the flip side is that such behaviour can amount to a 'mobocracy' in which sheer numbers can have a devastating impact on a person's life. The person may struggle to reply to or contextualise such information, which comes to define him publicly. With the lack of an identifiable agent, it is hard to pinpoint a specific abuse of power and liability in tort law may not be an effective form of redress.[89]

A further problem concerns the scope of the expectation of privacy. For example, a person may choose to share a photograph, with the world at large, of himself on a drunken night out. However, that person may not want it to be the first image for an indefinite period that anyone sees of him following a Google search. The person may not want the photo to be sent to prospective employers. Having been voluntarily shared, the information is not obviously private. Yet at the same time, the desire not to have a single image or piece of information entirely define a person's public profile touches on an aspect of privacy. The information only starts to interfere with privacy interests once it has been widely shared and made prominent.

Several years ago, Jonathan Zittrain described such phenomena as 'Privacy 2.0′ and warned that people will soon have to act like politicians running for high office.[90] The potential for pervasive and persistent scrutiny means that people will have to show restraint for fear of a possible public backlash. Even if most people are not subject to the worldwide ridicule bestowed on some unfortunate individuals, the potential can still have a deterrent effect. The current culture is one in which an ill-judged remark, joke or gaffe can result in sudden social and professional death.

The discussion shows that the capacity to invade privacy through unwanted publicity is no longer limited to powerful institutions. The concerns about informational privacy rights and the abuse of concentrated power do not always go together. The protection of privacy in *Campbell* was partly a method of making powerful media entities legally accountable for their actions. The question now arises as to how far such a tort should regulate the conduct of non-media institutions. If the focus is on abuse of institutional power, the scope of privacy protection should be more limited against non-powerful actors. To broaden the scope of

[88] J Ronson, *So You've Been Publicly Shamed* (Picador, 2015) 9. After setting out his initial view, the author makes clear the potentially disproportionate effects of such digital opprobrium.

[89] Parallel issues have arisen in contempt of court proceedings involving publications by multiple media defendants, in which the court has to consider each publication separately rather than the aggregate effects of all the media coverage. See *Attorney General v MGN* [1997] EMLR 284.

[90] J Zittrain, *The Internet and How to Stop It* (Allen Lane, 2008) 211–12.

tort liability would potentially interfere with ordinary social relations. On the other hand, when considering the impact on privacy rights, the potential for such information to be made persistently available and widely shared points to a broader scope for private information. The remedies and procedures associated with tort liability may be unsuitable to deal with this tension in many cases involving the threats to privacy posed by non-powerful actors. As a result, it may mean that for the most part, *Campbell* remains a tort that is largely focused on mass media defendants.

Alternatives to the *Campbell* tort

There are several responses that are typically advanced when discussing the new challenges to privacy. All options have pros and cons. One radical response is to consign privacy, as it is currently understood, to the past. The line of argument runs that we live in a society with greater transparency across the board. This brings many advantages in terms of freedom of communication and in acquiring information. Loss of privacy is one of the costs. The idea is that everyone will have certain things in their lives that they are embarrassed about, and having some unwanted publicity about things we would rather keep secret is simply one of life's vicissitudes. Versions of this view have, at various times, been attributed to people at the highest levels of the technology companies.[91] This is not the place to discuss the argument at any length, other than to note that it is a convenient position for technology companies to adopt. It currently seems doubtful that such a relaxation of attitude is taking place.[92] In any event, such an argument does not explain whether the change is desirable or not.

A second response is that people should take their own steps to protect privacy. For example, people may choose to engage a reputation management firm, which can take steps to ensure private information is found lower down search rankings. To do this, people may need to develop alternative websites and personal profiles, which will take priority over the intrusive sources in the rankings. The technique aims not to eradicate, but to bury the damaging information. There are, of course limits to this method. Employing such a firm may be costly and therefore not open to everyone. People may not want to construct a counter-narrative of their lives in order to deal with such issues.[93] The attack on privacy can thereby force a person to develop a public profile, yet the person might prefer not to undertake such a course of action. Part of privacy may be the freedom not to construct a public profile.

[91]For example, Mark Zuckerberg was reported to have said that the days of having different images among different groups was 'coming to an end pretty quickly': D Kirkpatrick, *The Facebook Effect* (Virgin Books, 2010) 199.
[92]For discussion of the transparency argument see Bernal (n 86) 48–50.
[93]See the account given by Ronson (n 88) 251–4.

A third response is that controls should be imposed on the recipient of the information, rather than the speaker. As US scholar Frank Pasquale argues, 'It may be that we cannot stop the collection of information, but we can regulate how it is used'.[94] For example, while it is difficult to stop private information seeping out of the social networks, maybe employers or recruiters, for example, could be subject to regulations controlling the use of such data in their hiring or other management decisions.[95] Under this strategy, the focus is not on disclosure, but on the *use* of private information and ensuring the use of fair procedures. Such a strategy comes with shortcomings. It does not address problems of hurt feelings caused by the embarrassment of publicity. In any event, it can prove very difficult to determine whether people have seen the private information and whether they have been able to eradicate it (consciously or unconsciously) from their decision-making processes.

Finally, different types of legal remedy targeting different actors may be appropriate. In particular, various intermediaries – search engines, social networks and other platforms – can find themselves becoming the targets for regulation and legal liability. Here the technology company is targeted not for its own data collection and monitoring of users, but for its role in facilitating invasions of privacy by other users. When private information is shared and published by hundreds and thousands of different sources, it is always more efficient to choke off the flow via the various gatekeepers, rather than target each speaker. In some respects, this approach is consistent with rationale underlying *Campbell*, in so far as the powerful actor is targeted. The ISP can be seen to take on the mantle of the new powerful gatekeeper, which can influence which voices are to be heard and made prominent. Of course, the ISP does not create the content, and so can be seen to bear less responsibility than the traditional media.

The type of control that is appropriate for intermediaries may in some instances differ from those applicable to the media. The right to be forgotten is an obvious example of an attempt to forge a new control on certain intermediaries to combat some of these newer problems.[96] In some ways, that right strikes a balance by permitting the disclosure of information, while at the same time seeking to limit its circulation. Such measures are controversial. In particular, there is a question of how the right to be forgotten is defined and what sort of information is protected under the right. There is a further question of whether the current right gives adequate protection for freedom of expression and the public's right to know. Finally, there are considerable reservations about the delegation of the decision on privacy protection to a private company, which may be tempted to err on the side of caution and remove more content to avoid liability. An ideal approach would at least allow for some system for claims to be independently adjudicated and for the relevant speaker to have an opportunity to contest

[94] F Pasquale, *Black Box Society* (Harvard University Press, 2015) 57.
[95] *ibid* 148–53.
[96] See *Google Spain SL v Agencia Espanola de Proteccion de Datos* [2014] QB 1022.

the claim. While intermediary liability raises difficult questions and needs to be approached with caution, it should not be dismissed. Some ISPs are powerful actors in the digital environment. While an ISP provides a platform for others and may not produce the offending content, it facilitates the widespread communication. Some form of regulation at least attempts to generate accountability for certain concentrations of power.

The discussion so far has not been to endorse any of these strategies, but to outline the various alternatives to the *Campbell* tort. Various strategies should be tested and subjected to experimentation to address different threats to privacy and strike the right balance. Such an approach continues the British tradition of piecemeal protection of privacy, albeit with new protections being developed to deal with the new threats.

Conclusion

This essay has considered the relationship between misuse of private information and concerns about media power. The decision in *Campbell* was made following longstanding complaints about the abuse of media power and the perceived failure of Parliament to address such issues. At the time, concerns about the abuse of media power and the infringement of privacy rights went hand in hand. No sooner did the new cause of action arrive, than the communications environment changed dramatically. Those changes should not be overstated, and the concerns about mass media power remain a key concern today. Unwanted publicity and intrusions can, however, come from a range of different sources. Privacy can now be infringed through channels of mass communication without the abuse of any concentrated institutional power. Furthermore, such infringements can occur through the aggregations of individual actions, none of which generate significant harm individually. Other types of power relation can still be found in the background, such as the gatekeeping power of the intermediary. The argument pursued here is that the justification and development of the tort in *Campbell* was focused on a mass media context. As the threat of unwanted publicity and intrusion moves beyond that context, the framework and approach to tort liability may not be so easily transferable, and other methods of protection may become more important as the distribution of communicative power continues to change.

Acknowledgements

With thanks to participants of the 'The Campbell Legacy' workshop at Newcastle Law School in April 2015.

Disclosure statement

No potential conflict of interest was reported by the author.

A just balance or just imbalance? The role of metaphor in misuse of private information

Rebecca Moosavian

This article undertakes analysis of misuse of private information (MPI) caselaw informed by deconstruction and wider literary and critical theory. It specifically considers the rhetorical effect of the 'balance' metaphor in MPI caselaw. It starts by providing an account of select theorists who explore the subtle but vital role that metaphor, traditionally viewed as a poetic or literary device, plays in non-literary texts. This account highlights the fundamental role of metaphor in legal discourse. Following this discussion, the article investigates the 'balance' metaphor in MPI judgments. It identifies and analyses two distinct ways in which the balance metaphor subtly benefits judicial reasoning. First, it creates an impression of certainty by drawing on connotations of the quantifiable and calculable. Second, it fosters the moral appeal of a decision by alluding to notions of justice and equilibrium. In doing so, the balance metaphor marginalises the non-rational, inexpressible aspects of judicial rights balancing.

In Demonstration, in Councell, and all rigorous search of Truth, Judgement does all … But for Metaphors, they are in this case utterly excluded. For seeing they openly professe deceipt; to admit them into Councell, or Reasoning, were manifest folly.[1]

What then is truth? a mobile army of metaphors, metonyms, and anthromorphisms, in short, a sum of human relations which were poetically and rhetorically heightened, transferred, and adorned, and after long use seem solid, canonical, and binding to a nation. Truths are illusions about which it has been forgotten that they are illusions, worn-out metaphors without sensory impact, coins which have lost their image and now can be used only as metal, and no longer as coins.[2]

[1] T Hobbes, *Leviathan* (Penguin Classics, 1985) Part I, Ch VIII, 136-7.
[2] F Nietzsche, 'On Truth and Lying in an Extra-Moral Sense' in *Friedrich Nietzsche on Rhetoric and Language* (Oxford University Press, 1989) 246–57, 250.

Introduction

Lawyers, like poets, are no strangers to metaphor. For example, legal discourse has adopted the notion of 'ripeness' for judicial review,[3] likened property rights to 'bundles of sticks',[4] excluded evidence as the 'fruit of the poisonous tree,[5] implicitly condemned claimants' 'fishing expeditions'[6] and retained Lockean agrarian imagery in copyright.[7] Law then, it seems, has its very own mobile army of metaphors. This article is concerned with one particular metaphor; that of 'balance'. The notion of balance is widely used within, and long associated with, law; in particular it constitutes 'one of the central features of postwar Western legal thought and practice'.[8] This article focuses on the role of the 'balance' metaphor in the specific context of misuse of private information jurisprudence.

Misuse of private information (MPI) is a relatively new doctrine that has emerged from a series of post-Human Rights Act 1998 legal disputes, many involving high profile claimants seeking to restrain publication of personal information by tabloid defendants.[9] The core of the action is an '*inter*right conflict'[10] between the Article 8 right of privacy[11] and the Article 10 right to free expression,[12] and to manage this conflict judges have created the 'balancing exercise'. Elsewhere, the author has undertaken deconstructive analysis of this binary opposition, examining how Articles 8 and 10 and their primary underlying dichotomy, 'public interest' versus 'interesting the public', are in some senses reversible, mutually reliant and not entirely distinct.[13] That analysis revealed some of the culturally-specific assumptions that silently shape understandings of the public interest dichotomy,

---

[3]James E Murray, 'Understanding Law as Metaphor' (1984) 34 *Journal of Legal Education* 714, 720–22.

[4]Thomas Ross, 'Metaphor and Paradox' (1989) 23 *Georgia Law Review* 1053, 1055–63.

[5]*ibid* 1067–69

[6]Elizabeth G Thornburg, 'Just Say "No Fishing": The Lure of Metaphor' (2006) 40 *University of Michigan Journal of Law Reform* 1.

[7]William Patry, 'Metaphors and Moral Panics in Copyright: the Stephen Stewart Memorial Lecture' [2008] *Intellectual Property Quarterly* 1, 8–10.

[8]Jacco Bomhoff, *Balancing Constitutional Rights, The Origins and Meanings of Postwar Legal Discourse* (Cambridge University Press, 2013) 1.

[9]Rebecca Moosavian, 'Charting the Journey from Confidence to the New Methodology' (2012) 34(5) *European Intellectual Property Review* 324–35.

[10]Jeremy Waldron, 'Rights in Conflict' (1989) 99 *Ethics* 503, 514.

[11]Article 8, European Convention on Human Rights and Fundamental Freedoms 1950. Art 8(1) states: 'Everyone has the right to respect for his private and family life, his home and his correspondence.'

[12]Article 10, European Convention on Human Rights and Fundamental Freedoms 1950. Art 10(1) states: 'Everyone has the right to freedom of expression. This right shall include freedom to hold opinions and to receive and impart information and ideas without interference by public authority and regardless of frontiers.'

[13]Rebecca Moosavian, 'Deconstructing "Public Interest" in the Article 8 vs Article 10 Balancing Exercise' (2014) 6 *Journal of Media Law* 234.

including Enlightenment-era ideals of intellectual debate, objective truth and democratic participation, and the related privileging of political over non-political speech. It was also found that the notion of the 'public' across MPI discourse is subject to varying constructions for rhetorical ends, shifting from empowered consumers to politically engaged citizens to the voyeuristic masses according to speaker, agenda and context. However, another strand of deconstructive thought has further insights to reveal in this area, namely its concern with the role of metaphor in discourse.

This article undertakes analysis of MPI case law informed by deconstruction and wider literary and critical theory. First, it provides an account of select theorists who explore the subtle but vital role that metaphor plays in non-literary texts. It pays particular attention to Derrida's work on metaphor, though academic interest in metaphor extends far beyond deconstruction. This discussion of the shared origins and history of metaphor and rhetoric is valuable here for three reasons. First, it highlights the various hierarchies operative across political-philosophical history; hierarchies that remain influential, particularly in law and therefore MPI specifically. Second, it shows that metaphors, often hidden, play a rhetorical role in discourses such as philosophy or science, with inevitable implications for claims based on truth, objectivity and reason. Third, it demonstrates the crucial role of metaphors in legal discourse generally, and the role of such metaphors in constituting and shaping our experiences. The second part of this article proceeds to investigate the use of 'balance' as a metaphor in MPI judgments. It considers the rhetorical effect of the rights-'weighting' process, asking what underlying subjectivities such metaphors might betray, and what rhetorically beneficial assumptions they might engender.

1. Metaphor, rhetoric and law

A metaphor is form of trope, the essence of which entails 'understanding and experiencing one kind of thing in terms of another'.[14] It is a device whereby a speaker refers to two different things at once, e.g. by a drawing a comparison, link or substituting one term for another, the second term being redeployed in a different context. In doing so metaphor draws upon similarities or resemblance between the two things. Metaphor has been traditionally viewed as a figurative or poetic form of expression, as distinct from literal, descriptive speech. Unlike the latter, it entails an open-ended form of communication, 'pregnant' with meaning and mystery, drawing links across contexts. Metaphors are seen as non-rational, appealing to the senses (especially visual senses) and playing on emotional responses. One such example is provided in the seminal *Illness as*

[14] George Lakoff and Mark Johnson, *Metaphors We Live By* (University of Chicago Press, 2003) 5.

Metaphor, where Sontag critiques the various metaphors that recur in literary depictions of cancer and tuberculosis.[15] She analyses cancer's portrayal as a parasite and a form of contamination, and the 'language of warfare'[16] with which it is depicted. For Sontag, such imagery cumulatively instils undue fear and dread regarding the disease and is therefore ultimately misleading. Despite this (or perhaps because of it) cancer comes to be adopted in turn as a metaphor in other disciplines. For example, in a political context cancer is a 'specifically polemical' disease;[17] describing an issue as a social cancer highlights the severity of the matter, raises the stakes and justifies drastic measures.[18]

1.1 *Classical views of rhetoric and metaphor*

The origins and characteristics of metaphor are closely entwined with those of rhetoric. Rhetoric, the art of using language to persuade an audience of a particular position, emerged to prominence with the sophists in classical Greek culture. Metaphor was viewed as a rhetorical device which could aid persuasion. Successful participation in the Athenian democratic system necessitated skills of persuasion on the political stage and particularly in the law courts.[19] The origins of rhetoric are thus at least partly legal.

Plato was highly critical of rhetoric as a practice[20] and denounced it in two of his dialogues *Phaedrus*[21] and *Gorgias*.[22] In the latter Plato condemned rhetoric as a mere knack or technique,[23] a form of flattery[24] that panders to the desire of its audience[25] and requires no specific expertise.[26] Instead it forms 'a phantom branch of statesmanship'.[27] Plato depicted rhetoric as inferior and opposed to philosophy in numerous respects. For example, rhetoric is concerned with attaining

[15]Susan Sontag, *Illness as Metaphor* and *AIDS and its Metaphors* (Penguin, 2002).
[16]*ibid* 65. See also 59, 86.
[17]*ibid* 74. See also 86.
[18]*ibid* ch 9, 82–83, 84.
[19]See HC Lawson-Tancred, 'Introduction' in Aristotle, *The Art of Rhetoric* (Penguin Classics, 2004) 8–14.
[20]This is linked to his hostility to the democratic system: Plato, *Republic* (Oxford University Press, 1998) 555b–562a.
[21]Plato, *Phaedrus* (Oxford University Press, 2009).
[22]Plato, *Gorgias* (Oxford University Press, 2008). For an illuminating reading of *Gorgias* see James Boyd White, *When Words Lose their Meaning: Constitutions and Reconstitutions of Language, Character and Community* (University of Chicago Press, 1984) ch 4.
[23]*Gorgias* (n 22) 462c.
[24]*ibid* 463a–b, 466a.
[25]Socrates: '[Flattery] isn't interested in the slightest in the best course of action, but she traps and deceives foolish people with the promise of maximising immediate pleasure, which makes her seem better than any alternative': *ibid* 464c–d. See also 502e; 518e–519a.
[26]*ibid* 459a–c, 462b. See also Plato, *Phaedrus* (n 21) 206a, 206c.
[27]Plato, *Gorgias* (n 22) 463d.

successful outcomes rather than engendering moral virtue;[28] it involves persuasion[29] rather than education,[30] manipulating[31] audiences in disregard of the truth.[32] Woven throughout Plato's account of rhetoric is a cynicism about the motives of rhetoricians and the capacities of their audiences,[33] a dynamic incidentally replicated in judicial understandings of the tabloid press and its readers.[34]

Aristotle also made a significant early contribution to the area, creating *The Art of Rhetoric*, a manual for effective speech. This aimed to put the practice of rhetoric on a more systematic, philosophical footing by attempting to organise discourse into a series of topics. Nonetheless, Aristotle's project still rested upon an implicit distinction between analytics and rhetoric.[35] Aristotle categorised rhetoric as deliberative (political),[36] forensic (legal)[37] or display. Each was directed to a particular audience[38] with the objective of 'bringing the giver of judgement into a certain condition'.[39] Aristotle made a significant distinction between deliberative and forensic (political and legal) oratory; the latter requires greater accuracy, precision and only 'the smallest amount of rhetoric' because the judgment it appeals to is 'pure'.[40] For Aristotle rhetoric is not inherently opposed to truth, but could be used to serve truth by mobilising audience support for it.[41] *Rhetoric* offered general guidance on matters such as understanding the character of an audience,[42] adopting a suitable style[43] and instilling appropriate emotion in

---

[28]*ibid* 506c–507e, 515a, 517b–c.

[29]Plato, *Gorgias*: 'I'm talking about the ability to use the spoken word to persuade – to persuade the jurors in the courts, the members of the Council, the citizens attending the Assembly – in short, to win over any and every form of public meeting in the citizen body' *ibid* 452e–453a.

[30]Socrates: 'A rhetorician, then, isn't concerned to educate the people assembled in lawcourts and so on about right and wrong; all he wants to do is persuade them *ibid* 455a. See also 454d–455a.

[31]Plato, *Phaedrus* (n 21) 267c–268a. On the ethics of persuasion see also James Boyd White, *Heracles' Bow: Essays on Rhetoric and the Poetics of the Law* (University of Wisconsin Press, 1985) ch 1.

[32]Plato, *Gorgias* (n 22) 521d–e; 526b–e. See also Plato, *Phaedrus* (n 21) 272e–273b.

[33]Stanley Fish, *Doing What Comes Naturally* (Clarendon Press, 1989) 473.

[34]Moosavian, 'Deconstructing' (n 13) 250–55.

[35]For an account of Aristotle's rhetoric see Peter Goodrich, 'Rhetoric as Jurisprudence: An Introduction to the Politics of Legal Language' (1984) 4 *Oxford Journal of Legal Studies* 88, 100–105.

[36]Aristotle (n 19) ch 1.4.

[37]*ibid* ch 1.10.

[38]*ibid* ch 1.3.

[39]*ibid* 1377b.

[40]*ibid* 1414a.

[41]*ibid* 1355a.

[42]*ibid* chs 2.12–2.17.

[43]'Experts in these [style and delivery] more or less carry off the prizes at the contests, and just as in the case of the tragedy actors now have more effect than the poets, so is it also in political contests, through the baseness of the citizenry' *ibid* 1403b.

speech.[44] Drawing upon his earlier work in *Poetics*,[45] Aristotle provided some discussion of metaphor as an ornamental, stylistic device and made recommendations for its use in rhetorical speech.[46] He viewed simile and metaphor as a fundamental aspect of style and, crucially, linked their use to a general psychology. The power of metaphor rests 'on the charm of unfamiliarity',[47] and to be effective metaphors must be used clearly and proportionately.[48] Goodrich summarises Aristotle's view of metaphor thus: 'Just as rhetoric is less than philosophy, so too metaphor is less than truth. Metaphor may be persuasive, pleasurable or pleonastic but it will seldom be necessary.'[49]

It is apparent from the preceding account that, as Fish argues, the classical philosophy/rhetoric divide is pervaded by a number of implicit (but contestable) hierarchies such as deep/surface, reason/passion, reality/illusion, fact/opinion and neutral/partisan.[50] Fish traces how the classic opposition rests on an innate privileging of apparently accurate, factual, transparent language over partisan, distorting, fictional language.[51] This classical suspicion of rhetoric and its associated qualities has remained influential. Goodrich charts the historical decline of rhetoric and its subordination to logic[52] and later Enlightenment-era empiricist, rationalist philosophies.[53] He shows how rhetoric has been consistently marginalised or dismissed as trivial, claiming it became 'the other of philosophy'.[54] Fish also shows how such oppositions have recurred across history in various guises,[55] spanning many disciplines, including law.[56] For example, a literal/metaphorical language divide informs criticisms of metaphor as deceitful and dangerous in the works

[44] *ibid* ch 2.1.

[45] Aristotle, *Poetics* (Penguin, 1996) ch 21, ch 25.

[46] For an account of Aristotle's metaphor see Goodrich, 'Rhetoric as Jurisprudence' (n 35) 106–107. Interesting discussion can also be found in Jacques Derrida 'White Mythology: Metaphor in the Text of Philosophy' in *Margins of Philosophy* (University of Chicago Press, 1984) 230–45; Paul Ricoeur, *The Rule of Metaphor* (Routledge Classics, 2003) Study 1.

[47] 'There lies behind Aristotle's whole account of style the unargued assumption that the essence of literary pleasure is the combination of the familiar with the exotic': HC Lawson-Tancred (n 19) 40. See also 42.

[48] *ibid* ch 3.2.

[49] Goodrich, 'Rhetoric as Jurisprudence' (n 35) 107.

[50] Fish (n 33) 474.

[51] *ibid* 474–75; 482–85.

[52] Peter Goodrich, 'Law and Language: An Historical and Critical Introduction' (1984) 11 *Journal of Law and Society* 173, 177; Goodrich, 'Rhetoric as Jurisprudence' (n 35) 100–104.

[53] Goodrich, 'Rhetoric as Jurisprudence' (n 35) 90.

[54] *ibid* 108.

[55] Fish (n 33) 478.

[56] *ibid* 474–75; 482–85. For an example of this distinction in law see e.g. Pierre N Leval, 'Judicial Opinions as Literature' in Peter Brooks and Paul Gewirtz (eds), *Law's Stories, Narrative and Rhetoric in the Law* (Yale University Press, 1996) 206–10. Here Justice Leval claims that literary devices in law have the potential for harm and deception, that

of thinkers such as Hobbes, Locke, Bentham and Kant. As Lakoff and Johnson claim, 'The fear of metaphor and rhetoric in the empiricist tradition is a fear of subjectivism – a fear of emotion and the imagination'.[57]

1.2 *Deconstruction and metaphor*

Deconstruction brought into question many of the assumptions of the classical philosophies outlined above. In general terms the deconstructive method of textual analysis entails drawing out multiple meanings, ambiguities and veiled ideologies.[58] Deconstructive strategies include an interest in metaphor which had been traditionally viewed as a literary or fictional device. Yet Derrida focused on the silent role of metaphor in philosophy; despite its claims to be a discipline based on reason and concerned with seeking higher truths, many leading texts were based on disguised metaphorical devices. The precursor to such deconstructive strategies is present in the work of Nietzsche, who claimed that human certainty rested on forgetting its origins in the 'primitive metaphor-world'.[59] For Nietzsche:

> the origin of language is not a logical process, and the whole material in and with which the man of truth, the scientist, the philosopher [and, one might add, the lawyer] works and builds, stems, if not from a never-never land, in any case not from the essence of things.[60]

In 'White Mythology'[61] Derrida continued this theme, highlighting the various ways in which metaphor is central to philosophical language. Derrida questioned whether philosophy can ever purge itself of metaphorical language, and indeed whether its leading metaphors can be identified in the first place. The very distinction between philosophy and literature itself rests on metaphor, and such metaphors can only be explained or challenged in metaphorical terms.[62] Derrida explained this circularity in the following terms:

---

rhetoric 'seduces the speaker as well as the audience' and sacrifices clarity for power (207–208, 210).

[57]Lakoff and Johnson (n 14) 191.

[58]I have provided an account of deconstruction elsewhere: Moosavian, 'Deconstructing' (n 13).

[59]Nietzsche, (n 2) 246–57, 252.

[60]*ibid* 249 (addition mine).

[61]Derrida, 'White Mythology' (n 46). An interesting discussion of this essay can be found in Ricoeur, *The Rule of Metaphor* (n 46) Study 8, Part 3.

[62]For example Derrida notes the texts of 'Renan, Nietzsche … Freud, Bergson, and Lenin, all of whom in their attentiveness to metaphorical activity in theoretical or philosophical discourse, proposed or practiced the multiplication of antagonistic metaphors in order better to control or neutralize their effect' *ibid* 214. See also Jonathan Culler, *On Deconstruction, 25th Anniversary Edition* (Routledge, 2008) 147; Anthony Reynolds, 'The Afterlife of Dead Metaphors: On Derrida's Pragmatism' (2009) 49 *Revista de Letras* 181, 184–85.

> The appeal to criteria of clarity and obscurity [of language] would suffice to confirm … this entire philosophical delimitation of metaphor already lends itself to being constructed and worked by 'metaphors'. How could a piece of knowledge or a language be properly clear or obscure? Now, all the concepts which have operated in the definition of metaphor always have an origin and an efficacity that are themselves 'metaphorical'.[63]

To acknowledge this casts doubt on whether philosophical language can objectively and accurately represent the nature of things. Indeed Derrida suggested that such an enterprise is impossible because, as Harrison explains, 'the metaphysician, to say what he wants to say, needs to view matters from a standpoint outside language, a standpoint in principle inaccessible to him'.[64] Influenced by Derrida, de Man also analysed metaphor to question the broad philosophy-literature divide, claiming that:

> All philosophy is condemned, to the extent that it is dependent on figuration, to be literary and, as the depository of this very problem, all literature is to some extent philosophical.[65]

In 'Plato's Pharmacy' Derrida undertakes analysis of Plato's medicine metaphor by deconstructing the sign 'pharmakon' as used in the dialogue, *Phaedrus*. The dialogue depicts a discussion between Socrates and Phaedrus about the nature of writing. Throughout the text writing is referred to as 'pharmakon', a Greek word with a dual meaning of both 'remedy' and 'poison',[66] and thus a term with a reversible and ambiguous structure.[67] Derrida traces silent, unwitting shifts in the meaning of 'pharmakon',[68] claiming that Plato's text 'manifests a series of slidings … that are highly significant'.[69] The sign 'pharmakon' is used to contain a selection of oppositions,[70] the most significant of which is that between speech (logos) over writing, a privileging seen throughout Western philosophy. Writing is seen (at once) as both a remedy and a poison via its association

---

[63]Derrida, 'White Mythology' (n 46) 252. See also 228.
[64]Bernard Harrison, '"White Mythology" Revisited: Derrida and His Critics on Reason and Rhetoric' (1999) 25 *Critical Inquiry* 505, 515
[65]Paul de Man, 'The Epistemology of Metaphor' (1978) 5 *Critical Inquiry* 13, 30.
[66]Jacques Derrida, *Dissemination* (University of Chicago Press, 1981) 70.
[67]*ibid* 112.
[68]*ibid* 71–72. He calls it a concept of 'malleable unity'. See also 95.
[69]*ibid* 83. For an interesting discussion of 'Plato's Pharmacy' see Jacques de Ville, 'Revisiting Plato's Pharmacy' (2010) 23 *International Journal for the Semiotics of Law* 315.
[70]Pharmakon 'constitutes the medium in which opposites are opposed, the movement and the play that links them among themselves, reverses them or makes one side cross over into the other … The pharmakon is the movement, the locus and the play: (the production of) difference. … It holds in reserve in its undecided shadow and vigil, the opposites … that the process of discrimination will carve out. Contradictions and pairs of opposites are lifted from the bottom of this diacritical, differing, deferring, reserve': Derrida, *Dissemination* (n 66) 127.

to pharmakon, a word that 'harbor[s] within itself [a] complicity of contrary values'.[71] Thus in one sense writing can be seen as a cure or beneficial remedy which aids memory and the growth of knowledge.[72] Yet writing can also be seen as a pernicious poison, making worse that which it claims to cure.[73] These non-rational qualities of Plato's philosophy have been widely acknowledged. Huizinga, for example, notes elements of 'the archaic sphere of play' across Plato's dialogues despite his denunciation of rhetoric,[74] and Goodrich also claims that Plato's defence of philosophy appeals to emotion rather than reason.[75]

Derrida returned to metaphor and related devices in the *The Beast & the Sovereign*, a series of lectures tracing the imagery of animals and beasts across a range of political philosophy texts, particularly those concerning sovereignty.[76] He discussed political philosophy as fable; though such discourse is presented as separate and different to fable,[77] Derrida sought to draw out its fable-like (or 'fabular') qualities. For example, noting the recurrence of the wolf across historical works, including mythology, The Bible and Rousseau's philosophy,[78] Derrida asked why certain political philosophers are compelled towards animal figures.[79] One reason may be the conventions of genre which involve the use of 'metaphors, metonymies or even [allegories], ..[and] animal fables'.[80] Derrida thus proposed that we pay attention to 'the logic of political unconscious' which is involved in these animal visions and note the 'symptoms [that] show up on the surface of political … discourse'.[81] Ultimately, *The Beast & The Sovereign* identifies further instances of philosophical models drawing upon metaphor and figurative, literary, non-rational devices. Deconstruction highlights the operation of such metaphors and the means by which they have been disguised, thus breaking down the apparent distinction between philosophy and literature.

[71]*ibid* 125.
[72]*ibid* 97.
[73]*ibid* 97–98, 102–103.
[74]Johan Huizinga, *Homo Ludens, A Study of the Play Element in Culture* (Martino, 2014) ch IX, esp 151.
[75]Goodrich, 'Rhetoric as Jurisprudence' (n 35) 101. See also: Lakoff and Johnson (n 14) 190.
[76]Derrida claims sovereignty is often depicted in animal terms: 'the essence of the political and, in particular of the state and sovereignty has often been represented in the formless form of animal monstrosity, in the figure without figure of a mythological, fabulous, and non–natural monstrosity, an artificial monstrosity of an animal': Jacques Derrida, *The Beast & the Sovereign, Volume I* (University of Chicago Press, 2009) 25.
[77]'[I]n the prevalent or hegemonic tradition of the political, a political discourse … should in no case come under the category of [fable] … a mythical narrative, without historical knowledge, a legend … in any case a fiction supposed to give something to be known' *ibid* 34.
[78]*ibid* First Session.
[79]*ibid* 80–81.
[80]*ibid* 81.
[81]*ibid* 82.

Within philosophical or other texts metaphors or tropes will often have a rhetorical effect, discreetly buttressing the arguments being made. 'Derrida's line of attack is to pick out … loaded metaphors and show how they work to support a whole powerful structure of presuppositions.'[82] An ideal example discussed by Derrida is Hobbes' *Leviathan* which depicts men in the lawless state of nature entering a social contract to found a sovereign who brings protection and order via laws that all must obey.[83] Despite his denunciation of metaphor, Hobbes envisages the sovereign state created by the social contract as a monstrous, artificial man-made animal[84] representing a copy of God's work.[85] Hobbes' extended metaphor sees sovereignty as the being's artificial soul,[86] and various state institutions as corresponding parts of the artificial body: 'The *analogistic* description of the *Leviathan* follows in the body of the state … the whole structure of the human body.'[87] This metaphor is supplemented by other science-based imagery in the text.[88] According to Derrida, the key human motivations that underlie Hobbes' account of humankind are fear, panic and terror.[89] His social contract represents men moving from one fear (of threat in the state of nature) to another (fear of the sovereign's punishment).[90] Thus, for Derrida, Hobbes' Leviathan is ultimately an 'animal-machine designed to cause fear … which runs on fear and reigns by fear'[91] Significantly, Derrida further claims that such 'fabular' dimensions in the rhetoric of political philosophy ultimately impact upon real world political actions regarding matters such as warfare or terrorism.[92]

Because of its implications for objective truth claims, and thus the very foundations of Western thought, deconstruction has been accused of detached, reckless nihilism or 'textual vandalism'.[93] However, these allegations have been rejected as misrepresentative by numerous commentators.[94] Culler, for instance, claims that deconstruction does not lead to destruction, but to reinterpretation or re-inscription

[82]Christopher Norris, *Deconstruction, Theory and Practice* (Routledge, 3rd edn 2006) 27.
[83]Derrida, *The Beast & the Sovereign* (n 76) 40–41.
[84]*ibid* 26–27.
[85]*ibid* 53–54.
[86]*ibid* 47.
[87]*ibid* 28.
[88]Midgley notes that Hobbes adopted ideas regarding matter, particles and motion from physics: Mary Midgely, *The Myths We Live By* (Routledge, 2011) 47–49, 71.
[89]Hobbes' *Leviathan* is just one political theory that 'has made fear or panic … an essential and structural mainspring of … [being a subject in political society]' Derrida, , *The Beast & the Sovereign* (n 76) 39.
[90]*ibid* 42.
[91]*ibid* 39–40. 'Sovereignty causes fear, and fear makes the sovereign', 40.
[92]*ibid* 35.
[93]'Deconstruction is not a form of textual vandalism designed to prove that meaning is impossible': Barbara Johnson, 'Introduction' in Derrida, *Dissemination* (n 66), vii-xxxiii, xiv.
[94]Harrison (n 64) 518–19.

of the relevant binary oppositions.[95] Such reinterpretation involves acknowledgement that the unspoken theoretical foundations of our thought systems are historically and culturally specific rather than universal, self-evident, objective or immovable:

> The deconstructive critique reminds us that our social vision and system of laws are not based on human nature as it really is, but rather upon an interpretation of human nature, a metaphor, a privileging.[96]

Derrida specifically made such observations in relation to the foundations of existing liberal legal systems. In 'The Force of Law' he claimed that legal discourse is based upon 'theoretically weak and crude [axioms]' and that its resulting limitations have 'massive and concrete' effects.[97] Yet here Derrida also expressly denied the charge of nihilism, arguing that deconstruction does not involve an abdication of questions of justice.[98] Rather it requires one to consider the history, development and limits of concepts such as justice and law; to consider the assumed 'values, norms and prescriptions that have been … sedimented there'.[99]

Fish defends anti-foundational outlooks such as rhetoric and deconstruction against classic, objectivist accusations. He rejects the distinction between literal and rhetorical speech, claiming that all languages (legal, scientific, poetic) are innately rhetorical because they occur within inescapable socially constructed paradigms.[100] This realisation need not entail cynicism and nihilism[101] because ultimately, for Fish,

> the radically rhetorical insight of Nietzschean/Derridean thought can do radical political work; becoming aware that everything is rhetorical is the first step in countering the power of rhetoric and liberating us from its force. Only if deeply entrenched ways of thinking and acting are made the objects of suspicion will we be able 'even to imagine that life could be different and better.'[102]

Derrida demonstrates that powerful metaphors can be found in unexpected places, and that despite appearances they can be employed for rhetorical effect remarkably effectively, prompting (perhaps subconscious) emotions and responses which

---

[95]Culler (n 62) 133. See also Johnson (n 93).
[96]JM Balkin, 'Deconstructive Practice and Legal Theory' (1987) 96 *Yale Law Journal* 743, 763, 760, 764.
[97]Jacques Derrida, 'Force of Law: The "Mystical Foundation of Authority"' (1989–90) 11 *Cardozo Law Review* 920, 965.
[98]*ibid* 953. For an interesting and clear account and analysis of Derrida's essay see Douglas Litowitz, *Postmodern Philosophy and Law* (University of Kansas Press, 1997) ch 5.
[99]Derrida, 'Force of Law' (n 97) 953.
[100]Fish (n 33) 486–88; 297–98.
[101]*ibid* 479–81.
[102]*ibid* 496.

contradict the stated ideals of the text. The potential implications of such strategies for legal discourse are patent.

1.3 *The rhetorical effects of metaphor in law*

Despite its legal origins, rhetoric is a technique or form of language that lawyers do not generally associate with the apolitical rationality of law. Yet the 1980s to 1990s saw renewed attention being given to law as a form of rhetoric. This interest was partly stimulated by the emerging law and literature movement which is not only concerned with representations of law *in* literature, but also reading law *as* literature.[103] The latter, of particular relevance to this article, raises questions about the implicit presence of literature (or literary devices such as metaphor) in law. Its general approach claims that literary theory – concerning matters such as interpretation, authorial intention, the construction of meaning – affords valuable insights into legal texts despite their crucial differences to fictional counterparts.[104] Judgments are thus understood as a 'quasi-literary genre',[105] an approach exemplified by White, who has written:

> in its hunger to connect the general with the particular, in its metaphorical movements, and in its constant and forced recognition of the limits of the mind and language, the law seemed to me a kind of poetry.[106]

But, crucially, the focus on legal judgments as rhetoric does not adopt the derogatory sense adopted by Plato. For example, White characterises rhetoric in a wider, positive sense as the study of how language and speech constitute our community and social world.[107] This is central to his conception of law, viewing it as 'an art essentially literary and rhetorical in nature'.[108] Like White, Goodrich provides a favourable account of rhetoric as the study of public speech, a discipline that emerged with democratic institutions and entailed collective dialogue about community needs.[109] Rhetoric's notion of persuasion was pragmatic, and in acting to

[103]Ian Ward, 'Law and Literature' (1993) 4 *Law and Critique* 44, 58–69; Paul Gewirtz, 'Narrative and Rhetoric in the Law' in Brooks and Gewirtz (n 56) 2–13, 3–4.
[104]White, *When Words Lose their Meaning* (n 22) ch 1; Fish (n 33); Sandford Levinson, 'Law as Literature' (1982) 60 *Texas Law Review* 373.
[105]John Hollander, 'Legal Rhetoric' in Brooks and Gewirtz (n 56) 176–86, 186. See also White, *Essays on Rhetoric* (n 31) ch 6 ('The Judicial Opinion and the Poem').
[106]White, *When Words Lose their Meaning* (n 22) xii.
[107]*ibid* xi.
[108]'[Law] is most usefully and completely seen as a branch of rhetoric. But 'rhetoric' … should be seen not as a failed science nor as an ignoble art of persuasion (as it often is) but as the central art by which culture and community are established, maintained and transformed. This kind of rhetoric – I call it 'constitutive rhetoric' – has justice as its ultimate subject': White, *Essays on Rhetoric* (n 31) 28.
[109]Goodrich, 'Law and Language' (n 52), 175–78.

decentralise power over meaning it was 'a great leveller of discourse'.[110] Goodrich therefore advocates introducing a critical rhetoric into law as an alternative to the 'authoritarian monologue'[111] of dominant legal discourse which depicts itself as clear, technical and formal, but whose language rests on unarticulated exclusions that reflect power.[112]

One need not subscribe to Goodrich and White's defences of rhetoric, to recognise its pertinence to legal judgments. That such texts are concerned (at least partly) with persuasion is reasonably uncontroversial. Gewitz identifies a judicial opinion as serving three primary functions, the third of which is 'to persuade the court's audiences that the court did the right thing'.[113] Similarly, Levinson claims that judgments are 'rhetorical performances'[114] whose cogency is based upon both the court's inherent authority and the persuasiveness of their text. Interestingly, such views also raise the related question of who constitutes the audience to be persuaded. There may be multiple potential audiences including: the losing side; opposed citizens; lawyers; fellow judges; academics; the reporting media and the wider populace.[115]

Metaphors are a common trope in law and their rhetorical effect is no less operative in legal than philosophical discourse. In 'The Metaphysics of American Law', Peller argues that socially-constructed metaphors pervade law. Such metaphors are contingent in numerous ways. First, only certain metaphors are adopted whilst other possible alternatives are neglected.[116] One interesting example is put forward by Scales who questions the preponderance of sports metaphors in law and legal academia, claiming they are inherently gendered, pro-rule and trivialise legal power. Why, she asks, use sports metaphors rather than, for example, mothering metaphors?[117] Second, metaphors highlight certain similarities whilst suppressing others: 'Representational metaphors abstract particular features from the otherwise thick texture of the world. But there is no necessary reason to abstract some features rather than others.'[118] Peller's claim here is consistent with Lakoff and Johnson's leading account of metaphor. They claim that metaphors operate by highlighting certain similarities between two things, and therefore inevitably mar-

[110]Goodrich, 'Rhetoric as Jurisprudence' (n 35) 95, 99, 100.
[111]*ibid* 90, 99.
[112]Goodrich, 'Law and Language' (n 52) 173–75.
[113]Gerwitz (n 103) 10.
[114]S Levinson, 'The Rhetoric of Judicial Opinion' in Brooks and Gewirtz (n 56) 187–205, 187.
[115]*ibid* 196–200. See also Haig Bosmajian, *Metaphor and Reason in Judicial Opinion* (Southern Illinois University Press, 1992) 28–34.
[116]Gary Peller, 'The Metaphysics of American Law' (1985) 73 *California Law Review* 1151, 1175.
[117]Ann C Scales, 'Surviving Legal De-Education: An Outsider's Guide' (1990) 15 *Vermont Law Review* 139, 149–52.
[118]Peller (n 116) 1167.

ginalising others.[119] There will thus remain parts of a metaphor that remain unused.[120] The act of metaphoric representation, then, can only ever be an interpretation reflecting a specific culture, context and politics. Peller provides the salient example of consent in rape cases as a supporting example. 'Consent' is a product of interpretation, projected onto events, drawing on 'external signals' and ultimately based on a view of coercion founded on a mind/body distinction.[121]

Crucially, alluding perhaps to Nietzsche's 'worn coins', Peller claims that the metaphorical nature of concepts is gradually effaced and their terminology ultimately comes to be institutionalised, viewed as 'common sense' and merely reflecting an already present objective reality.[122] But Peller claims that rather than *reflecting* reality, legal metaphors actually *constitute* reality because they act to mediate and filter[123] our experience of social events. In this regard, Peller's claim is broadly consistent with Lakoff and Johnson's arguments that the human conceptual system is fundamentally metaphorical in nature,[124] and that metaphors thus 'create our realities'.[125] Similarly, for Peller, legal metaphors *construct* our 'reality' in the process of representing it,[126] and thus influence our actions and social arrangements.[127] Ultimately, like philosophy, 'legal discourse can present itself as neutral and determinate only to the extent that it denies its own metaphoric starting points and instead pretends to reflect the positive content of social relations'.[128]

So despite mainstream liberal understandings of law as a neutral, rational discipline, law is as reliant upon tropes as literature or philosophy are. According to Goodrich, law as an institution relies 'upon an unconscious reservoir of institutional connotations, metaphoric structures [and] long-term deployments of meaning which develop in the indefinite time of precedent'.[129] Thus exploring figurative and symbolic devices in apparently rational, technical judgments may

[119]Lakoff and Johnson (n 14) ch 3.
[120]*ibid* 109.
[121]Peller (n 116) 1187–91.
[122]*ibid* 1289–90.
[123]*ibid* 1155.
[124]Lakoff and Johnson (n 14) 6. An interesting account of recent cognitive research on metaphor relevant to lawyers is outlined in Linda Berger, 'Metaphor and Analogy: The Sun and Moon of Legal Persuasion' (2013) 22 *Journal of Law and Policy* 147.
[125]Lakoff and Johnson (n 14) 158, 145.
[126]Peller (n 116) 1176.
[127]*ibid* 1151. It should be noted that Peller's metaphors across the article take the form of fundamental binary oppositions such as mind/body, subject/object, knowledge/power etc.
[128]*ibid* 1182.
[129]Peter Goodrich, 'Jani anglorum, Signs, Symptoms, Slips and Interpretation In Law' in Costas Douzinas, Peter Goodrich and Yifat Hachamovitch (eds), *Politics, Postmodernity and Critical Legal Studies* (Routledge, 2004) 107–144, 127.

show that they are beset at some level by certain unarticulated politics, emotions or subjectivities that they explicitly claim to avoid. As Douzinas states:

> A concern with the figures of the legal text or with the symbolic structure and context of law ... is a concern with a series of highly political yet largely unquestioned aspects of legal governance. The critical scholar attends to the marginal, the peripheral or the surface precisely so as to recapture the politics which has escaped the text, or has been hidden beneath its ritual paraphernalia.[130]

The preceding discussion in this part affords illuminating insights pertinent to the balance metaphor in misuse of private information case law. It has highlighted the often-suppressed figurative, imaginative nature of legal discourse, and indicated that these essential characteristics are at odds with law's self-presentation. It has also revealed the unavoidable historically- and culturally-specific hierarchies that inform legal discourse and thus modern rights-balancing techniques. Finally, the discussion here suggests that the balance metaphor does not merely represent – but may actually *constitute* – judicial understandings of rights conflicts in MPI case law. It is to that case law that discussion now turns.

2. The balance metaphor in misuse of private information

The modern judicial technique of balancing competing rights or interests emerged in the late 1950 to 1960s via a series of broadly parallel decisions by the US Supreme Court and German *Bundesverfassungsgericht*.[131] In his comparative study of these developments, Bomhoff argues that despite their shared terminology, the US and German understandings of balancing have their own respective intellectual origins[132] and meanings specific to their national legal-jurisprudential cultures.[133] But nonetheless, these US and German traditions have influenced contemporary understandings of balance, the latter playing a particularly prominent role in the metaphor's European meaning.[134] The role of 'balance' in misuse of private information case law must be viewed against the backdrop of such influences.

It should be noted that a number of salient metaphors populate MPI case law in addition to that of 'balance'. Note for example the recurring vigilant media 'watchdog',[135] an idealisation that implicitly 'casts the media as observer,

[130]Costas Douzinas, 'Introduction' in Douzinas, Goodrich and Hachamovitch, *ibid*, 1–31 16.
[131]Bomhoff (n 8) 28, 72.
[132]*ibid* ch 2.
[133]*ibid* ch 3 (Germany), ch 4 (United States).
[134]*ibid* 29–30, 238–39.
[135]*Campbell v MGN* [2004] UKHL 22 [107]; *Von Hannover v Germany* [2004] EMLR 21 [63]; *ETK v News Group Newspapers Ltd* [2011] EWCA Civ 439 [13]; *Mosley v UK* (App 480009/08) May 2011, ECtHR [114]; *Spelman v Express Newspapers* [2012] EWHC 355 [48].

scrutiniser and also guardian, protector of the public'.[136] Another highly significant metaphor in MPI cases, and indeed wider law, is the metaphor of line-drawing as adopted in *Flitcroft*[137] and *Browne.*[138] This line-drawing device, an integral feature of adjudication, has the effect of implying a clear, distinct divide wherever the line is situated; it envisages an issue in spatial terms, definitively splitting it into two clear 'areas' or categories, where a case or set of facts will fall on one side or the other. Yet, it is arguable that 'balance' is the most prominent and influential metaphor in MPI and its metaphorical nature has been acknowledged by leading commentators, though not subject to further metaphor-based scrutiny.[139]

2.1 *'Balance'*

In misuse of private information judgments the notion of 'balance' plays a crucial role. The balancing exercise is reflected in the second of Lord Steyn's four principles that form a key part of the new methodology ('where the values under the two articles are in conflict, an intense focus on the comparative importance of the specific rights being claimed in the individual case is necessary').[140] This requires a relative weighting of each right responsive to the specific facts, though it offers no further guidance on how the mechanics of such a weighting should proceed. Subsequent ECtHR judgments, particularly *Axel Springer*[141] and *Von Hannover No 2*[142] have provided further elaboration of guiding principles.

The term 'balance' is French but has Latin origins, having evolved from an amalgamation of 'bi' (meaning double) and 'lanx' (meaning a metal dish or pair of scales).[143] 'Balance' has the following dictionary meanings:

> [noun] (1) Equilibrium; what is needed to produce equilibrium ... (2) harmony among the parts of anything; (3) stability of body or mind; (4) equality or just proportion of weight or power ... (5) the act of weighing two things; (6) an instrument for weighing, usu formed of two dishes or scales hanging from a beam supported in the middle;[144]

> [transitive verb] (7) to set or keep in equilibrium ... (8) to weigh in a balance; (9) to settle (eg an account)[145]

---

[136] Moosavian, 'Charting the Journey' (n 9) 249.
[137] *A v B (Flitcroft)* [2002] EWCA Civ 337, 208 (D).
[138] *Browne v Associated News* [2007] EWHC 202 (QB) [45].
[139] See e.g. Gavin Phillipson, 'Leveson, the Public Interest and Press Freedom' (2013) 5 *Journal of Media Law* 220, 236.
[140] *Re S (A Child) (Identification: Restrictions on Publication)* [2004] UKHL 47 [17].
[141] *Axel Springer AG v Germany* [2012] ECHR 39954/08).
[142] *Von Hannover v Germany (No 2)* [2012] ECHR 40660/08.
[143] *Chambers Dictionary* (Chambers, 10th edn 2006) 111.
[144] *ibid* (numbers added).
[145] *ibid* (numbers added).

In media privacy case law the term 'balance' is primarily used in two key senses. First and foremost, it is used as a transitive verb (definition (7)), i.e. to depict the process of balancing objects, in this case the 'objects' being rights. Related to this, judgments use 'balance' to refer to the specific act of weighing two things (as in definition (5)). It is interesting to note that in each of these meanings, the act of balancing produces equilibrium; this is discussed further in part 2.3 below. Second, 'balance' is employed to refer to a set of scales, an instrument for weighing (as per definition (6) and the term's Latin origins); this use is significant and now warrants further attention.

Balance: the scales metaphor

Actual references to 'scales' in the weighing process are present across case law, including *Douglas*,[146] *Theakson*,[147] *Campbell*,[148] *Prince of Wales*[149] and *ETK*.[150] Additionally, repeated references to 'scales' are present in the leading text, *Tugendhat and Christie*, as in the following passage:

> a claim to privacy in respect of information about health or sexual life is likely to *weigh more heavily in the scales* than a claim to protect information which, though private in character, is intrinsically less intimate.[151]

There are numerous other instances of judicial use of the term 'balance' to indicate 'scales' in case law. In *Prince of Wales v Associated Newspapers* the Court of Appeal stated that ensuring that parties upheld their duties of confidence was 'a significant element to be weighed in the balance'.[152] Elsewhere, in *Hutcheson* the Court of Appeal stated that the public dimension of family was 'a factor to be weighed in the balance'.[153] An identical use of 'balance' in the scales sense

146 *Douglas and Others v Hello! Ltd* [2001] QB 967 (CA) [171]. Here Keene LJ, discharging an interim injunction, stated: 'When [the claimants'] organised publicity is balanced against the impact on the defendants of an injunction restraining publication, I have no doubt that the scales come down in this case against prior restraint.'

147 *Theakston v MGN Ltd* [2002] EWHC 137 [76]. Here Ouseley J stated 'I consider that the scales would be likely to come down in favour of the freedom of expression of the newspaper and of the prostitutes unless it was clear that there was a strong case for inhibiting it'.

148 *Campbell* (n 135) [29]. Disagreeing with the earlier judgment of Morland J, Lord Nicholls stated 'the judge seems to have put nothing into the scales'.

149 *Prince of Wales v Associated News* [2006] EWHC 522 [133] where Blackburne J spoke of 'considerations that must be weighed in the scales'.

150 *ETK* (n 135) [20]: 'the additional rights of children are to be placed in the scale.'

151 Tugendhat and Christie, *The Law of Privacy and the Media* (Oxford University Press, 2nd edn 2011) 5.131. Other references to 'scales' can be found at 12.125, 12.144.

152 *HRH Prince of Wales v Associated Newspapers Ltd* [2006] EWCA Civ 1776 [76].

153 *Hutcheson v News Group* [2011] EWCA Civ 808 [47](iv): the public dimension of family 'is a factor to be weighed in the balance'.

is evident in *Campbell*,[154] *CDE*,[155] *ETK*,[156] *WXY v Gewanter*,[157] *AAA v Associated Newspapers*[158] and *Rocknroll v News Group*.[159] Similarly, in *Ferdinand* Nicol J made reference to 'the art 8 *side* of the *balance*', later stating that publication of an 'unexceptionable' photo of the claimant and a woman with whom he had an adulterous affair '[did] not *tip* the *balance*' in the claimant's favour.[160] In each of these extracts the meaning of 'balance' has subtly shifted, to represent a set of measuring scales.

From these case law extracts, it is apparent that 'balance' forms, in Lakoff and Johnson's terms, a conventional structural metaphor expressible as ADJUDICATING RIGHTS IS BALANCING SCALES.[161] It is conventional in that it forms part of our culture's ordinary conceptual system, as reflected by its widespread usage in legal – and indeed wider political – discourse.[162] Furthermore it is structural in nature because it allows lawyers to orient, quantify, discuss and structure rights adjudication.[163] As is common in other structural metaphors, the balance metaphor enables this because the defining concept (BALANCING SCALES) is 'more clearly delineated in our experience and typically more concrete'[164] than the defined concept (ADJUDICATING RIGHTS). The MPI case law and commentary indicate that privacy/free expression disputes are envisaged as BALANCING SCALES in a number of ways. Disputes occur in binary terms and the opposing sides are 'balanced'. The metaphor is extended with frequent references to the 'weight' of rights representing the cogency of each side's supporting arguments. Further extension occurs with repeated references to sets of scales. Further discussion in parts 2.2 and 2.3 will indicate that the structural metaphor ADJUDICATING RIGHTS IS BALANCING SCALES is supplemented by additional metaphors.

---

[154] *Campbell* (n 135). Lord Hope discussed the 'weight' to be given to Art 8, claiming 'As for the other side of the balance, a person's right to privacy may be limited by the public's interest in knowing about central traits of her personality and certain aspects of her private life': [120]. Lord Carswell also used such terminology, stating 'I would not myself attempt to isolate which ... [element of the defendant's publication] is more harmful or tips the balance': [170].

[155] *CDE and another v MGN Limited* [2010] EWHC 3308 [7].

[156] *ETK* (n 126) [15] (quoting the original unreported judgment of Collins J).

[157] *WXY v Gewanter* [2012] EWHC 496 (QB) [110]: 'An additional factor to be weighed in the balance ... is the claimed public interest.'

[158] *AAA v Associated Newspapers Ltd* [2013] EWCA Civ 554 [55]: 'It is not in dispute that the legitimate public interest in the father's character is an important factor to be weighed in the balance against the Claimant's reasonable expectation of privacy.' See also [10].

[159] *Rocknroll v News Group Ltd* [2013] EWHC 24 [39].

[160] *Ferdinand v MGN Ltd* [2011] EWHC 2454 [70], [102].

[161] This follows Lakoff and Johnson's presentational format featuring metaphors in capital text (n 14).

[162] *ibid* 139.

[163] *ibid* 61 (and ch 13 generally).

[164] *ibid* 108–109

Part 1 discussed the analysis of the rhetorical effect of metaphor across various discourses. Informed by the literature discussed, it is arguable that the balancing metaphor discreetly brings two distinct but related rhetorical advantages that will now be discussed in turn.

2.2 *The certainty of the quantitative*

First, the balancing exercise connotes a seemingly objective,[165] scientific[166] and precise[167] weighting process; one to be undertaken in relation to two objects, two 'things' with a physical presence. Gauging weight is a quantitative process and this language thus gives a sense of the quantifiable[168] or, in Derrida's terms, the 'calculable'.[169] It is arguably influenced by Aristotle's notion of rectificatory justice, that form of particular justice whereby a judge restores the precise status quo when an injustice has occurred between parties. Aristotle's account of rectificatory justice also draws upon quantitative imagery, viewing it in terms of unequal lines, the longer of which has its excess halved and transferred to the shorter.[170] The likely influence of German jurisprudence should also be noted here. Bomhoff traces similar 'scientific' tendencies through the works of influential German thinkers, for example the *Interessenjurisprudenz* scholars, including Heck, who viewed balance as a neutral method[171] and later authors, such as Forsthoff, who sought to render balancing more scientific by structuring and formalizing it.[172] A prominent contemporary manifestation of this tradition is the work of Alexy on balancing, optimization and

[165]'The scales affirm that the workings of justice are both objective and impartial. The process of judgment must be independent of the whim of any individual; judgment is concerned with the objective weighting of issues in the balance. ... this objective standard which is reflected through law': Martin Loughlin, *Sword and Scales: An Examination of the Relationship Between Law and Politics* (Hart, 2000) 56. See also Dennis Curtis and Judith Resnik, 'Images of Justice' (1987) 96 *Yale Law Journal* 1727, 1765; Martin Jay, 'Must Justice be Blind?' in Costas Douzinas and Lynda Nead (eds), *Law and the Image, The Authority of Art and the Aesthetics of Law* (University of Chicago Press, 1999) ch 1, 21.

[166]'The image [of balancing] is of a highly objective process (two weights in a scale, suggesting both science and Blind Justice)': Duncan Kennedy, *A Critique of Adjudication* (Harvard University Press, 1998) 148.

[167]Loughlin (n 165) 56.

[168]Waldron also notes that 'balance' involves 'connotations of quantity and precision' and entails 'quantitative imagery': Jeremy Waldron, 'Security and Liberty: The Image of Balance' (2003) 11 *Journal of Political Philosophy* 191, 192.

[169]Derrida, 'Force of Law' (n 97) 963, 965, 971. Derrida claims that the 'calculable' is the concern of law, in contrast to justice which is incalculable.

[170]Aristotle, *Nicomachean Ethics* (Oxford University Press, 2009) book V, ch 4, esp 1132a–1132b.

[171]Bomhoff (n 8) 60–64.

[172]*ibid* 87–89.

proportionality.[173] According to Bomhoff, the image conveyed by Alexy's account is that of 'a finely calibrated balance ... where all values and interests can receive their *exact* due'.[174]

Crucially, the balancing metaphor also acts to reify rights because it inevitably leads one to view the rights being balanced as tangible objects. Such reification can be seen in MPI cases where the courts include the rights of additional family members in the balancing exercise. In *ETK v News Group* for example, the Court of Appeal recognised the rights of the claimant's wife and children as separate objects with weight in themselves.[175] Their addition to the 'balance' implied more 'quantity', adding weight to the claimant's Article 8 arguments.[176] The balance metaphor thus also entails the ontological metaphor that A RIGHT IS A PHYSICAL OBJECT OF VARIABLE WEIGHT. Ontological metaphors depict experiences in terms of corporeal items which, according to Lakoff and Johnson, brings numerous advantages: 'Once we can identify our experiences as entities or substances, we can refer to them, categorize them, group them, and quantify them – and, by this means, reason about them.'[177] This seems particularly apt to rights; is it possible to deal with conflicting rights detached from notions of balance and weight? Yet, as discussed in part 1.3, such reifying metaphors necessarily entail limitation, closure and exclusion.[178]

Despite judgments drawing heavily on this quantitative metaphor, the balancing exercise involves judges making qualitative assessments, particularly about the social value of the defendant's proposed publication.[179] So despite involving qualitative evaluations, MPI case law repeatedly draws upon the quantitative imagery of balancing. For example, in *Ferdinand* Nicol J stated 'I have to decide where the balance lies between these competing rights as an *objective* matter'.[180] This gives the impression that the weighting process can be undertaken scientifically, mathematically, despite the fact that the Art 8/10 rights are not material objects. Yet elsewhere in MPI discourse, there is isolated acknowledgement in case law that the balancing exercise is not a precise science. For example in *Campbell* Lord Carswell conceded that the weighting process may lead different people to different conclusions.[181] In *A v B (Flitcroft)* the Court

[173]For Alexy balancing is an inherently rational process that can be aided by the formation of scales of degree and methods of quantification. See *ibid* 195, 219; Robert Alexy, 'Constitutional Rights, Balancing, and Rationality' (2003) 16 *Ratio Juris* 131.
[174]Bomhoff (n 8) 201 (emphasis added).
[175]*ETK v News Group* (n 135) [14].
[176]'I cannot agree that the harmful effect on the children cannot tip the balance' *ibid* [18] (Ward LJ).
[177]Lakoff and Johnson (n 14) ch 6.
[178]Peller (n 116) 1157–58.
[179]For a discussion of this see Moosavian, 'Deconstructing' (n 13) 243–50.
[180]*Ferdinand* (n 158) [103] (emphasis added).
[181]*Campbell* (n 135) [168].

of Appeal similarly acknowledged that subjectivities and ambiguities may plague the process of balancing conflicting rights by stating:

> We are suggesting that frequently what is required is *not* a technical approach to the law but a balancing of the facts. The weight which should be attached to each relevant consideration will vary depending on the precise circumstances. *In many situations the balance may not point clearly in either direction.*[182]

Even allowing for the fact that the *Campbell* and *Flitcroft* judgments were provided at the earliest stages of the emerging MPI doctrine, these passages are revealing. The latter passage candidly acknowledges that 'balancing' in this context is actually variable, non-technical and, by implication, subjective. Furthermore, in '*many*' cases the outcome will be uncertain, with scope for the process to be legitimately conducted in numerous different ways. This latter point is demonstrated by the split 3:2 Law Lords decision in *Campbell* and the dissenting judgment of Judge Lopez Guerra in *Axel Springer* in the ECtHR.[183] This undermines the impression subtly fostered by the metaphor that the balancing exercise is scientific or objective in nature. Furthermore, it indicates that the balancing exercise is fundamentally different in nature to the balancing of objects in scales, despite the recurrent use of that image; unlike theoretical, metaphysical rights balancing, using scales allows the weight of a particular item to be factually quantified with certainty. Yet such mixed judicial statements also perhaps reflect an ambiguity inherent in the balance metaphor: are the rights weighed with reference to an 'external', objective scale, or relative to one another? The imagery of scales suggests both.

The enduring influence of 'balance' in modern human rights discourse is perhaps a reflection of our broader political-bureaucratic culture, with its emphasis on reductive rationalities, binary ends/means trade-offs and social-scientific approaches to crucial community issues.[184] Yet, as White argues, the work of lawyers is inherently creative[185] and legal reasoning works by a range of methods, many of which are distinctly non-scientific.[186] The balance metaphor in MPI is particularly paradoxical; a literary device that discreetly draws on the stature of science. Yet even this quantitative, reifying metaphor entails a subtle rhetoric of its own, its power resting on its implicit claims to be *non*-rhetorical.

---

182 *Flitcroft* (n 137) 210 (D)–(E).

183 *Axel Springer* (n 141). Dissenting opinion of Judge Lopez Guerra, joined by Judges Jungwiert, Jaeger, Villiger and Poalelungi.

184 White, *Essays on Rhetoric* (n 31) ch 2, esp 32. White's preferred method entails 'reading law as a kind of literature (as opposed, for example, to reading law as a kind of policy science or economics or social process)': 122.

185 *ibid* 34.

186 '[O]ne reasons not only with 'propositions' but with metaphors, analogies, general truths, statements of feeling and attitude … and one moves not only by logic but by association and analogy and image, by what seems natural and right': White, *When Words Lose their Meaning* (n 22) 12. See also 14. See also Murray (n 3).

In Fish's terms, 'Impersonal method [e.g. of the balancing sort] … is both an illusion and a danger (as a kind of rhetoric it masks its rhetorical nature)'.[187]

Exposing the connotations of calculability and certainty sedimented in the balance metaphor necessarily entails facing uncertainty. Yet, for White, this is an inevitable feature of life, and the lawyerly

> process of meaning-making and community-building … requires him or her to face and accept the condition of radical uncertainty in which we live: uncertainty as to the meaning of words, uncertainty as to their effect on others, uncertainty even as to our own motivations.[188]

Thus perhaps 'balance' acts as a convenient fiction which overlays an inherently creative, subjective and, to some extent, inexpressible interpretive activity.[189] Ricoeur, for example, notes 'the capacity of metaphor to provide untranslatable information'.[190] Perhaps what the term seeks to represent remains a process the core of which will inevitably elude attempts to articulate, categorise or systematise it. This possibility is embraced by White, who writes:

> In forcing us to the limits of expression and of our minds, [reading law as literature] is a commitment to openness, to the recognition of mystery, to the value of what no-one has yet found the words to say or do. In all of this we must perpetually acknowledge that we have something to learn.[191]

2.3 *The allure of reconciliation*

The second advantage of 'balancing' is its capacity to foster the moral appeal of a decision in a number of discreet but powerful ways. For example, 'balance' contains a trace reference to the traditional symbol of justice: the scales. In this sense it constitutes an image-based metaphor which plays on the visual aspect of 'balance'.[192] Daube confirms that the symbol of the scales in decision-making

---

[187]Fish (n 33) 485.

[188]White, *Essays on Rhetoric* (n 31) 39–40. See also 128,130.

[189]'We require our complexity to be explicit, spelled out, and we call it an aesthetic value and a test of truth. But in its own way this can itself be a kind of simplemindedness – an avoidance of the complexity that underlies and is evoked by some simple texts, or a denial of the importance of what matters most': *ibid* 120.

[190]Paul Ricoeur, 'The Metaphorical Process as Cognition, Imagination and Feeling' (1978) 5 *Critical Inquiry* 143, 143. See also Ross (n 4) 1071–72.

[191]White, *Essays on Rhetoric* (n 31) 124. See also: Ricoeur, 'The Metaphorical Process' (n 190) 143. Ricoeur states that 'metaphorical meaning compels us to explore the borderline between the verbal and non–verbal': 151.

[192]For a really interesting discussion of the dominance of visual metaphors in legal discourse as a reflection of dominant power, and the more recent shift towards aural metaphors associated with challenging that power, see Bernard J Hibbitts, 'Making Sense of Metaphors: Visuality, Aurality, and the Reconfiguration of American Legal Discourse' (1994) 16 *Cardozo Law Review* 229.

has ancient origins, with references dating back to the Egyptian Book of the Dead (circa 1400 BC).[193] This depicted the ritual judgment of each individual in the afterlife (Duat) by weighing their heart in a set of scales in order to judge their past conduct.[194] The deceased's heart was weighed against a feather of Maat which represented order, truth and justice. The ideal outcome was equilibrium; an exact balance between heart and Maat. The balancing process entailed purification. The good went to paradise, the evil faced the punishment of being devoured by a hybrid crocodile-headed beast called Ammit. Scales as a form of judgement also feature in *The Iliad*, where Zeus consulted his golden scales to decide who would die in battle, a process termed 'kerostasia', the weighing of souls. Zeus placed keres (death spirits) in each pan and the heavier sank to Hades.[195] In this context the scales represent death and destruction and, interestingly, there is no moral dimension to the judgment,[196] though Huizinga identifies an element of chance or play within the metaphor.[197] References to judgment via scales are also present in religious texts such as the Old Testament and the Koran.[198] Loughlin claims that 'the imagery of the scales has assumed an almost universal significance',[199] perhaps, most prominently, by virtue of the scales held by Lady Justice in legal iconography.[200] These brief historical examples indicate that though the subject matter being weighed has changed over the millennia to reflect the ideals and culture of the day, the image of the set of scales representing (or 're-presenting') judgment has endured. Ancient mystic death spirits and feathers of truth are now replaced with twenty-first-century legal rights.

Though 'balance' in MPI judgements refers to either the process of balancing or a set of scales, a further meaning becomes significant in this context; balance as equilibrium and harmony (as in the dictionary definitions (1)-(4)). These additional meanings of 'balance' refer to a state of affairs and, in the context of MPI case law, imply that equilibrium, an optimum outcome, is capable of being achieved. In this sense, the scales form a recurring figurative device conveying an implicit message; that via the balancing exercise order is achieved, equilibrium

[193]David Daube 'The Scales of Justice' (1951) 63 *Juridical Review* 109, 113–20. Though references to the process of weighing the heart on scales have been found in the Coffin Texts, circa nineteenth century BC: John Taylor (ed), *Journey Through the Afterlife: Ancient Egyptian Book of the Dead* (British Museum Press, 2010) 205.

[194]The process is detailed in Taylor (n 193) ch 9 (Judgment).

[195]Homer, *The Iliad* (Penguin Classics, 1965) 146–47, 310, 359–60, 402.

[196]BC Dietrich, 'The Judgment of Zeus' in *Rheinisches Museum fur Philiologie*, Nue Foge, 107 Bd 2 H (1964) 97, 125

[197]Huizinga (n 74) 79.

[198]Daube (n 193) 113–20.

[199]Loughlin (n 165) 56.

[200]For a discussion of the image of Lady Justice, Justitia, through history see Curtis and Resnik (n 165). This article is more specifically focused on the device and meaning of the blindfold on Justitia, but provides some passing discussion of the scales.

restored. Deconstructive readings consider the effect of 'traces' of other meanings within terms employed; the implicit meanings of 'balance' in its other senses (e.g. scales, order, equilibrium, harmony, stability)[201] are also at play in media privacy judgments and their influence cannot be discounted.[202] Judicial use of 'balance' draws silently upon these meanings, thus leaving an accretion of subconscious clues or indicators which cumulatively instil the impression that the conflict between Arts 8 and 10 can be neatly solved. This is supported by select judicial and academic comments which seem to indicate that the Art 8/10 conflict can be enigmatically ameliorated by going through the balancing process. For example, in *Campbell* Lord Hoffmann asked 'How are they to be *reconciled* in a particular case?'[203] He furthermore appeared to suggest that if one understood the case in terms of the HRA, such opposition was not actually present:

> If one takes this approach [of balancing privacy and free expression], there often is *no real conflict.*[204]

This particularly interesting statement seems to claim that through the HRA lens the privacy-free expression conflict disappears, or (perhaps) that it was never there in the first place. Lord Hoffmann's comment may have been influenced by Fenwick and Phillipson's arguments that justifications for free expression can actually be employed to undermine and restrict privacy-invading speech. The authors claim, 'at the level of principle … the rights to freedom of speech and to privacy are in many respects "*mutually supportive*"'[205] and 'it will only be in a fairly narrow category of cases that any *real conflict* will arise'.[206] In other words, properly conceived, there is actually no conflict between privacy and free expression at the level of principle in most cases; true conflict only occurs in cases involving privacy-invading speech which actually serves the public interest. Waldron makes a similar Dworkin-influenced point. He proposes viewing *inter*right conflicts via the 'internal relation' between rights rather than as a simple clash of interests. Taking this 'more systemic' approach, argues

[201]Loughlin (n 165) 56: 'The symbol of the scales of justice seems first to embody the idea that justice is primarily concerned with the maintenance of equilibrium, an idea which was central to Greek thought. The Greeks believed that the world exhibits a deep, underlying unity which is revealed through logos, nomos and taxis (reason, legality and order).' Kennedy (n 166) 149 also notes the link between 'balance' and equilibrium: 'In the force field model, policies vary in strength from one fact situation to another, and different rules 'draw lines' by balancing – that is, by finding the point of equilibrium.'
[202]Bomhoff (n 8) 57–59 notes the presence of equilibrium in the works of French writer François Gény, one of the earliest jurists to adopt the ideas and language of balance.
[203]*Campbell* (n 135) [55] (emphasis added).
[204]*ibid* [56].
[205]Gavin Phillipson and Helen Fenwick, 'Breach of Confidence as a Privacy Remedy in the Human Rights Act Era'(2000) 63 *Modern Law Review* 660, 684 (emphasis added).
[206]*ibid* 685.

Waldron, allows free expression conflicts to be viewed in a way which relates disputes back to the animating principles for the rights in question. For example, a dispute between two conflicting free expression arguments should be viewed 'in terms of each person's interest in participating on equal terms in a form of public life in which all may speak their minds'.[207] In doing so, 'What looked like a *brute confrontation* between two *rival* interests ... turns out to be resolved by considering the internal relation that obtains between our understanding of the respective rights claims'.[208] These arguments display marked similarities to earlier German balancing discourse which reflected a constitutional culture that emphasised the unification and harmonisation of conflicting values or interests;[209] that 'favoured synthesis and reconciliation over contestation and conflict'.[210] Crucially, this culture entailed the view that such conflicts 'could be reframed so as to lessen their impact, or even so as to overcome them entirely'.[211] The approaches of Lord Hoffmann, Fenwick, Phillipson and Waldron all underplay the degree of conflict in MPI cases; they foster the impression that the Art 8/10 conflict might *prima facie* look intractable and brutal, but it is ultimately underpinned by coherent, harmonious principles. Yet it must be remembered that this coherence is created (or rather *imposed*) by the interpretation, a constructive interpretation.[212] At the level of abstract value the authors are selecting *one particular* conception of free expression from many, [213] and *one particular* conception of privacy from many, in order to find them mutually supportive. This choice, though certainly justifiable, is also eminently contestable. An alternative view is that the 'brute confrontation' between Arts 8 and 10 also inescapably occurs at the level of principle. What judgments provide is certainly a resolution, but it is arguably *not* one that successfully eradicates the conflict between Arts 8/10 at a more fundamental level. Instead the resolution rests on merely one interpretation that has been preferenced over many other possible interpretations, and as such it represents a political choice.

The efficacy of 'balancing' as a precise technique is questioned by Frug in his deconstruction of bureaucratic models in American law. He considers two judicial review cases involving 'the modern judicial technique of "balancing"' where courts '"weigh" the interests to determine which is the most important'.[214] He

---

[207]Waldron, 'Rights in Conflict' (n 10) 518.
[208]*ibid* 517–18 (emphasis added).
[209]Bomhoff (n 8) 105, 108–109.
[210]*ibid* 222.
[211]*ibid* 110, 109–110. Lord Hoffmann's comment in *Campbell* that there is no real conflict bears similarities to the German *Spiegel* case, where the court 'den[ied] the existence of such a conflict altogether': *ibid* 111.
[212]Ronald Dworkin, *Law's Empire* (Hart, 1998).
[213]In Wragg's terms, 'Article 10 represents a particular conception of freedom of speech rather [than] the concept': Wragg, 'Mill's Dead Dogma: The Value of Truth to Free Speech Jurisprudence' [2013] *Public Law* 363, 385.
[214]Gerald Frug, 'The Ideology of Bureaucracy in American Law' (1984) 97 *Harvard Law Review* 1276, 1349.

claims that such balancing functions as a reassuring 'abstraction or reification' because it indicates that 'tensions' between issues can be resolved. But in fact the technique can only fluctuate between two opposing policy aims based upon questionable distinctions. Frug claims that once this is acknowledged, 'the *image* of judicial *balancing* loses its *power to persuade*'.[215] Such critique is equally applicable to MPI case law which also, despite its claims, demonstrates an inability to reconcile rather than simply preference one of two particular rights in any given case.

Mainstream comments indicating that adjudication within the HRA framework can fully solve disputes and somehow render Arts 8 and 10 (for the most part) compatible should be questioned. Can the balancing exercise provide reconciliation *per se* if it must ultimately rest on the privileging of one of the rights in any given circumstances? By the end of the adjudicative process in each case the Art 8/10 rights will have been situated in a temporary hierarchy. Eady J in *Mosley* stated that the balancing exercise was a matter of 'determin[ing] which [right] should take *precedence* in the particular circumstances'.[216] In *Hutcheson* (CA) Gross LJ quoted the following passage by Posner: 'when cases are difficult to decide it is usually because the decision must strike a balance between two legitimate interests, one of which must give way',[217] i.e. be subjugated. Both of these statements acknowledge that one right will, or indeed *must*, be privileged over the other. So from a starting point of equality, one right must be prioritised or viewed as hierarchically superior in that case. Thus the balancing exercise inevitably results in an *im*balance. This ultimate imbalance entails a further orientational metaphor which fosters the understanding of experiences in spatial terms.[218] Lakoff and Johnson identify up/down as a crucial metaphor that pervades human thought, with 'up' being associated with positive experiences (happy, conscious, in control, more) and 'down' with negative (sad, unconscious, under control, less).[219] In the MPI balancing exercise, the successful litigant will be the party whose right is the weightiest. The imbalance represents victory for the party whose scale is 'down', in direct contrast to the common tendency of up/down orientations. This ideal outcome of the balancing exercise can also be contrasted with Zeus' golden scales (where 'down' represented destruction) and with the Egyptian weighing of souls (where equilibrium was the ideal).

So ultimately 'balance' constitutes a disguised metaphorical device that has key beneficial rhetorical effects in MPI judgments. It evokes ideals and draws upon a reassuring cluster of properties (order, equality, equilibrium etc) that are inconsistent with the methods of reasoning employed (which involve conflict,

[215] *ibid* 1351 (emphasis added).
[216] *Mosley v News Group Newspapers Ltd* [2008] EWHC 1777 [11] (emphasis added).
[217] *Hutcheson* (n 153) [28].
[218] Lakoff and Johnson (n 14) ch 4.
[219] *ibid* 15–17.

privileging, imbalance etc). The balance metaphor instils a sense of elegance, justice and thus confidence in the process. In this sense, perhaps the balancing exercise merely conceals or underplays the conflict. Perhaps its '"resolutions" are achieved only by sleight of hand'[220] or, in Rosenfeld's terms, by distortion and suppression.[221] The rhetoric of 'balance' cannot truly *resolve*; it can only *justify* the imposed legal outcome, reflecting Goodrich's claim that 'The telos [end goal] of rhetorical speech is *victory* rather than *cure*'.[222] Yet herein lies a vital ambiguity at the heart of the balance metaphor. Alongside its connotations of moral appeal and equilibrium balance simultaneously represents the inescapably binary nature of judicial decisions.[223] For Daube the scales express 'a deep-rooted tendency to see no shades between black and white, to admit no degrees of right and wrong, to allow no distribution of loss and gain among several litigants, to send a party away either victorious or defeated'.[224] In the end, legal disputes necessitate an inevitable outcome or 'answer' that judgment must provide; for Loughlin, this is a crucial connotation of the scales imagery.[225]

Conclusion

The balancing of Articles 8 and 10 is an integral part of MPI case law and the 'balance' metaphor fulfils a discreet but crucial persuasive role in two ways. First, it marginalises the non-rational, inexpressible, even mysterious, aspects of judicial rights-balancing and constructs the process by emphasising the quantifiable, concrete properties of 'balancing' rights. Second, it simultaneously highlights *and* mitigates the zero-sum outcome of litigation. In doing so, 'balance' transgresses the implicit divides between the rational and the imaginative, the quantifiable and unquantifiable, objective and subjective. It forms an important rhetorical device that benefits each individual judgment, the institution of law

[220] Clare Dalton, 'An Essay in the Deconstruction of Contract Doctrine' (1985) 94 *Yale Law Journal* 997, 1109.

[221] Michel Rosenfeld, 'Deconstruction and Legal Interpretation: Conflict, Indeterminacy and the Temptations of New Legal Formalism' in Drucilla Cornell, Michel Rosenfeld and David Gray Carlson (eds) *Deconstruction and the Possibility of Justice* (Routledge, 1992), 152–210, 153.

[222] Goodrich, 'Jani anglorum' (n 129) 111 (emphasis added).

[223] Curtis and Resnik (n 165) 1755 write: 'The scales, like the sword, have potential for absolute rather than compromised outcomes; souls are weighed and sent to eternal life or damnation.'

[224] Daube (n 193) 8. This is a particularly interesting point in the context of MPI where disputed stories are often 'split' into parts, the balancing process being undertaken in relation to each respective part.

[225] 'However novel, complex or ambiguous the issue of contention, the one clear duty of the judge is to provide an answer … Above all, then, the symbol of the scales is a symbol of order and certainty: the first principle of legal justice is that an answer will be given to all disputes which arise between citizens': Loughlin (n 165) 57.

more generally and, in turn, parties or interests the law may tend to favour. This is significant in light of the wider influence of the balance metaphor beyond media-privacy disputes, particularly in counter-terrorism discourse for example.[226]

This article does not claim that the subjugation of either privacy or free expression in particular cases is a 'bad thing' *per se*. Waldron defends 'rights trade-offs' of the sort found in MPI case law. His quite reasonable point is that moral conflicts between parties are an unavoidable fact and

> it is important not to saddle the proponent of [rights] trade-offs with responsibility for the actual existence of moral conflicts … [A] hard choice has to be made on any account, and the only way of mitigating its hardness is to diminish the concern we feel about one or both of the options. It is not the fault of the theorist [or presumably judge] who proposes trade-offs.[227]

This article does not seek to 'blame the judge' charged with deciding the case as it comes before them, but it does use MPI case law to question more generally law's narrative about itself. It also invites us to become more attuned to the presence and influence of metaphors across legal discourse more generally, and the paradoxes they may both express and obscure.[228] As Ross claims, 'we cannot stay in the shelter of our unexamined metaphors'.[229]

Judicial reference to balance and scales is a recurring metaphor in MPI case law. Again, this is not a criticism *per se*; metaphors such as this are an inherent part of human thought, and the notion of balance and its associated qualities are intuitively appealing ideals. But nevertheless we should not necessarily accept 'balance' as an accurate representation of what occurs in these judgments, or indeed assume that the process *is* fully representable; perhaps the precise instance of balance must always remain in the sphere of play, eluding rationalisation, classification and articulation. Rather than precisely gauging the exact weight of individual rights and creating equilibrium and order, the judgments entail political choices where certain values are suppressed at the expense of others, and *im*balance inevitably results. Deconstructive interpretation de-mythicizes the balancing metaphor and warns us not to assume that equilibrium is ultimately achieved via

[226]Consistent criticisms have been made of the liberty v security 'balance' metaphor by MacDonald, though he does not undertake a metaphor–based analysis. He claims 'balance' obscures and simplifies and the complex relation between liberty and security, for example by assuming a basic, binary hydraulic relation between the two (i.e. when one goes up, the other goes down). The balancing metaphor is also insensitive to the issues being weighed and it prevents the opening up of decision–making to consideration of other perspectives: Stuart MacDonald, 'Why we Should Abandon the Balance Metaphor: A New Approach to Counterterrorism Policy' (2008) 15 *ISLA Journal of International and Comparative Law* 95.

[227]Waldron, 'Rights in Conflict' (n 10) 508.

[228]Ross (n 4) 1053, 1077–80.

[229]*ibid* 1053, 1083–84.

the balancing process. It disputes the impression that an intractable inter-right conflict can be made to conveniently disappear, or interpreted away. So, despite the rational, technical language of MPI case law, it engages in unavoidable 'textual violence',[230] even where the results may be justifiable or morally appealing.

Disclosure statement

No potential conflict of interest was reported by the author.

[230]For an interesting discussion of the relationship between legal interpretation and violence see Robert Cover, 'Violence and the Word' (1986) 95 *Yale Law Journal* 1601. But note that Cover's chosen examples, the sentencing of defendants and the death penalty, are textbook examples of law's coercive force.

Protecting private information of public interest: *Campbell's* great promise, unfulfilled

Paul Wragg

According to the House of Lords decision in Campbell v MGN Ltd, a misuse of private information claim may succeed even though public interest expression is at stake. The post-Campbell jurisprudence, however, does not reflect this central tenet. Cases are not determined by balancing the weight of each claim but by a binary approach in which claims succeed or fail depending on whether public interest expression is present or not. By charting this development, this article argues that a greater sense of proportionality would be achieved if cases were decided not by the quality of expression but by the harm caused by it. By re-imagining Campbell as a four-part test, it will show how the current paternalistic and idiosyncratic influences on decision-making may be reduced significantly.

1. Introduction

Campbell v MGN Ltd[1] remains a momentous decision. It shows the sort of judicial activism that Lord Irvine claimed would define the Human Rights Act era: enabling British judges to pioneer effective rights protection and influence European human rights law.[2] In *Campbell*, the House of Lords elevated the status of privacy to the same standing as freedom of expression such that either right could be protected where of greater comparative importance. In this way, the Art 10 ECHR right of the press to publish public interest expression was preserved but qualified. Thus *Campbell* created not just a quasi-privacy right but a strong one at that: one capable of protecting privacy *despite* the presence of a competing

This article stems from a paper read to participants at 'The *Campbell* Legacy: a Decade of "Misuse of Private Information"', Newcastle Law School, 17 April 2015. It also builds upon two short papers published by *Inforrm* and the *Gazette of Law and Journalism* (Australia).

[1] [2004] 2 AC 457.

[2] Lord Irvine of Lairg, 'Constitutional Reform and a Bill of Rights' (1997) *European Human Rights Law Review* 483, 485.

public interest claim. This outcome is all the more remarkable given the reported effect of privacy-invasion on Ms Campbell. The House of Lords placed greater reliance on her sense of outrage at the invasion than its actual effect on her treatment for narcotics dependency. The Court was satisfied that her recovery *could* have been compromised.[3] This is not to belittle her complaint. But it does suggest the fact of privacy intrusion was more important than the actual effect. This further evidences the great promise inherent in the *Campbell* decision.

Yet *Campbell* poses a question that it does not answer. If cases are to be determined by 'balancing' the respective claims then what is the unit of measurement by which the extent of public interest in expression is assessed? After all, determining the level of public interest at stake is very different to the more usual responsibility of classifying speech as being of public interest or not. The former question is not a task that judges are familiar with. Yet, it seems this issue has not been sufficiently recognised by the courts, and, as a result, the misuse of private information ('MOPI') jurisprudence lacks a method of determining the weight of a public interest claim. Although the need to balance claims is mentioned frequently enough, the mechanics of resolving disputes in practice do not fulfil the term: judges do not balance but, instead, apply the simple rule that public interest expression trumps privacy, and so claims fail where it is at stake. After showing this in the next section, the paper explores how a greater sense of balancing may be achieved. It does so, first, by explaining the reasons why balancing based upon the significance of expression cannot be achieved, at least not in the manner *Campbell* foreshadows. Inevitably, it would engender judicial paternalism and idiosyncrasy concerning the nature and value of public interest expression, as has happened. Instead, it will be argued that the spirit of *Campbell* is better realised by limiting protection according to the effect of the expression on the claimant. On doctrinal and theoretical grounds, this ought to be where speech is unjustifiably coercive. The final section, therefore, proposes a revised four-part test that would protect public interest expression but allows for its restriction where privacy invasion had a devastating effect. This safeguard for privacy interests would be subject to the narrow caveat that behaviour particularly damaging to societal concerns warrants coercion.

2. The balancing act and its failings

The exceptional level of privacy protection envisaged by *Campbell* is meant to be realised through the proportionality exercise at stage two of the *Campbell* test (stage one being the threshold question of whether there is a reasonable expectation of privacy), which is often referred to as the 'balancing act'. Here, the courts decide whether the privacy claim is stronger than the competing free speech claim. This process is best illuminated by the four propositions that, in

[3] *Campbell* (n 1) [158], discussed below.

the contemporaneous House of Lords decision in *Re S*,[4] Lord Steyn derived from the *Campbell* decision:

> First, neither article [8 nor 10] has as such precedence over the other. Secondly, where the values under the two articles are in conflict, an intense focus on the comparative importance of the specific rights being claimed in the individual case is necessary. Thirdly, the justifications for interfering with or restricting each right must be taken into account. Finally, the proportionality test must be applied to each. For convenience I will call this the ultimate balancing test.

The need for an 'intense focus' on the actual rights at stake is often referred to by courts when determining MOPI claims. The analysis, though, has a fatal superficiality to it. Although judges may talk at length about the privacy interests and free speech interests, typically the observations are compartmentalised. There is usually little or no real comparison of the two. Allied to this, when judges discuss the free speech claim, they do not measure its weight. Consequently, judges do not *balance* the competing claims, at least not in the way that *Campbell* foreshadows. They do not decide which is greater in a specific way but rather in a generalised way, according to whether there is a public interest in the expression. Thus, they employ a binary approach to determining stage two of the *Campbell* test. They subdivide each claim into its elemental parts and then classify accordingly: either the privacy claim fails because there is a public interest in publication or it succeeds because there is no such public interest at stake. In other words, at stage two, the claim is disposed of by deciding whether there is a public interest in disclosing each of the matters revealed. This is not balancing in *Re S* terms, as in the process of deciding whether the extent of privacy-invasion merits the degree of public interest to be derived from publication. It is, instead, a process of applying a simple rule: that free speech trumps privacy where public interest expression is at stake. Since privacy, therefore, can only succeed where public interest expression is not at stake, freedom of expression occupies a privileged position, rendering the prospective equality of the two rights largely redundant.

This thesis can be seen at work in *Campbell* itself – that there was a public interest in the first two categories of information (relating to the fact of her drug addiction and treatment) but not in the final three (relating to details of her treatment at Narcotics Anonymous and photographs of her departing a meeting). It was largely on this binary issue that the House of Lords was divided: Lords Nicholls and Hoffmann felt that there was a public interest in allowing newspapers to publish details about her treatment, and Hoffmann also thought there was in the photograph (Lord Nicholls felt it failed at stage one), whilst Lord Hope, Lord Carswell and Baroness Hale disagreed. It can also be seen in many other cases,[5]

[4] [2005] 1 AC 593 [17].

[5] See discussion in Paul Wragg, 'The Benefits of Privacy-Invading Expression' (2013) 64(2) *Northern Ireland Legal Quarterly* 187 and 'The Legitimacy of Press Regulation' (2015) *Public Law* 290, 299–304.

including, more recently, the Court of Appeal decision in *AAA v Associated Newspapers Ltd*,[6] which concerned an article about the identity of AAA's father. The claim, at first instance, had been sub-divided into two categories: photographs of AAA and disclosure of his father's identity. The Court of Appeal agreed with the High Court: there was no public interest in the publication of the photograph of AAA, therefore that portion of the claim succeeded, but there was a public interest in knowing his father's identity given he was a prominent public official, and therefore that part failed.

Yet neither case demonstrates the proportionality exercise at work. For example, in *Campbell*, why was there a public interest in knowing that Naomi Campbell took drugs and why did this outweigh the harm caused? Admittedly, counsel for Ms Campbell conceded this point early on in proceedings but what is interesting is the general consensus amongst their Lordships that counsel was right to do so. Baroness Hale put this most strongly where she said 'the possession and use of illegal drugs is a criminal offence and a matter of serious public concern. The press must be free to expose the truth and put the record straight.'[7] It is understandable, perhaps, that a judge would not want to condone drug use but the criminal law treats use differently to possession and supply, and possession is usually treated as less serious. To suggest that *any* drug use is a matter of *serious* public concern surely exaggerates the issue. Also, Baroness Hale's analysis sits in sharp contrast to the approach that Eady J would later take in *Mosley* where he was unconvinced that the commission of any crime is always a matter of public interest meriting publication.[8] Of course, with Campbell, there was the additional point of exposing her public lie: that she did not take drugs. Yet it is also not clear why this public interest outweighed the privacy invasion that this information constituted. Why did the public need to know this? Or rather, why was this more important than her entitlement to keep this aspect of her private life away from public scrutiny or the detrimental effect this public knowledge might have on her rehabilitation? As Fenwick and Phillipson have previously said, this concession comes 'perilously close to destroying' the notion of informational autonomy underpinning the privacy right.[9] Likewise, in *AAA*, it is not clear why the identity of the child's father was of such public interest that it would outweigh the child's privacy claim. At first instance, the court put it in these terms:

> [i]t is said that such information goes to the issue of recklessness on the part of the supposed father, relevant both to his private and professional character, in particular his fitness for public office. I find that [it does].

---

[6] [2013] EWCA Civ 554.
[7] *Campbell* (n 1) [151].
[8] *Mosley v News Group Newspapers Ltd* [2008] EWHC 1777 (QB) [117].
[9] Helen Fenwick and Gavin Phillipson, *Media Freedom under the Human Rights Act* (OUP, 2006) 804.

What is the value of this information, though, to the electorate and why does it matter? If the courts are serious about the proportionality exercise then we should expect to see this value quantified more explicitly.

As a result, the process of balancing often seems quite superficial. For example, in *In Re Guardian News and Media Ltd*,[10] the Supreme Court agreed that anonymity orders protecting five applicants suspected of terrorist activity disproportionately interfered with press freedom. Since the applicants were challenging the designation process (and the freezing orders that accompanied it) the Court declared that the public had a 'legitimate interest in not being kept in the dark' about these individuals and were entitled to receive information supplementing that already in the public domain so that they might know the 'true position' of the challenge to the freezing order system. In this way, the public might make 'informed judgment[s]' about the applicants and the current law.[11] The deleterious effect of identification, though, was dismissed in short order. Although the press might be 'outrageously hostile', the risk of abuse was not a 'sufficient reason' to deny publication.[12] Even from this brief excerpt, it can be seen the 'intense focus' on comparative rights in this case pitted a speculative public benefit (public discourse will be enriched, somehow) against a dismissive evaluation of the detriment (some abuse may follow but that is the price of freedom). Objectively, the marginal benefit to public discourse seems disproportionate when set against the immediate harmful consequences of being labelled a suspected terrorist.

The issue in these cases, though, is not simply that the courts made judgments that others might not have made. It is much more fundamental than that. Neither the *Campbell* test nor *Re S* elucidation is expansive enough. It is all or nothing. Neither contains the analytical tools that would enable courts to compare the benefits and harms of the rights at stake. As Barak has argued, the proportionality test requires an evaluation not of the societal importance of one right compared to another but the marginal social importance of the rights at stake.[13] In other words, the courts should evaluate the specific consequences caused by the actual interference with either right. Yet the *Campbell* test and *Re S* elucidation do not provide the means to do so. Criteria like 'proportionality', 'comparative importance' and 'justified interference' are too deeply value-laden to operate as functional guidance of themselves. As the European Court of Human Rights (ECtHR) has made plain, it is for domestic courts to 'interpret' these criteria in light of local conditions.[14] Further explication is required. Since this has not happened, judges are left to shoehorn claims uncomfortably into two narrow questions that leave other questions unanswered and largely unanswerable. Often the finding of a public interest

[10] [2010] UKSC 1.
[11] ibid [68]–[69].
[12] ibid [72].
[13] Aharon Barak, *Proportionality* (CUP, 2012) 340–349.
[14] *Handyside v UK* (1979–80) 1 EHRR 737 [48] –[50].

at stake is understandable, but the idea that a privacy claim should be defeated as a consequence does not ring true. Likewise, the finding that there is no public interest at stake (because the court has concluded the expression is unimportant or simply prurient) can equally seem idiosyncratic and unprincipled. This can cause decisions to feel quite artificial. It makes comparisons between cases, and of identifying objective justifications for different outcomes, very difficult. For example, in *Goodwin*, it was held that there was a public interest in knowing about the fact of Fred Goodwin's affair with a colleague because

> there should be public discussion of the circumstances in which it is proper for a chief executive (or other person holding public office or exercising official functions) to be able to carry on a sexual relationship with an employee in the same organisation.[15]

This seems all the more remarkable because in the earlier case of *K*, a case involving an extra-marital affair between colleagues, the Court of Appeal rejected the notion there was a public interest in publishing even the fact of the affair, despite noting that the woman involved was dismissed as a result (to placate her former lover and colleague), a decision that left her 'upset and angry'.[16] The public interest in *Goodwin* seems little different to the issues raised in *K* – if anything they seem more heightened in *K*: why was the woman dismissed and not the man? One obvious difference is that *K* did not involve, so far as one can tell, actual or quasi public office holders, but this is distinctly unsatisfying as an explanation. It seems the employment had some public context – there is passing reference to a public announcement of her departure[17] – and, as is well-established, the notion of a public figure is very broadly defined in the MOPI jurisprudence.[18] Indeed, the inclusion of Fred Goodwin, a chief executive at a PLC, shows something of this flexibility.

The courts' failure to employ proportionality in a satisfying manner, therefore, can be attributed to a fundamental problem with both the *Campbell* test and *Re S* elucidation. Neither articulates a test in the proper sense of the word. Instead, both establish a framework for determining rights conflicts that a test must satisfy, without providing the test itself. So, this framework says that conflicts will have to be settled in a manner that respects both sets of rights, in terms of both the merits and limitations of the respective claims, and should interfere with either only in a proportionate way. The need to articulate such a test has not been judicially recognised, at least not as regards the balancing act. It has been recognised for the threshold question at stage one, and therefore, partially recognised in respect of identifying the extent of privacy intrusion. Thus, in *Murray*, the Court of Appeal found the test requires the court to evaluate all the circumstances, including:

[15] *Goodwin v NGN Ltd* [2011] EWHC 1437 (QB) [133].
[16] *K v NGN Ltd* [2011] 1 WLR 1827.
[17] ibid [7].
[18] *A v B plc* [2003] QB 195.

> the attributes of the claimant, the nature of the activity in which the claimant was engaged, the place at which it was happening, the nature and purpose of the intrusion, the absence of consent and whether it was known or could be inferred, the effect on the claimant and the circumstances in which and the purposes for which the information came into the hands of the publisher.[19]

This passage is the leading authority on this point, as the Supreme Court recently confirmed.[20] It allows the court to make precise judgments about the strength of the privacy claim. Yet since a comparable evaluation cannot take place for the free speech claim, courts are left to conclude the balancing act by reference to two stark evaluations, the extent of the privacy-invasion and the bare classification of the expression as being of public interest or not, with no obvious means of comparing the two. This feature of the MOPI jurisprudence renders the 'intense focus' impotent once the expression is classified as being of public interest. Even though freedom of expression is not assumed to be of greater importance than privacy before the assessment starts, it acquires supremacy once that classification occurs. From that point, the *Campbell* test does remarkably little to protect the claimant.

This renders the common reference to Lord Hoffmann's remark in *Campbell* that the ultimate question must be 'whether there is sufficient public interest … to justify curtailment of the conflicting right'[21] little more than rhetorical. Neither *Campbell* nor *Re S* explains how to calculate sufficiency nor identifies legitimate justifications to interfere with public interest expression. This has left subsequent courts without the analytical means of determining the answer meaningfully. Instead, courts tend to answer a different question dressed up as that one. For example, in *K*, the Court of Appeal answered it by asking itself this:

> Is a debate about the reasons why X's employment terminated a matter of such public interest? … The reasons for her leaving may interest some members of the public but the matters are not of public interest.[22]

Yet this is an evaluation about classification passed off as one about degree. This sleight of hand is not uncommon. In *Ntuli v Donald*, Eady J said this at first instance:

> I am not persuaded that there is any substantial argument for publication based on public interest … it seems to me that there is no reason to suppose that the revelation of the relationship would in any way contribute to a debate of general interest. Nor would it serve to prevent the public being misled or lead to the exposure of hypocrisy.[23]

[19] *Murray v Express Newspapers plc* [2009] 1 Ch 481 [36].
[20] *Re JR38* [2015] UKSC 42.
[21] *Campbell* (n 1) [56].
[22] *K* (n 16) [23].
[23] [2010] EWCA Civ 1276 [19].

In other words, it was not simply that Eady J could identify no *substantial* public interest, he could find none at all. The Court of Appeal, though, endorsed this approach, stating it could detect 'no analytical deficiency'.[24] The problem of identifying the extent of the public interest is also revealed by the language employed by the judges to describe it. On those rare occasions where the courts say there is an insufficient amount at stake, they use some variant of the word 'modicum'. For example, in *YXB v TNO* (a 'kiss and tell' about a premiership footballer), the court held that there was 'a modest degree of public interest in putting before the public the other side of the story'.[25] In *HRH Prince of Wales v Associated Newspapers Ltd* the contribution of Prince Charles's private journal to matters of public interest was found to be 'minimal'.[26] Yet to find there is a modicum of public interest is to say there is none at all. *De minimis non curat lex.*

Since press freedom is typically interpreted as an audience interest, the notion of proportionality is particularly difficult to realise. It would require judges to evaluate the effect caused by depriving the audience of the information or by imposing a financial penalty on the speaker (which may (or may not) modify the speaker's future behaviour). It is an empirical claim that a court simply cannot determine objectively. A court cannot say what the marginal social effect would be of depriving the audience of particular instances of public interest expression.[27] For example, if a court decides that public criticism of Rio Ferdinand's affair is a matter of public interest then it cannot say what the effect would be on public discourse if that condemnation could not take place. It could not evaluate how worse off society would be compared to how better off Rio Ferdinand would be without relying upon speculation and personal inclination. As Tugendhat J said in *Terry*, 'it is not for the judge to express personal views on such matters, still less to impose whatever personal views he might have'.[28] This sort of moralising, though, is apparent in the case law. For example, in *CTB* (the Ryan Giggs case), Eady J was particularly dismissive of the public interest value that 'kiss and tell' stories have:[29] 'As in so many "kiss and tell" cases, it seems to me that the answer, at stage two, is not far to seek.'[30] In *Ferdinand*, though, Nicol J was much more sympathetic.[31] The courts lack an independent principle that would allow them to explicate the significance of public interest expression in objective terms. Imagining the public interest as occupying a scale of zero to ten, the courts lack the language to say what would count as a public interest claim with a magnitude of seven, or four, or whatever.

---

[24] ibid [25].
[25] *YXB v TNO* [2015] EWHC 826 (QB) [61 (viii)].
[26] [2008] Ch 57, 126 [72].
[27] A point apparently recognised by Laing J in *AMC v News Group Newspapers Ltd* [2015] EWHC 2361 (QB) [27].
[28] *Terry v Persons Unknown* [2010] EMLR 16 [101].
[29] *CTB v News Group Newspapers Ltd* [2011] EWHC 1232 (QB) [26].
[30] See, similarly, *AMC* (n 27).
[31] *Ferdinand v MGN Ltd* [2011] EWHC 2454 [26].

The difficulties inherent in balancing, what are essentially, two incommensurate rights have not gone entirely unnoticed by the judiciary. The Court of Appeal has previously explained away the problem in this way:

> In many cases, this balancing exercise is difficult. This is partly because the two rights are rather different in their constituent factors, partly because there are often powerful arguments pointing in opposite directions, partly because each case depends very much on its own particular facts, and partly because the exercise can involve a significant degree of subjectivity.[32]

This, though, is an unsatisfying account. The exercise involves not just a 'significant degree of subjectivity'. In some cases it seems to rely upon nothing but subjectivity. It sits uneasily with the view expressed by the House of Lords in *Scott v Scott* (the original privacy claim about the embarrassment caused by public knowledge of the defendant's impotence).

> the power of an ordinary Court of justice to hear in private cannot rest merely on the discretion of the judge or on his individual view that it is desirable for the sake of public decency or morality that the hearing should take place in private. If there is any exception to the broad principle which requires the administration of justice to take place in open Court, that exception must be based on the application of some other and overriding principle which defines the field of exception and does not leave its limits to the individual discretion of the judge.[33]

The context is different but similar observations can be made about the MOPI jurisprudence. It relies upon 'mere discretion' and lacks an 'overriding principle' that determines how and when 'sufficient public interest' is established. Moreover, despite the recognition by the Supreme Court in *In Re Guardian News and Media* that absolute protection for public interest expression is not warranted (it can be interfered with, albeit 'scarcely'), the jurisprudence offers no meaningful method of ensuring protection *is* qualified. Without such a principle 'the field of exception' referred to in *Scott* is left undefined. This cuts both ways, leaving public interest expression over- and under-protected. The public interest expression may be vulnerable if a judge has a preconceived mind-set toward particular types of speech. For example, in *YXB v TNO*, Warby J concluded that in disposing of the application he must bear 'in mind that the case is of the "kiss-and-tell" variety, and that there is in general no public interest in the disclosure of details about matters of this kind'.[34] If MOPI cases are dealt with on specifics and not generalities (as they should be)[35] then this vulnerability is problematic.

---

[32] *JIH v News Group Newspapers Ltd* [2011] EWCA Civ 42 [3].
[33] *Scott v Scott* (1913) AC 417 435.
[34] *YXB v TNO* (n 25) [60].
[35] *Ntuli v Donald* (n 23) [54].

The need to identify the principle by which 'sufficient' is established is not simply of academic interest. The courts' propensity, of late, to define the term 'public interest' generously has seriously weakened the value of the MOPI claim. The failure by the House of Lords in *Campbell* to define the public right not to be misled in clear terms has caused difficulties in later cases, particularly *Hutcheson v NGN*,[36] *Ferdinand v NGN*[37] and *McClaren v NGN*[38] where this 'right' was used to justify publications concerning fairly trivial immorality by well-known (and less well-known) individuals. In addition, the courts have also employed the nebulous concepts of 'role model' status and 'freedom to criticise' to justify interferences with privacy.[39] These devices have protected the press where the claimant's private life has been judged inconsistent with their public persona or incompatible with their chosen career or harmful to it. More generally, it allows newspapers to advance successful public interest claims on the basis the claimant's behaviour was socially or morally 'wrong'.[40]

Having established the limitations of the judicial approach to balancing, the following seeks to outline reasons why at least some of these difficulties cannot be overcome. In particular, it will be argued that there are cogent and compelling reasons why balancing as a process of determining the significance of expression cannot be realised in a principled manner. The *Campbell* test and *Re S* elucidation rely too heavily upon abstract terms, or else have been interpreted in this way. To be sure, abstract principles (particularly those derived from philosophical theories) are vital to better understanding both rights but, as will be argued shortly, invite unwarranted paternalism to determine outcomes. Instead, it will be argued that a more pragmatic approach is advisable. As Solove has argued, a contextual approach to privacy, with specific problems and outcomes in mind, is more likely to yield reliable solutions.[41] Thus it will be argued that judges should not balance by means of assigning hypothetical values to each claim and deciding which is greater. The courts can, however, make judgments about the effect of the expression on the claimant and decide whether those effects are excessive. This would be balancing, but of a different kind. This argument is set out in the final section.

3. Problems in evaluating the significance of the public interest at stake

The *Re S* formulation, at stages two and three, presupposes that the weight of the free speech claim is equivalent to the degree of engagement with the values underpinning Art 10. In *Campbell*, Baroness Hale advocated the adoption of a

[36] [2011] EWCA Civ 808.
[37] See n 31.
[38] [2012] EWHC 2466 (QB).
[39] For further discussion see Wragg, 'The Benefits of Privacy-Invading Expression' (n 5).
[40] *Terry* (n 28); cf *AMC* (n 27).
[41] Daniel J Solove, *Understanding Privacy* (Harvard University Press, 2008).

hierarchical approach to this process. She noted that 'some [types of expression] are more deserving of protection in a democratic society than others' and 'top of the list is political speech'.[42] This taxonomical approach is well-established in the academic literature. It is advocated by US scholars like Meiklejohn,[43] Sunstein[44] and Fiss.[45] Meiklejohn, for example, argued that to be self-governing, citizens must receive information and ideas necessary for democratic decision-making. It also chimes with Lord Justice Leveson's appraisal of press freedom: that the importance of a free press lies in its capacity to enable democratic participation and act as a check on power.[46] These conceptions prioritise information vital to the process of electing and monitoring government. On this view, a judge might take into account the proximity of both the claimant's occupation and their pernicious behaviour to the political process. For example, it is well-established that politicians are expected to show greater tolerance to intrusions into their private lives than ordinary members of the public.[47] In this way, exposing the extra-marital affairs of an England footballer might be held to be less significant than exposing corruption in public office. Also, a judge might make distinctions based upon the extent of public accountability involved in the claimant's employment. Utilising this calculus, there would be a greater public interest in knowing of a politician's involvement in embezzling public money than the misdemeanours of low-level public servants.

Exclusive reliance on the democratic participation value, though, is problematic. There are other values that Art 10 champions. The ECtHR has consistently said that 'freedom of expression … constitutes one of the essential foundations of a democratic society, indeed one of the basic conditions for its progress and for the self-fulfilment of the individual'.[48] The UK courts have identified similar values, of which Lord Steyn's view in *ex parte Simms* is particularly well known:

> Freedom of expression is, of course, intrinsically important: it is valued for its own sake. But it is well recognised that it is also instrumentally important. It serves a number of broad objectives. First, it promotes the self-fulfilment of individuals in society. Secondly, in the famous words of Holmes J. (echoing John Stuart Mill), 'the best test of truth is the power of the thought to get itself accepted in the competition of the market' ... Thirdly, freedom of speech is the lifeblood of democracy. The free flow of information and ideas informs political debate.[49]

[42]*Campbell* (n 1) [148].
[43]Alexander Meiklejohn, *Free Speech and its Relation to Self-Government* (Harper, 1948).
[44]Cass R Sunstein, *Democracy and the Problem of Free Speech* (Free Press, 1995).
[45]Owen M Fiss, *Liberalism Divided* (Westview Press, 1996).
[46]Lord Justice Leveson, *An Inquiry into the Culture, Practices and Ethics of the Press: Report* (HC 780, 2012) 64–65.
[47]*Lingens v Austria* (1986) 8 EHRR 407.
[48]*Vereinigung Bildender Kunstler v Austria* [2007] ECDR 7 [26].
[49]*R v Secretary of State for the Home Department ex parte Simms* [2000]2 AC 115, 126.

Exposure of a footballer's affair may not further democratic participation (though see below) but could be said to engage values relating to truth, self-fulfilment and autonomy. Indeed, this seemed to be Tugendhat J's view in *Terry v Persons Unknown*:

> There is much public debate as to what conduct is or is not socially harmful. Not all conduct that is socially harmful is unlawful, and there is often said to be much inconsistency in the law ... The fact that conduct is private and lawful is not, of itself, conclusive of the question whether or not it is in the public interest that it be discouraged. There is no suggestion that the conduct in question in the present case ought to be unlawful, or that any editor would ever suggest that it should be. But in a plural society there will be some who would suggest that it ought to be discouraged ... Freedom to live as one chooses is one of the most valuable freedoms. But so is the freedom to criticise (within the limits of the law) the conduct of other members of society as being socially harmful, or wrong.[50]

This is a far broader set of values than are apparent in Meiklejohn's and Leveson's conceptions.

Neither can it be said that the domestic and supranational jurisprudence advocates the prioritisation of democratic participation value. Whilst speech enabling democratic participation is particularly important to protect, there is nothing to suggest that the Art 10 values are ranked. Admittedly, both UK and Strasbourg courts have emphasised the importance of protecting political expression. The Supreme Court, for example, has said that political communications 'sit at the top of the hierarchy of free speech'[51] and, recently, the High Court has said that 'freedom of political expression is one of the most important freedoms'.[52] Likewise, the ECtHR has said that interferences with the expression of elected officials 'call for the closest scrutiny'.[53] Yet, the ECtHR has made it clear that 'political expression' is not limited to information about government but includes matters of 'public interest and concern'.[54] Also, in articulating the press's 'public watchdog role', which it describes as 'vital', it refers to the duty to disseminate 'public interest expression'.[55] Given how broadly the term 'public interest expression' has been interpreted in the UK, it must be that the other values underpinning Art 10 – truth, autonomy and self-fulfilment – are also capable of falling within this category of higher order expression.

Alternatively, even if the democratic participation value was prioritised, it is such an elastic concept that it could not be confined to narrow understandings of the term, such as the process of public decision-making. As Greenawalt has memorably said, political speech cannot be 'hermetically sealed' from other concerns: 'speech that is

---

[50] *Terry* [2010] EWHC 119 (QB), [104]

[51] *R (Lord Carlile of Berriew)v Secretary of State for the Home Department* [2014] UKSC 60 [61].

[52] *Barron v Collins* [2015] EWHC 1125 (QB) [12].

[53] *Castells v Spain* (1992) 14 EHRR 445 [42].

[54] *Steel & Morris v UK* [2005] EMLR 15 [88].

[55] *Thorgeir v Iceland* (1992) 14 EHRR 843 [63].

not explicitly political often has political implications.'[56] Or, as has been said of the First Amendment, 'a politically based approach … abandons history, precedent, and important values in pursuit of a legitimacy that is founded on controversial question begging'.[57] For example, speech falling within Tugendhat J's freedom to criticise may be treated as a form of political expression by virtue of expressing views about societal morality. As another commentator has argued:

> it is simply confused to try to effect a separation between moral vision and political vision, between moral sensibilities and political sensibilities. To express a moral vision is inevitably to express a political vision.[58]

Accordingly, stories about the promiscuity of professional footballers and its effect on impressionable minds may be said to further the democratic participation value.[59] Such discussion contributes to public debate about the appropriateness of footballers as figures of influence.

It is doubtful whether the judiciary could confine the term 'public interest' to democratic decision-making or something narrower. Admittedly, the ECtHR has consistently said[60] that expression is not of public interest where the 'sole purpose is to satisfy the curiosity of a particular readership regarding the details of a public figure's private life … In such conditions, freedom of expression calls for a narrower interpretation'.[61] Subsequent ECtHR decisions, however, have cast doubt on the restrictiveness of this principle, as *Von Hannover (No 2)* shows: in that case photographs of the applicant on holiday at a time when her father was gravely ill contributed to a debate of public interest about how members of the royal family deal with such matters.[62] As a result, the principle seems no more meaningful than the familiar UK rendition:

> it is important not to overlook the fact that what may be in the public interest to know and thus for the media to publicise in exercise of their freedom of speech is not to be confused with what is interesting to the public and, therefore, in a newspaper's commercial interest to publish.[63]

---

[56]Kent Greenawalt, *Speech, Crime, and the Uses of Language* (OUP, 1989) 45.
[57]Steven Shiffrin, 'The First Amendment and Economic Regulation: Away from a General Theory of the First Amendment' (1983) 78 *Northwestern Law Review* 1212, 1239.
[58]Michael J Perry, 'Freedom of Expression: An Essay on Theory and Doctrine' (1984) 78 (5) *Northwestern University Law Review* 1137, 1149.
[59]For further discussion of the theoretical support for this position see Wragg, 'The Benefits of Privacy-Invading Expression' (n 5).
[60]See *Von Hannover v Germany* (2005) 40 EHRR 1 [65] and, more recently, *MGN v UK* (2011) 53 EHRR 5 [143].
[61]*Von Hannover* (n 60) [65]–[66].
[62]*Von Hannover v Germany (No 2)* (2012) EMLR 16 [117].
[63]*HRH Prince of Wales v Associated Newspapers Ltd* [2006] EWCA Civ 1776 [118].

This comparison of polar opposites may be useful in obvious cases of unjustified privacy-invasion but not in others. Ultimately, it relies upon – or otherwise encourages – the use of paternalism to decide what is important for the public to know and what is not. Yet the maxim lacks analytical bite. The phrase has become a sort of refuge in which to make idiosyncratic judgements about the quality of speech, usually accompanied by the stern moral disapproval that it is of prurient interest only.[64] This, though, is not a particularly helpful analytical tool to distinguish between, say, knowledge of adulterous behaviour that is in the public interest (eg, the extra-marital affairs of Steve McClaren, John Terry, and Rio Ferdinand) and that which is not (eg, the extra-marital affair of the claimant in *CC v AB*).[65] Further, the phrase 'genuine public interest',[66] often employed in the domestic case law, is a gloss that does nothing to clarify what is otherwise replica public interest. Without employing paternalism there is no way of knowing what constitutes the substandard form.

Also, it may be argued that the softer approach to the definition of public interest is defensible, not least for its consistency with the treatment of the term found elsewhere in the case law. For example, defamation law has long treated it generously. In *London Artists Ltd v Littler*, Lord Denning MR considered that 'whenever a matter is such as to affect people at large, so that they may be legitimately interested in, or concerned at, what is going on; or what may happen to them or to others; then it is a matter of public interest … '.[67] Thus the issue on the facts – a published letter alleging a plot to force a successful play to close – was a matter of public interest. *Per* Edmund Davies LJ:

> Just as the presentation of a new play is of public interest, so also, in my judgment, is the sudden and surprising closure of a play enjoying a highly successful run … For example, it might well lead to a discussion of whether the paucity of West End theatres is such that even highly successful plays have to be taken off to make way for new ones awaiting production, or to an examination of theatre finances, or to an assessment of the virtues and vices of the starring system, all such comment springing from and primarily illustrated by the abrupt taking off of one highly praised and successful production.[68]

This broad approach is consistent with the decision in *Campbell v Spottiswoode*:

> Nothing is more important than that fair and full latitude of discussion should be allowed to writers upon any public matter, whether it be the conduct of public

[64] See, eg, *BBC v Roden*, UKEAT/0385/14/DA [37]; *W v M* [2012] EWHC 1679 (Fam) [25]; *K* (n 16) [23]; *Independent News and Media Ltd v A* [2010] EWCA Civ 343 [22]; *Leeds City Council v Channel Four* [2005] EWHC 3522 (Fam) [33].

[65] [2006] EWHC 3083 (QB).

[66] See, eg, *McKennitt v Ash* [2006] EMLR 178 [57] or, more recently, *ZYT v Associated Newspapers Ltd* [2015] EWHC 1162 (QB) [14].

[67] [1969] 2 WLR 409, 418.

[68] ibid, 421.

> men, or the proceedings in courts of justice or in Parliament, or the publication of a scheme or of a literary work.[69]

Similarly, in the more recent case of *Branson v Bower*, Eady J noted:

> In a modern democracy all those who venture into public life, in whatever capacity, must expect to have their motives subjected to scrutiny and discussed. Nor is it realistic today to demand that such debate should be hobbled by the constraints of conventional good manners – still less of deference.[70]

Given its doctrinal heritage, a narrowing of the common law's generous interpretation of the term 'public interest' seems unlikely.

There are issues, then, in evaluating the strength of public interest expression by ranking the values apparently furthered by it. Even if all values are treated as equal, problems remain in evaluating the degree to which those values are furthered. Inevitably, such an approach invites courts to specify the importance of the expression as if it were some quantifiable commodity. Such observations can be found in the case law. For example, in *Belfast City Council v Miss Behavin' Ltd*, the House of Lords accepted that pornography engages Art 10 but only 'at a very low level':[71] 'The right to vend pornography is not the most important right of free expression in a democratic society'[72] and 'comes well below celebrity gossip in the hierarchy of speech which deserves the protection of the law'.[73] In *Connolly v DPP*, a woman was prosecuted for sending unsettling images of aborted foetuses to her local chemist to dissuade them from selling the 'morning after' pill. The court found the prosecution was proportionate because, amongst other things, her campaign was 'hardly an effective way of promoting the anti-abortion cause'.[74] Similarly, in *R (Prolife) v BBC*, Lord Hoffmann, in determining a judicial review case about a party political broadcast, found it 'relevant to consider whether it has any impact upon the particular democratic interest which [it] was intended to advance'.[75] He concluded that since Prolife was a single-issue party seeking election in six Welsh constituencies, in which they gained very few votes, the impact was negligible.[76]

These sorts of judgments about the societal significance of expression are problematic. First, since there is no independent means of determining the value of speech to the audience, idiosyncratic and/or paternalistic assessments will occur.

---

[69](1863) 3 B & S 769, 778.
[70][2002] QB 737 [25].
[71][2007] UKHL 19 [16].
[72]ibid.
[73]ibid [38].
[74]*Connolly v DPP* [2007] EWHC 237 (Admin) [31].
[75]*R (Prolife) v BBC* [2004] 1 AC 185 [67].
[76]ibid [67]–[68]. See criticism in Eric Barendt, 'Free Speech and Abortion' [2003] *Public Law* 280.

This problem is well recognised in the academic literature. Alexander, for example, has argued forcefully that there is 'no metaphysical basis' for determining units of value.[77] Similarly, Redish has said that the fetish for public decision-making is not only arbitrary but also confused since it overlooks entirely the more powerful individual need for informed private decision-making.[78] Meanwhile, Fish, adopting a more extreme position along the same spectrum, has insisted that the protection of 'important' speech is flawed because such judgments 'will always reflect a *political* decision to indemnify some kinds of verbal behaviour and devalue others'.[79] It is for reasons like this that Schauer has concluded that free speech clauses are best founded upon a deep mistrust of government (including courts) to appraise the value of speech reliably.[80] For obvious reasons, judges should not be foisting their own view of importance upon society at large. Secondly, this sort of approach undermines the long-standing principle that Art 10 protects unimportant expression, even that which 'shocks, offends or disturbs'.[81] If speech is protected to the extent of its 'importance' then it is inevitable that speech which is irresponsible, juvenile or unpersuasive will fare badly on this metric. 'Bad' speech, even that which is overtly political, will enjoy little or no protection at all. Yet the ECtHR has consistently said that, on matters of public interest, Art 10 allow for 'recourse to a degree of exaggeration or even provocation, or in other words to make somewhat immoderate statements'.[82] Indeed, the Court has even said that Art 10 'as such does not prohibit discussion or dissemination of information received even if it is strongly suspected that this information might not be truthful'.[83] There is also the issue of editorial autonomy that both Strasbourg and the domestic courts recognise as an equally important principle to respect when determining Art 10 claims. The ECtHR has said that since 'methods of objective and balanced reporting may vary considerably' it is not 'for this Court, nor for the national courts, to substitute its own views for those of the press as to what technique of reporting should be adopted'.[84] In their dissenting opinions in *Campbell*, both Lord Hoffmann and Lord Nicholls[85] recognised this point. Lord Hoffmann expressed it this way: 'One must … ask whether the journalists exceeded the latitude which should be allowed to them in presenting their story.'[86] Requiring courts to evaluate the

[77]Larry Alexander, *Is There a Right to Freedom of Expression?* (CUP, 2005) 139.
[78]Martin Redish, 'The Value of Free Speech,' (1982) 130 *University of Pennsylvania Law Review* 591.
[79]Stanley Fish, *There's No Such Thing as Free Speech* (OUP, 1994) 15.
[80]Frederick Schauer, *Free Speech: A Philosophical Enquiry*, (CUP, 1982).
[81]*Handyside* (n 14).
[82]See, most recently, *Maguire v UK* (2015) 60 EHRR 12.
[83]*Salov v Ukraine* (2007) 45 EHRR 51 [113].
[84]*MGN v UK* (n 60) [141].
[85]*Campbell* (n 1) [29].
[86]ibid [68].

significance of speech, though, invariably causes considerable tension with this principle, for it invites judicial comment on the form of the expression.

Finally, the weighing of public interest claims also sits uncomfortably with Strasbourg principle, because it envisages the possibility of 'weak', 'average' or 'imperfect' public interest claims (or any other description of strength sitting on the spectrum between 'modicum' and 'genuine'). Although it is intuitively appealing to believe that a strong privacy claim would trump a weak public interest claim, such an approach ignores the crucial normative and doctrinal point that public interest expression is always a strong form of free speech claim (for which interference is 'scarcely justified').[87] As the ECtHR has consistently said:

> it is incumbent on [the press] to impart information and ideas on matters of public interest. Not only does it have the task of imparting such information and ideas: the public also has a right to receive them. Were it otherwise, the press would be unable to play its vital role of 'public watchdog'.[88]

This does not mean the public has an absolute right to receive the information since, as noted, Art 10 is a qualified right. Yet the Strasbourg jurisprudence suggests that the permissibility of interference must be determined by the nature of the legitimate aim at stake rather than the quality of the expression.[89] Admittedly, the ECtHR is not as emphatic on this point as it could be. In *MGN v UK*, for example, the Court approved the approach taken by the House of Lords in *Campbell* by noting its consistency with the established principle that, in resolving Art 8/Art 10 disputes, the domestic court 'must balance the public interest in the publication of a photograph and the need to protect private life'.[90]

Yet, the balancing approach adopted by the ECtHR does not seem reliant upon a valuation of the public interest at stake. Instead, when asking whether the interference met a 'pressing social need', the Court's inquiry is confined to examining the effect of the expression on the victim. For example, in *MGN v UK*, the ECtHR supported its position on balancing by relying on[91] the case of *Hachette Filipacchi Associates v France*,[92] which concerned photographs of a murder scene and of the deceased in an article about the murder. The family of the victim complained successfully, in their domestic court, of a breach of Art 8. In finding that no violation of Art 10 had occurred, the ECtHR made no attempt to evaluate the significance of the photograph in public interest terms. Instead, having noted it was public interest expression,

[87] *In re Guardian News and Media Ltd* [2010] UKSC 1 [51].
[88] *MGN v UK* (n 60) [141].
[89] See, eg, *Hadjianastassiou v Greece* (1993) 16 EHRR 219 [39]; *Markt Intern v Germany* (1990) 12 EHRR 161 [26]; *Muller v Switzerland* (1991) 13 EHRR 212 [27]–[28].
[90] *MGN v UK* (n 60) [142].
[91] ibid (n 34).
[92] (2009) 49 EHRR 23.

it concluded that it 'intensified' the trauma and grief suffered by the family to such a degree that the interference with Art 10 was justified.[93] This approach is evident in other ECtHR cases. For example, in *Krone Verlags v Austria*,[94] a case about comparative advertising, the ECtHR resolved the case without determining the extent of the public interest at stake; instead, it determined that there was a public interest at stake and no convincing reason was established by the domestic court to interfere with it. In other words, it was the effect of expression on the claimant that the Court was most interested in.

For these reasons, it would be a mistake for judges to determine the weight of the public interest expression by assigning some value to it. Inevitably, such judgments would be paternalistic, idiosyncratic and unprincipled. Yet public interest expression should not enjoy absolute protection. In the final section, it will be argued that the overriding principle to determine its limits should be based on the specific effects of the speech upon the claimant, as intimated by the Strasbourg jurisprudence.

4. Achieving greater proportionality in MOPI claims

As noted above, following *Murray*, the courts may make some fine distinctions about the extent of privacy invasion. It is clear that, to pass the threshold test, the claimant must establish that their Art 8 interests are actually, not prospectively, affected, and sufficiently seriously, as both *Terry*[95] and *YXB* show. *YXB* is particularly illustrative of how strictly this principle is applied. Here, the claimant, following a newspaper report, wished to conceal his identity as the unnamed premier league footballer who had engaged in adulterous sexual conduct after his club's Christmas party. Indeed, the court added a few extra details, which had not appeared in the newspaper report:

> In the early hours of 16 December 2014, during a party … the defendant performed oral sex on the claimant. They have never met again, but a month later the claimant initiated an exchange of messages between the two, via their mobile phones, in the course of which he wrote to her, and she to him, about having sex together. The claimant sent the defendant explicit images, including photographs of his erect penis, and video of himself masturbating. She also sent him images, but nothing so intimate.[96]

Yet the claimant failed to provide evidence of the effect that identification would have, which Mr Justice Warby was particularly critical of:

> The claimant's own attitude to the privacy rights relied on is a relevant, and important, factor. When applying an intense focus to the specific rights at issue in the individual case, the court can hardly be expected to attach great weight to the privacy

[93] ibid [49].
[94] (2006) 42 EHRR 28.
[95] *Terry* (n 28).
[96] *YXB* (n 25) [1].

> rights asserted on the claimant's behalf if he fails, without justification, to give any evidence himself. The most remarkable feature of this case is the complete absence of any evidence from the claimant ... What has been said by [counsel] on instructions suggests that the concern is embarrassment, and mainly directed at the images, which are to be protected anyway. This lends support to [opposing counsel's] submission that the claimant has not shown any great concern about privacy for his sexual conduct.'[97]

This is an apparent departure from *Campbell*. Here, the House of Lords examined the quality of the privacy invasion and concluded that it was of a type which, viewed objectively, interfered with privacy interests. It was less concerned with examining the actual effect. For example, Baroness Hale said

> The trial judge ... could tell whether the impact of the story on her was serious or trivial. The fact that the story had been published at all was *bound* to cause distress and *possibly* interfere with her progress. But he was best placed to judge whether the additional information and the photographs had added significantly both to the distress and the *potential* harm. He accepted her evidence that it had done so.[98]

The use of inference here illustrates the court's more relaxed attitude toward the actual effect. There was no great scrutiny of that evidence in the balancing process. Instead, it was accepted that the information was *capable* of having a deleterious effect.

YXB may also be contrasted with *Weller v Associated Newspapers Ltd*,[99] which concerned the publication of photographs of Paul Weller, his 16-year-old daughter and infant twins shopping in Los Angeles. The photographs revealed nothing embarrassing or controversial. The court, however, was satisfied that since publication had caused shock, anger and embarrassment the action for misuse of private information was made out. In short, then, in these two cases the privacy claim failed in one because extreme information had a trivial effect on the claimant and succeeded in the other because trivial information had an extreme effect.

YXB may be further contrasted with *EF v AB*,[100] which concerned similar facts (and, coincidently, was handed down on the same day) but decided by the employment appeal tribunal. Unlike in *YXB*, the interim relief application succeeded. In both, the parties involved had engaged in adulterous but lawful sexual activity and had exchanged intimate images. Although the differing outcomes might be justified (or criticised) on a number of grounds, the evidence of the potential effect that publication would have on the claimants varied significantly. In *EF* the distressing effect of privacy-invasion on EF, his wife and his child influenced

---

[97] ibid [61 iii, c].
[98] *Campbell* (n 1) [158] emphasis added.
[99] [2014] EWHC 1163 (QB).
[100] UKEAT/0525/13/DM.

the outcome strongly.[101] This sort of subjective approach has doctrinal authority. As Lord Hope said in *Campbell*, 'the mind that has to be examined is that, not of the reader in general, but of the person who is affected by the publicity'.[102]

If, as seems increasingly clear, MOPI is concerned to protect privacy based not on an objective assessment of the nature of the information disclosed but upon the effect of disclosure on the claimant[103] then the limits of public interest expression must lie where this effect would be so unbearable that the court feels compelled to protect the claimant. This approach is consistent with the judicial treatment of other free speech claims, particularly where governed by statute. For example, in contempt of court cases, the court focuses upon the effect upon the administration of justice (including open justice) that the expression would have.[104] In claims under the Protection from Harassment Act 1997, the court must decide, under s 7, whether the effect of the speech would be alarming or distressing.[105] Similarly, the Obscene Publications Act 1959 requires the court to decide, under s 1(2), whether the publication would 'deprave and corrupt' the audience.[106] There is, therefore, considerable judicial experience of determining the outcome of free speech claims based upon the effect of expression without resorting to speculation about its inherent worth.

Further, this sort of approach is entirely consistent with established liberal principle. John Stuart Mill, for example, claimed social pressure to conform loses its legitimacy where it amounts to coercion.[107] In Mill's sense, this means 'compulsion and control' and includes 'the moral coercion of public opinion'.[108] It is the point where forceful argument is exceeded. Society is always justified in seeking to persuade an individual to change their lifestyle but cannot force change unless harm would otherwise occur. Solove, endorsing Mill's argument, notes that 'privacy is a recognition that in certain circumstances, it is in society's best interest to curtail the power of its norms'.[109] Coercion in this context does not only mean the use of unauthorised physical force or legal compulsion. It can also extend to the use of authority to compel an individual to comply. As Tugendhat J commented in *Terry*, newspapers remain a source of authority by which public opinion is formed.[110] And evidence given to the Leveson

[101]ibid, eg, [65] and [84].
[102]*Campbell* (n 1) [99].
[103]See also *Rocknroll v News Group Newspapers Ltd* [2013] EWHC 24 (Ch), [39]; and in a different context, *Z v News Group Newspapers Ltd* [2013] EWHC 1150 (Fam), [59] and [77]; *In Re E* [2014] EWHC 7 [53].
[104]See, eg, *Attorney General v Random House* [2009] EWHC 1727 (QB).
[105]See, eg, *Thomas v News Group Newspapers Ltd* [2002] EMLR 4.
[106]See, eg, *DPP v Whyte* [1972] AC 849.
[107]John Stuart Mill, *On Liberty* in John M Robson (ed), *Collected Works of John Stuart Mill*, Vol XVIII (University of Toronto Press, 1977) 213.
[108]ibid, 225.
[109]Solove (n 41) 95.
[110]*Terry* (n 28) 104.

enquiry plainly attests to the dreadful effect that unwanted press scrutiny can have. Moreover, Leveson refers to the large body of evidence that reveals those who complain about press treatment are often made an example of through further privacy-invasion: 'it is legitimate to conclude that the aim was to "pay back" or "punish" for the disagreement by causing distress, embarrassment or discomfort'.[111]

In distinguishing coercion from persuasion, a court should have regard to the form of expression as well as its effect. It should be satisfied that the expression exceeded persuasive debate. Interference with public interest expression on such grounds seems to be anticipated by the ECtHR in the hints it has given about the limits of the right. For example, the Court has found interferences with public interest expression to be unjustified because the speech was 'not excessive'[112] or did not 'constitute a gratuitous personal attack'.[113] Similarly, as noted above, Art 10 permits 'a degree of exaggeration or even provocation'.[114] In a recent case, the Court said

> while some of the remarks ... portrayed the institution embodied by the King in a very negative light, with a hostile connotation, they did not advocate the use of violence, nor did they amount to hate speech, which in the Court's view is the essential element to be taken into account.[115]

These comments show it is the effect rather than significance of the expression that determines the limits of protection.

Applying this sort of approach to MOPI, the domestic court must be satisfied that the public interest expression exceeded robust criticism and that the claimant was severely affected by it. This would require a relatively high threshold if the strong protection for public interest expression is to be preserved. This might be evidenced by an effective withdrawal from society or the modification of behaviour simply to bring the unwanted scrutiny to an end. In both instances it may be concluded the individual is no longer autonomous because they have been deprived of genuine choice on how to act.[116] In other words, the individual did not change their ways because they were persuaded by what the press said (because, say, they accepted what they did was wrong and were repentant) but because submission brought the unwanted press attention to an end. This might be the case where press attention is particularly invasive in the detail revealed, or in its intensity (say, where press reporting continues over a prolonged period). This sort of thinking is evident in *Mosley* where Eady J remarks

[111] Leveson (n 46) 482 [2.42].
[112] *Standard Verlags GmbH v Austria* (2008) 47 EHRR 58 [55].
[113] *Unabhangige Initiative Informationsvielfalt v Austria* (2003) 37 EHRR 33 [43].
[114] *Prager and Oberschlick v Austria* (1996) 21 EHRR 1 [38].
[115] *Mondragon v Spain* (2015) 60 EHRR 7 [54].
[116] See John Gray, *Mill on Liberty: A Defence* (2nd edn, Routledge1996) 73–86.

> Everyone is naturally entitled to espouse moral or religious beliefs to the effect that certain types of sexual behaviour are wrong or demeaning to those participating. That does not mean that they are entitled to hound those who practise them or to detract from their right to live life as they choose.[117]

In some cases there may be an element of harassment (and overlap with harassment claims) as in *Othman v The English National Resistance*[118] where the court heard evidence that near constant demonstrations outside Abu Qatada's house left his wife and children in fear of their lives. This was also the case in *Green Corns Ltd v Claverley Group Ltd*[119] where local fury about the provision of care homes for troubled teenagers resulted in angry scenes, criminal damage and terrified residents transferred to other facilities by the police. Although in both cases the court decided that there was no public interest expression at stake (though this seems debatable), even if it had, the coercive effect of publication ought to have been sufficient to negate the free speech claim. The same principle could be applied to the *Mosley* case: even if the information had revealed a public interest matter, publication had a traumatic effect on Max Mosley. As Eady J noted, '[h]e is hardly exaggerating when he says that his life was ruined'.[120] The effect of publication may be even more profound where the press victim has no experience of press attention. In some cases, this can have tragic consequences, as with trans primary school teacher Lucy Meadows who suffered miserably from unwanted press attention about her transition.[121] Three months later she committed suicide.

To be sure, what is being proposed here is that, to succeed with a MOPI claim where public interest expression arises, the court must be satisfied that the intense public scrutiny caused severe harm to the claimant, such as his enforced conformity to end unwanted scrutiny, or caused him/her to withdraw from society, or otherwise impacted severely on his/her mental health. This behaviour may result from the frequency of privacy-invasion or the severity of it. This approach is consistent with the *Re S* elucidation. It is a justification that legitimises interference with public interest expression at stage three of the *Re S* test. To develop the law more explicitly in this way offers a meaningful method of strengthening privacy protection, albeit it would be a weaker version of the *Campbell* promise. It would not restore the presumptive parity of Art 8 and Art 10 entirely but would afford a means of tempering the supremacy of public interest expression. It would also ensure that public interest expression is only 'scarcely' interfered with.

---

117 *Mosley* (n 8) [127].
118 [2013] EWHC 1421 (QB).
119 [2005] EWHC 958 (QB).
120 *Mosley* (n 8) [236].
121 See discussion in Paul Wragg, 'Leveson and Disproportionate Public Interest Reporting' (2013) 5(2) *Journal of Media Law* 241, 247–248.

Admittedly, there might be occasions where even coercive public interest expression ought to be protected despite the interference with privacy rights. This possibility is also anticipated by liberal principle. For example, Mill argues that an individual should be unmolested by state or general society where their behaviour harms no one but themselves (self-regarding behaviour) but may be interfered with where it harms others (other-regarding behaviour). Thus, the invasion of privacy to expose behaviour harmful to society might be justified even though coercive in nature. Harm, though, should be given a high threshold. Since Mill's chief concern is that individuality should not be undermined by a moralising and 'tyrannical' majority, the fact that other people disagree with particular behaviour does not make it wrong nor justify interference with it. As Lord Denning has previously said, extra-judicially,

> What matters in England is that each man should be free to develop his own personality to the full: and the only duties which should restrict this freedom are those are necessary to enable everyone else to do the same.[122]

The coercive force of newspapers, therefore, is not justified if

> a person's conduct affects the interests of no persons besides himself, *or needs not affect them unless they like it* ... In all such cases, there should be perfect freedom, legal and social, to do the action and stand the consequences.[123]

This seems particularly apposite for the role model analysis. Members of society might choose role models but no one is forced to. So, for example, in the typical claim where a disappointed public learns their beloved role model is a philanderer, and not the wholesome character they believed, it could not be said this level of harm had been reached if the public could shun the claimant and take their business, devotion, etc, elsewhere. Similarly, individuals are not harmed simply because they believe the actor's behaviour to be 'foolish, perverse or wrong'.[124] As Ten has said of Mill's position, this means that morality-dependent distress suffered from knowing of a person's immorality does not constitute harm sufficient to justify coercion.[125] Translated to MOPI, this means that although there may be a right to criticise others for behaviour that a newspaper (or wider society) thinks wrong or morally repugnant, there is no right to force a person to change their ways.

The harm, therefore, must be explicable in terms extending beyond morality-dependent distress or harm to interests over which the public has no control. It is justified, for example, where the police publish images asking the public to

[122]Sir Alfred Denning, *Freedom under the Law* (Stevens & Sons, 1949) 4–5.
[123]Mill (n 107) 276 (emphasis added).
[124]ibid 226.
[125]CL Ten, 'Mill's Defence of Liberty' in John Gray and GW Smith (eds), *JS Mill On Liberty in Focus* (Routledge, 1991) 212–238.

identify a person committing a public order offence.[126] The recent shaming of Lord Sewel, including claims he used his Parliamentary allowance to buy cocaine and prostitutes, which led to his resignation as deputy speaker of the House of Lords, may also be an example where such coercion is justified despite the gross interference with privacy.[127] Whether this level of harm is realisable where the claimant engages in immoral rather than illegal behaviour is doubtful. Certainly, there seems no obvious justification that would explain why a newspaper should be able to force an individual into submission where the law is not being broken. Given that coercion is the ultimate interference with individual autonomy, the courts are entitled to scrutinise closely the justification offered by the press for doing so. Laing J seemed to recognise this in *AMC* where she noted, caustically, of the claimant's alleged adultery:

> I do express a suitably diffident doubt whether this conduct was socially harmful. It caused private pain; but no-one was corrupted or co-erced. The conduct had no ramifications beyond [that]. It did not affect society in any way.[128]

One factor that might be relevant is whether the coercion was a direct or indirect consequence of the expression. For example, if a newspaper exercises its campaigning role in order to agitate legal reform, the claimant may be constantly discussed as a vivid example of why change should happen. Something of this nature occurred recently with the heated debate over the rehabilitation of rapist professional footballers following Ched Evans's release from prison. The popular response has made it near impossible for him to return to the game. Similarly, there has been much debate about tax avoidance schemes involving well-known companies and celebrities. Comedian Jimmy Carr became a major discussion point when his involvement in such a scheme was revealed. Amid intense press coverage, and despite the scheme being entirely legal, he publicly apologised for a 'terrible error of judgment' and was said to have exited the scheme shortly afterwards.[129] In January 2015, the *Mirror* reported that he had paid £500,000 in taxes and hailed him as a 'reformed tax avoider' who was now paying his 'full share'.[130]

In situations like this, the court is capable of asking the defendant why it was necessary to hound a particular individual, especially if their behaviour was immoral rather than illegal. It would not be an unjustified interference with

---

[126] *Re JR38* (n 20).

[127] Of which pictures of him topless and wearing a bra seemed particularly extreme. See Stephen Moyes, 'Kate McCann and Holly Christodoulou' [Busted] *The Sun on Sunday*, (26 July 2015).

[128] *AMC* (n 27) [27].

[129] Patrick Wintour and Rajeev Syal, 'Jimmy Carr apologises for 'terrible error of judgment' over tax scheme' [SIC]*The Guardian* (21 June 2012).

[130] Nigel Pauley, 'Reformed tax-avoider Jimmy Carr paid £500,000 bill last year after bumper profits' *The Mirror* (31 January 2015).

editorial autonomy to require a newspaper to demonstrate that no less intrusive measures were available. For example, if the newspapers sought ultimately to reform the law then this may be done without coercing particular individuals. Coercion of this sort is comparable to the use of subterfuge or covert surveillance. The Editors' Code of Conduct states, in clause 10, that such behaviour 'can generally be justified only in the public interest and then only when the material cannot be obtained by other means'. The Press Complaints Commission has previously upheld complaints where the press could offer no such persuasive reasons even though there was a public interest at stake in the information disclosed.[131]

This revised approach to MOPI claims would utilise a different sort of balancing to that of weighing the respective claims by assigning some hypothetical value to them. Instead, it would allow judges to hold that although public interest expression is important to protect, it cannot be (and should not be) protected absolutely. The balance is achieved, therefore, by denying protection where the effect of the expression is so severe as to cause the claimant to become a pariah – unless the press is justified in doing so. Despite falling readership, newspapers continue to hold great authority. Condemnation by them can ruin lives. It is appropriate in those circumstances that the courts have the power to intervene and offer meaningful protection to victims, especially where they have engaged in immoral rather than illegal behaviour. This approach should appeal to the judiciary. It does not compromise the principle that public interest expression is the highest form of expression deserving of strong protection. Instead, it focuses the courts on a task more suited to their expertise: it requires them to determine the extent of interference with privacy based upon evidence, both of impact on the claimant and the degree to which this effect could have been anticipated by the defendants.

5. Conclusion

In the privacy/free speech dichotomy, public interest expression is supreme. *Campbell*'s great promise has not been realised because the MOPI case law lacks an overriding principle to limit, effectively, the protection afforded to it. Redressing this balance, though, should not rely upon paternalistic judgments about its meaning or extent. Instead, judges should interfere where its effect is particularly severe and, it is submitted, amounts to coercion. This is a high threshold to reach, as it should be if robust protection for public interest expression is to be preserved. Yet it cannot command absolute protection. There will be cases where interference based on effect amounts to an 'egg shell skull' rule, especially, it may be imagined, where ordinary members of the public are claimants. So be it. Journalists and editors are perfectly capable of anticipating such consequences prior to publication. They can, for example, identify whether their target has experience of

[131] *Liberal Democrat Party and The Independent*, 10 May 2011. See also, *Haldimann v Switzerland* (21830/09), reported (2015) EHRLR 323.

unwanted press attention, in order to gauge their resilience. This principle should be qualified only in circumstances where society's interests are harmed by the private behaviour, in a manner greater than morality-dependent distress or where members of society cannot protect their interests by transferring them somewhere else (such as finding a different role model, etc). This development would recast the *Campbell* framework into a four-part test in which the court should ask: first, is there a reasonable expectation of privacy at stake? Secondly, is there a public interest at stake in the privacy-invading expression? Thirdly, if there is, is the effect of that expression coercive, such that the victim is forced to withdraw from society or conform simply to end the harm caused by the expression? Finally, if the expression is coercive, is it nevertheless justified because the claimant's private behaviour is harming a valid societal interest? This revised test would not always realise *Campbell*'s great promise. But it would come much closer than the present law does.

Acknowledgements

I am grateful to Iain Christie, Gavin Phillipson, Thomas Bennett, Daithi Mac Sithigh, David Campbell, Eric Descheemaeker, Alastair Mullis and the anonymous reviewer for *JML* for helpful comments and discussion about an earlier version.

Disclosure statement

No potential conflict of interest was reported by the author.

Privacy, third parties and judicial method: *Wainwright*'s legacy of uncertainty

Thomas D. C. Bennett

A year before the seminal *Campbell* case, the House of Lords' decision in *Wainwright v Home Office* emphatically ruled out the recognition of general privacy tort. In so doing, the House aimed to preserve legal certainty by restricting the development of privacy rights in the common law: development was to occur only on a piecemeal, narrowly incremental basis. A dozen years after *Wainwright*, however, it is evident that this restrictive approach has not secured the certainty desired. This is particularly apparent in the burgeoning doctrine relating to the relevance of the privacy interests of third parties to the determination of claims for misuse of private information. This article scrutinises key cases in that body of doctrine and highlights the novelty of the issues posed and the path taken by the courts in resolving them.

Introduction

In the aftermath of the House of Lords cases of *Wainwright v Home Office*[1] and *Campbell v MGN*,[2] privacy law in England developed in a distinctly fragmentary fashion. In *Wainwright*, the House disavowed the possibility of recognising a general tort of privacy, prioritising the maintenance of legal certainty by limiting the development of the law.[3] In keeping with this desire to limit the expansion of privacy law, the subsequent and seminal case of *Campbell* gave birth to English law's private facts tort, known as 'misuse of private information' (MPI).[4] This essay calls into question the legacy of the *Wainwright* decision. It argues that,

[1] *Wainwright v Home Office* [2003] UKHL 53, [2004] 2 AC 406 ('*Wainwright*')
[2] *Campbell v MGN Ltd* [2004] UKHL 22, [2004] 2 AC 457 ('*Campbell*')
[3] See *Wainwright* (n 1) [26] (Lord Hoffmann). I do not defend this conception of the judicial role – indeed it seems to me to be deeply problematic in a system of common law that hopes to keep up with societal changes. Nevertheless, it is quite clearly the primary concern underpinning the *Wainwright* ruling. On the ineffectiveness of such a rigidly formal conception of the judicial role, see generally EW Thomas, *The Judicial Process* (CUP, 2006).
[4] *Campbell* (n 2) [14].

in opting to leave the law to develop in a fragmentary fashion (rather than recognise a 'blockbuster'[5] privacy tort), it has left open the door to inconsistency and incoherence. Judges have demonstrably been anxious to secure justice for vulnerable individuals. However, with *Wainwright* requiring the courts to force all informational privacy claims into (the sometimes ill-fitting) tort of MPI, the judiciary has stretched and developed that tort in ways that were not only unforeseeable, but which undermine some of the core features of private law that have long been taken for granted.

In order to highlight the issue, this essay focuses on one particular aspect of post-*Campbell* doctrine. This is the way in which the interests of unrepresented third parties (usually the children of claimants) have come to occupy a central place in MPI method. The development is portrayed by the courts as a straightforward application of existing doctrine. However, a detailed examination of these cases reveals that the issue is anything but straightforward.

The significance of making third party interests relevant becomes apparent when one considers that, traditionally, private law claims are bilateral disputes; the only parties whose interests are relevant are the represented parties (the claimant and defendant). This is particularly true in equitable breach of confidence cases which, traditionally founded on a relationship between the parties akin to a trust, necessarily excluded the interests of others.[6] In tort law, the bilateral nature of the claim is no less acute. As Ernest Weinrib observes, tort law is based upon 'the bipolar procedure that links [claimant] and defendant', in which 'the [claimant] sues the defendant and, if successful, is entitled to the defendant's performance of a remedial act'.[7]

This essay is concerned with ostensibly 'pure' private law cases – specifically those brought in the tort of MPI which do not feature public bodies as parties to the litigation.[8] In the cases of *CDE v MGN* and *K v NGN*, upon which the analysis will

[5] *Wainwright v Home Office* [2001] EWCA Civ 2081, [2002] QB 1334 [60] (Mummery LJ).

[6] The precise nature of the relationship between equitable confidentiality and the tort of MPI has not been conclusively established. Recently the High Court and Court of Appeal have concluded that the two actions exist in parallel (see *Vidal-Hall v Google* [2014] EWHC 13 (QB) and *Google v Vidal-Hall* [2015] EWCA Civ 311), and the Supreme Court has recently refused permission to appeal that aspect of the matter any further. However, the reasoning in both the High Court and Court of Appeal judgments is regrettably lacking a detailed explanation of MPI's doctrinal roots. As such, there is still scope for debate as to whether MPI ought *properly* to be considered an extension of equitable confidentiality or a freestanding tort inspired by the older doctrine but based on different underlying principles (or, indeed, something else entirely). For a helpful survey of earlier responses to this particular issue, see Rebecca Moosavian, 'Charting the Journey from Confidence to the New Methodology' (2012) 34(5) *European Intellectual Property Review* 324.

[7] Ernest J Weinrib, 'Understanding Tort Law' (1989) 23 *Valparaiso University Law Review* 485, 494.

[8] There are also some cases in which ostensibly private law actions take on a primarily public focus because they are brought by public bodies. In *Commissioner of Police of the Metropolis v Times Newspapers Ltd*, [2011] EWHC 2705 (QB), [2014] EMLR 1, the

focus, the interests of unrepresented third parties – most notably the children of the claimants – were considered relevant by the courts to the determination of the main claim.[9]

In traditional private law claims, third party interests would not be considered relevant to the resolution of the dispute.[10] By contrast, the impact of court orders on third parties has long been relevant in areas of public and family law.[11] The waters are muddied slightly by the influence of policy considerations upon findings of liability (and the extension of heads of liability) in English tort law, since this entails considering the impact of liability upon persons other than the parties. However, taking into account broad-brush policy considerations (often based on a rather speculative idea of what best serves the public interest) differs from the phenomenon we observe in the third party interest cases. For, in these cases, *specific* interests of *particular* individuals are taken into account (and, in effect, *specific* rights are granted to them). Even if this distinction were not as significant as I suggest, policy considerations that are openly acknowledged are far less objectionable than instances (such as in the third party cases) where such interests are taken into account in a manner that obscures the fact that a *development* is

---

claimants, both public bodies, brought an action for breach of confidence (alongside actions for breach of the Data Protection Act 1998 and conversion) in respect of leaked operational documents. The defendant newspaper intended to use the documents in its defence to a libel action brought by another individual. In making their case, the claimants made extensive reference to the potential for harm to come to unrepresented third parties should the documents be used and reported in open court. As Tugendhat J notes in that case, however, '[c] laims for breach of confidence [brought] by public authorities are different from claims by individuals' ([15]). The reason for the difference was spelt out by Lord Goff in *Attorney General v Observer Ltd (No 2) ('Spycatcher')* [1988] UKHL 6, [1990] 1 AC 109. There is a 'continuing public interest that the workings of government should be open to scrutiny and criticism … in such cases, there must be demonstrated some other public interest which requires that publication should be restrained' (283C–D, 285H). The claimants, moreover, considered that the interests of third parties, in particular their Article 8 rights including the control of personal data, triggered the claimants' s 6 HRA obligation to act compatibly with Convention rights and thus mandated their bringing the claim. *Commissioner v Times*, then, is an unusual breach of confidence case; it is brought by the claimants exclusively on the basis of third party interests. That is, however, an inevitable consequence of the claimants' status as public bodies. The fact that they brought the claim under a cause of action traditionally considered part of private law does not alter the fact that this is a case with a primarily public focus.

[9] *K (formerly 'ETK') v News Group Newspapers Ltd* [2011] EWCA Civ 439, [2011] 1 WLR 1827 ('*K*'); *CDE v MGN Ltd* [2010] EWHC 3308 (QB) ('*CDE*').

[10] Rather, those who experience losses and might be classed as third parties can, in some instances, initiate their *own* claims, such as under the Contracts (Rights of Third Parties) Act 1999. See also *Dobson v Thames Water Utilities Ltd* [2007] EWCA Civ 28, [2009] 3 All ER 319, [2009] UKHRR 617 and discussion, below.

[11] For avoidance of doubt, in this essay I treat family law cases as distinct from those which I refer to as traditional private law claims (by which I primarily mean cases in tort, equity and contract).

taking place in the law. Moreover, because the developmental dynamic present here is obscured, the normative rationale underpinning it is also hidden from view. We cannot immediately see *why* the courts may be justified in making this move. This, I argue, is highly unsatisfactory. For assuming the essay correctly shows that the courts were not *obliged* as a matter of formal law to take these interests into account, the decision to do so anyway must have a normative dimension. But this dimension is one which has never been made plain and which thus causes uncertainty and invites speculation.

This third party issue is thus significant because the courts' treatment of it alters the traditionally bilateral structure of a particular type of tort claim (MPI). It does so seemingly in the name of securing the ECHR rights of vulnerable parties. This may have profound implications. It suggests that, potentially, *any* tort may be developed in such a way as to accommodate third party interests. This sets the courts' approach in the MPI cases upon which we will dwell substantially apart from that in other torts.[12]

None of the issues raised by the third party cases upon which the essay focuses are necessarily irresolvable. Indeed, the essay will propose and discuss two theories (the 'incremental accommodation' theory and the 'inseparability' theory) that may be inferred from the case law and may provide ways of understanding the third party cases. Central to the first of these is the concept of 'incrementalism' – the manner in which the common law is developed. The second theory involves reworking and broadening our understanding of the nature of the Article 8 right itself to embrace the integrity of the whole family unit. Both theories are, however, problematic. Finding a workable solution is a more complex matter than the courts appear to have appreciated. The courts, then, have treated as straightforward a matter that is – in reality – anything but.

The analysis which follows casts serious doubt on the efficacy of *Wainwright*'s attempt to secure legal certainty in privacy law going forward. Although it will point up problems with their reasoning at a formal level, this essay is not intended as an attack on the third party interests line of cases. Rather it is an attack on *Wainwright* itself for creating an environment so formally restrictive that the courts have been left with little option but to develop the law in ways that necessarily end up undermining legal certainty if they are inclined to secure justice for vulnerable parties. In essence, it suggests that forcing the courts to attempt to achieve just outcomes for vulnerable parties through a tightly circumscribed mechanism – the informational tort of MPI – does more harm than good. It is, to use a colloquialism, an instance of the proverbial chickens coming home to roost. For the courts are committed to protecting the vulnerable – particularly children – and this is no bad thing in itself. Their efforts to do so, however, result in an unpredictable stretching of MPI that even goes so far as to rewrite the basic, bilateral structure of the claim.

---

[12]See *Dobson v Thames Water* n (10) (and accompanying text, below).

Having set out the aims of the essay, we will begin with an analysis of the third party cases. Whilst the cases of *CDE* and *K* deal with essentially the same issue, they do so in quite different ways and so the essay will deal with each in turn, starting with *CDE*.

The relevance and importance of third party interests: the cases

CDE v MGN

The first claimant, CDE, was a man who regularly appeared on television, and the second claimant, FGH, was his wife. They sought an injunction restraining the defendants from publishing details of a 'quasi-relationship' between CDE and another woman, X. The first defendant was publisher of the tabloid *The Mirror*. X was the second defendant, who wished to sell her story. As is the case with so many of these privacy cases, the application was for interim injunctive relief. This requires the court to determine, often on the basis of limited evidence, whether it is 'likely' that the claimant will succeed in obtaining a permanent injunction at trial.[13] If the court is not convinced that is likely, no injunction will generally be granted.

In his judgment, Eady J asserts that third party interests have relevance to his decision-making in the following terms:

> [P]ublication is likely to prove distressing to the Claimants, and almost certainly to their children … Although there can be little doubt that the coverage contemplated would be intrusive upon the Claimants' family life and bring bewilderment and distress to their children, it is correspondingly true also of the Second Defendant's family. She too has a young daughter (and another who is now an adult). I have no doubt that these are all persons whose Article 8 rights are currently engaged …[14]
>
> In this case, it is a question of balancing the rights of the Claimants (and/or their family) under Article 8 and Article 6, on the one side, with those of the Defendants under Article 10.[15]

The defendant's primary objection to the court considering the interests of third parties was that it disregarded the traditional bilateralism of private law claims:

> As I understand the attitude of the newspaper, it is simply that a married man cannot be accorded greater rights or consideration by the court than a single man and, in so far as there may be any impact on his family, that is too bad.[16]

Eady J, however, was swift, emphatic and explicit in his rejection of that argument:

---

[13] Human Rights Act 1998 s 12(3). See also *Cream Holdings v Banerjee* [2004] UKHL 44; [2005] 1 AC 253 [23].
[14] *CDE* (n 9) [6].
[15] *ibid* [83].
[16] *ibid* [7].

> Yet it is now well established that the first question a court has to address on applications of this kind is whether Article 8 rights are engaged. As to that, the threatened publication would undoubtedly engage the Article 8 rights of all the persons I have identified. The fact that the First Claimant has a wife and children simply means that there are more persons whose rights have to be taken into account. They cannot simply be ignored on the basis of traditional arguments along the lines of who has a cause of action and who does not. Since they would at least potentially be affected by the exercise of the Defendants' Article 10 rights, their Article 8 rights have to be weighed in the balance.[17]

Eady J's aim (to take seriously the interests of the children) is noble; it is certainly morally appealing. But that does not mean that it is grounded firmly in existing law. There is a subtle but important (and rather clutch-less) shift in this segment of his judgment. For he states that it is 'well established' that the courts begin with an assessment of whether Article 8 rights are engaged.[18] From this he moves to determine whether *anyone's* Article 8 rights are engaged, not just those of the claimants. It is certainly well established that the court must begin with an assessment of whether the claimants' Article 8 rights are engaged. But it is far less clear whether the law requires that the search for engaged Article 8 rights be broadened beyond that. When the MPI tort was first recognised in *Campbell*, Lord Nicholls phrased the engagement test thus: '[e]ssentially the touchstone of private life is whether in respect of the disclosed facts *the person in question* had a reasonable expectation of privacy.'[19] The reasonable expectation of privacy question, moreover,

> is a broad one, which takes account of all the circumstances of the case. They include the attributes of the claimant, the nature of the activity in which the claimant was engaged, the place at which it was happening, the nature and purpose of the intrusion, the absence of consent and whether it was known or could be inferred, the effect on the claimant and the circumstances in which and the purposes for which the information came into the hands of the publisher.[20]

Nothing in this well established test even suggests the relevance of third party interests. Rather, it reflects the traditional, bilateral framework of tort litigation. Likewise, the refinement set out by Lord Steyn in *Re S* expressly limits the court to conducting 'an intense focus on the comparative importance of the specific rights *being claimed*'.[21] It might be said that Lord Nicholls, when he stated in *Campbell* that '[t]he values embodied in articles 8 and 10 are as much applicable in disputes between individuals … as they are in disputes between individuals and a public authority',[22] was seeking to harmonise the approaches to

---

[17] *ibid* [7].
[18] *ibid.*
[19] *Campbell* (n 2) [21] (emphasis added).
[20] *Murray v Express Newspapers* [2008] EWCA Civ 446, [2009] Ch 481 [36].
[21] *Re S (A Child)* [2004] UKHL 47, [2005] 1 AC 593 [17] (emphasis added).
[22] *Campbell* (n 2) [17].

adjudicating public and private privacy claims. Eady J in *Mosley* picked up on this when he said:

> as Lord Nicholls at [17]–[18] and Lord Hoffmann at [50] observed in *Campbell* in 2004 ... private individuals and corporations (including the media) ... are obliged to respect personal privacy as much as public bodies. It is not merely state intrusion that should be actionable.[23]

However, one must understand *Campbell* in context. At that time, there was much debate about the extent to which the HRA had 'horizontal effect'.[24] For instance, one influential commentator had denied the possibility of *any* horizontal application of human rights law.[25] A more conservative reading of Lord Nicholls' statement might take it as simply making clear that the HRA does indeed have some, indirect horizontal effect. On that matter the whole House was in agreement. Moreover, it is inescapable that Lord Nicholls' statement – howsoever it is read – recognises the need for a violation to be 'actionable'. It is well established that a person whose informational privacy is violated is entitled to seek redress as much against the media as against the state, but that person must *bring* the action. It does not directly follow from any of these authoritative statements of law that third party interests can be relied upon by claimants seeking to bolster their own claim.

The only authorities Eady J cites in support of his broad reading are *Secretary of State for the Home Department v AP (No 2)*[26] and *Donald v Ntuli*.[27] The fact he points to just two cases must call into question the extent to which his reading is in fact 'well established'.[28] The passage from *AP* was a repetition by Lord Rodger of

---

[23]*Mosley v News Group Newspaper Ltd* [2008] EWHC 1777 (QB), [2008] EMLR 20 [126].

[24]For key contributions to this debate, see: Murray Hunt, 'The 'Horizontal Effect' of the Human Rights Act' [1998] *Public Law* 423; William Wade, 'Horizons of Horizontality' (2000) 116 *Law Quarterly Review* 217; Anthony Lester and David Pannick, 'The Impact of the Human Rights Act on Private Law: The Knight's Move' (2000) 116 *Law Quarterly Review* 380; Deryck Beyleveld and Shaun Pattinson, 'Horizontal Applicability and Horizontal Effect' (2002) 118 *Law Quarterly Review* 623; Jonathan Morgan, 'Privacy, Confidence and Horizontal Effect: "Hello" Trouble' [2003] *Cambridge Law Journal* 444; Nicole Moreham, 'Privacy and Horizontality: Relegating the Common Law' (2007) 123 *Law Quarterly Review* 373; Gavin Phillipson, 'Clarity Postponed: Horizontal Effect after Campbell' in H Fenwick, G Phillipson and R Masterman (eds), *Judicial Reasoning under the UK Human Rights Act* (CUP, 2007); Gavin Phillipson and Alexander Williams, 'Horizontal Effect and the Constitutional Constraint' (2011) 74(6) *Modern Law Review* 878, 143–73.

[25]Richard Buxton, 'The Human Rights Act and Private Law' (2000) 116 *Law Quarterly Review* 48.

[26][2010] UKSC 26, [2010] 1 WLR 1652 [7] ('*AP*').

[27][2010] EWCA Civ 1276, [2011] 1 WLR 294 ('*Donald*').

[28]The notion that this is well established resurfaces in more recent cases, such as *AAA v Associated Newspapers* [2012] EWHC 2103 (QB), [2013] EMLR 2 (at first instance) and [2013] EWCA Civ 554 (on appeal). However, these more recent pronouncements are based upon the authorities cited in *K v NGN*, rather than those relied upon by Eady

what he himself had said six months earlier in *In re Guardian*.[29] He stated that, when balancing individual privacy against freedom of expression, the court had to ask the following question:

> Is there a sufficient general, public interest in publishing a report of the proceedings which identifies the person concerned to justify any resulting curtailment of his right and his family's right to respect for their private and family life ... ?[30]

In re Guardian was not a bilateral private law case, and did not concern the misuse of private information. It was a case concerning the media's right to name publicly the applicants in judicial review proceedings in which the applicants were challenging their designation as suspected terrorists. Section 6 HRA does not discriminate between the Convention rights of represented and unrepresented parties to such proceedings, because the decision whether or not to grant anonymity is a procedural, rather than a substantive, matter.

What muddies the water somewhat is the obligation on the courts themselves not to act incompatibly with ECHR rights, which is imposed by virtue of s 6(1) and s 6(3)(a) of the HRA. Alison Young (drawing on the work of Ian Leigh) makes a helpful distinction between 'procedural' and 'remedial' forms of horizontality, both of which are derived from the s 6 obligation.[31] She explains:

> *Procedural horizontality* occurs when the court, as a public authority, exercises its inherent or statutory powers to regulate its own procedures by managing cases or granting court orders, which create obligations on private individuals bound by such court orders ... *Remedial horizontality* occurs when courts exercise their discretionary powers to grant remedies, where ... they must ensure that the remedy in question is not contrary to Convention rights. A discretionary remedy may include an injunction to prevent a private individual from acting in a manner incompatible with Convention rights.[32]

J. We will return to the *K* authorities below. But the fact that Eady J asserts that this is well established by authorities which have not been taken to provide evidence of its being well established in later cases weakens his position (in formalist terms) considerably.

[29] *In re Guardian News and Media Ltd* [2010] UKSC 1, [2010] 2 AC 697, [2010] 2 WLR 325. *AP* was a case concerning the identification in court of a suspected terrorist who had been made subject to a control order. The applicant wished to maintain his anonymity and the Home Secretary concurred. Moreover, the applicant did not at any point assert any third party interest that might bolster his case; the matters weighing in favour of maintaining anonymity related to him and him alone. The statement of law repeated in *AP* therefore did not apply in any way to third parties in that case and, insofar as it refers to third parties, it is clearly *obiter*.

[30] *In re Guardian*, ibid [50–52], cited in *AP* (n 26) [7] and *CDE* (n 9) [85].

[31] Alison Young, 'Mapping Horizontal Effect' in David Hoffman (ed), *The Impact of the UK Human Rights Act on Private Law* (CUP, 2011), 16–47, 22. Young draws on Ian Leigh, 'Horizontal Rights, the Human Rights Act and Privacy: Lessons from the Commonwealth?' (1999) 48 *International and Comparative Law Quarterly* 57.

[32] *ibid*, 22 (emphasis is original).

Young cites *Re S (a child)* as an example of procedural horizontality. In that case, the House of Lords granted an injunction prohibiting the publication of the name of a defendant in a criminal case who was charged with the murder of one of her sons, in order to protect the privacy interests of her surviving son (who might otherwise have been easily identified).[33] Because the litigation concerning the prohibitory injunction was separate from the criminal trial, the case is rightly classified by Young as procedural.[34] Most MPI cases, by contrast, exhibit remedial horizontality, since the application for an injunction is part and parcel of the primary litigation itself (albeit dealt with as a preliminary matter). This is because very few MPI cases ever go to trial; for the vast majority, the granting of an interim injunction is, in practice, sufficient to prevent publication of the private information ever occurring. There are two reasons for this. First, because the newsworthiness of the information often diminishes quickly so that media defendants are less interested in publishing it further down the line. Second, because the test applied by the court in determining whether to grant the injunction is whether 'the applicant's prospects of success at the trial are sufficiently favourable'.[35] In other words, an interim injunction will (generally) be granted only where it is likely that a permanent injunction will be awarded following a trial of the issues. It is not controversial that, in either of these sorts of circumstances, the court must consider the impact of its decision upon the Convention rights of the *named* parties; that is the nature of the s 6 obligation.

The jurisdictional basis for the granting of injunctions in procedural and remedial circumstances is, however, not identical. In procedural cases, the court is the primary decision-maker and the parties have a statutory right (under s 6) to have their Convention rights taken into account. In remedial cases, the court is the arbiter of a dispute between the parties. Its power to grant an injunction is, like in procedural cases, discretionary. But it does not *solely* derive from its inherent or statutory powers. It requires *also* that the claimant have some right *at common law* to the injunction (i.e. because the defendant has breached a common law right of the claimant's, such as the right to the non-misuse of private information). Unless that underlying common law right is present, the power to grant a remedial injunction has nothing upon which to bite. Moreover, the court's obligation is, as Young states, to 'ensure that the *remedy in question* is not contrary to Convention rights'.[36] The remedy is claimed by one (and

[33] *Re S* (n 21).
[34] The recent cases of *F v G* (2012) UKEAT/0042/11/DA and *EF v AB* (2015) UKEAT/0525/13/DM are examples of third party interests being correctly considered in the context of procedurally-generated injunctions. Both involved anonymity orders relating to Employment Tribunal cases relating to allegations of sexual impropriety in the work place, publication of the details of which would have enabled the identification of third parties who were indirectly involved.
[35] *Cream Holdings* (n 13).
[36] Young (n 31) 22 (emphasis added).

awarded against the other) party. Thus where a third party has no common law right to claim a remedy, and therefore there is no possibility of granting them an injunction, there is no *formal compulsion* upon the court under the HRA to take that third party's Convention rights into account.

This is the same basic rationale that justifies the courts in not developing the common law in such a way as to give third parties their own claim *irrespective* of that which the parent might have.[37] The rationale derives from the ethos of indirect horizontality: that the (bilaterally structured) common law is the mechanism through which Convention rights are addressed horizontally. So long as the courts apply the common law (and, if necessary, develop it incrementally) in a manner that is compatible with the Convention rights of the named parties, the s 6 obligation is satisfied. The s 6 obligation does not require the courts to amend further the common law in order to act compatibly with (or secure) the Convention rights of individuals *who are not parties to the litigation* and *to whom the common law grants no right to a remedy* in the instant case.

Thus whilst it may be necessary for the court to develop the common law in order to ensure the *named* parties' Convention rights are afforded a sufficient degree of protection, the court is not *formally required* by the HRA to consider the Convention rights of third parties.[38] Moreover, if the court *does* decide to consider the Convention rights of third parties, it ought to recognise that it is *developing* the common law. Such a development may not necessarily be objectionable (a matter to which we shall return, below), and indeed it is not the aim of this essay to object to it. But such a development ought to be recognised for what it is. With great respect, Eady J does not seem to have appreciated this in his wholesale adoption of the *In re Guardian* statement.

Eady J also cites the Court of Appeal's judgment in *Donald v Ntuli* as supporting his decision to take into account third party interests. Yet this does not actually provide much in the way of clear, reasoned confirmation of his approach. *Donald* was an appeal from a decision of Eady J himself in the High Court in which he had granted a so-called 'super injunction' to a claimant prohibiting the defendant from disclosing various private details about a relationship they had previously had.[39] The Court of Appeal upheld Eady J's decision in part, although it discharged the anonymity and the restriction on publishing the details of the judgment itself. Apart from repeating the same phrase from *In re Guardian* (which the court likewise attributed to *AP*), the Court of Appeal's only reference to third party interests came when Maurice Kay LJ stated that Eady J 'had proper regard to the possible impact of publicity on the parties' respective children'.[40]

[37]See the Court of Appeal's rejection of the claimant's (the child of the subject of the private information) attempt to secure an injunction in MPI to prevent publication in *O v A (previously OPO v MLA)* [2014] EWCA Civ 1277, [2015] EMLR 4, discussed below (see n 94).
[38]This is the approach taken in *Dobson v Thames Water* (n 10) (and see below, n 88).
[39]Eady J's original decision in *Donald* is unreported.
[40]*Donald* (n 27) [24].

There is nothing that suggests the issue of propriety in this regard was argued before the Court of Appeal, and no authority was cited by the court explaining its assertion that Eady J's regard for third party interests was 'proper'. Eady J's reference to *Donald* in *CDE* thus amounts to the mere citation of a bare affirmatory statement from the Court of Appeal upholding, in part, one of his own decisions.

It is also relevant that in *Ambrosiadou v Coward*,[41] which actually pre-dates *CDE* by five months, Eady J similarly held that the interests of the parties' 13-year-old son were of 'particular significance' in an application for injunctive relief in respect of information, some of which directly concerned the son (a point of distinction from *CDE*). In that case, Eady J made his position on third parties plain when he stated that '[the son's] rights under Article 8 of the Convention certainly need to be borne in mind throughout – even though he is not a party to his litigation'.[42] Indeed, the judge insisted that 'it must be right … to take into account the rights of the son'.[43] However, unlike the more developed reasoning in *CDE*, Eady J cited no authority whatsoever for the relevance of third party interests on that occasion, suggesting that, prior to *CDE*, whilst he had come to the view that third party interests *were* relevant, he had yet to identify any supporting authority.

The decision by Eady J to take into account third party interests in *CDE* thus appears to be on less than entirely solid formal ground. In the light of this, we will now turn our attention to our second case, *K v NGN*.[44]

K v NGN

K concerned information pertaining to an adulterous affair conducted between a well-known male in the entertainment industry and a work colleague. In *K*, the Court of Appeal held that the Article 8 ECHR interests of the claimant's children, who were not parties to the proceedings (and did not give evidence), were amenable to being taken into account when weighing and balancing the competing Convention rights of the claimant and defendant. The issue and conclusion are thus very similar to those in *CDE*, although in *K* we have the benefit of a somewhat more detailed judgment on these points.

The judgment indicates that, when conducting the balancing exercise, the court 'should accord particular weight to the Article 8 rights of any children likely to be affected by the publication, if that would be likely to harm their interests'.[45] Ward LJ (with whom Laws and Moore-Bick LJJ agreed) placed a high value on the interests of the claimant's children in this particular instance:

---

[41] [2010] EWHC 1794, [2010] 2 FLR 1775 ('*Ambrosiadou*').
[42] *ibid* [29].
[43] *ibid* [33].
[44] *K* (n 9). For a summary of the key issues in *K*, see TDC Bennett, 'The Relevance and Importance of Third Party Interests in Privacy Cases' (2011) 127 *Law Quarterly Review* 531.
[45] *K* (n 9) [19].

> the benefits to be achieved by publication in the interests of free speech are wholly outweighed by the harm that would be done through the interference with the rights to privacy of all those affected, *especially where the rights of the children are in play.*[46]

The potentially detrimental effect that publicising their father's extra-marital affair might have on his children, particularly in the context of their school lives, looms large in Ward LJ's judgment. He is concerned by the 'ordeal of playground ridicule … that would inevitably follow publicity'.[47] He asserts that 'the playground is a cruel place where the bullies feed on personal discomfort and embarrassment'.[48] He accords this sort of harm 'particular weight'. It is worth noting that there is no indication that Ward LJ heard any evidence on the level of cruelty the children could expect to encounter in their school playground – indeed the language he uses makes plain that he is assuming this apparently 'inevitable' hardship.[49]

Ward LJ relies upon three cases, and two subtly different legal justifications, to support his assertion that the children's interests are relevant. The first, which he acknowledges takes place in 'another context',[50] is *Beoku-Betts v Secretary of State for the Home Department*,[51] wherein Baroness Hale commented, in a short judgment, that

> the central point about family life … is that the whole is greater than the sum of its individual parts. The right to respect for family life of one necessarily encompasses the right to respect for the family life of others, normally a spouse or minor children, with whom that family life is enjoyed.[52]

Beoku-Betts was a deportation case, and it ostensibly centres on the issue of third party interests. The appellant appealed against the decisions of the Court of Appeal and the Immigration Tribunal which had overturned the determination of the immigration adjudicator and upheld the Home Secretary's decision to deport him. The adjudicator had, in determining that he should not be deported, directed himself to 'consider whether the interference with the appellant's family rights, which would obviously interfere with the family as a whole, is justified'.[53] He therefore considered the adverse impact upon third party family members, concluded that the interference with the rights of the family was not proportionate

[46]*ibid* [22] (emphasis added).
[47]*ibid* [17].
[48]*ibid.*
[49]Indeed, in *K*, the interests of the claimant's children did not even form part of claimant counsel's submissions. I am grateful to Hugh Tomlinson QC (who acted for the claimant) for this insight.
[50]*K* (n 9) [17].
[51][2008] UKHL 39, [2009] AC 115 ('*Beoku-Betts*').
[52]*ibid* [4].
[53]Quoted in *Beoku-Betts* (n 51) [12].

to the legitimate aim of controlling immigration, and allowed the appeal. The Home Secretary appealed this decision and was successful in both the Immigration Appeal Tribunal and the Court of Appeal, both of which found that the adjudicator had misdirected himself in law and that he ought only to have considered the impact upon the appellant's Article 8 rights in isolation from other family members.

The House of Lords held that the third party interests were relevant and should have been taken into account by the Home Secretary when making the decision on deportation. The House accepted the appellant's arguments that, if the case were appealed to the ECtHR, that is the approach that would be taken there. Moreover, to do otherwise would leave the remaining family members with no option but to initiate their own proceedings under s 7 HRA.

The issue of the relevance of third party interests in deportation cases has an apparently complex judicial history since the coming into force of the HRA 1998. We need not concern ourselves with the detail of it, save to note that there was no clear determination of the law's requirements either way until the House decided *Beoku-Betts*.[54] What must be remembered, however, is that – as with all deportation cases – this was a 'vertical' human rights appeal against a decision of a public authority. The Home Secretary was bound by s 6 HRA not to act incompatibly with Convention rights – an obligation which does not discriminate between primary litigants and third parties. The Home Secretary need only ask herself whether her decision engages *any* Article 8 rights – *engagement* is the touchstone in that instance that ought to put her on alert.

This is significantly different from a case in misuse of private information. In MPI, the first question for the court is not a straightforward one of engagement of Article 8, but rather the question whether the claimant has a reasonable expectation of privacy. This covers much of the same ground as the engagement question – indeed if the answer is 'yes' then clearly the claimant's Article 8 rights are engaged – but it is not the *same* question.[55] For if the *claimant*'s Article 8 rights are *not* engaged, the case falls at that point. No third party interests would ever be considered, since they have been brought into play (in cases like *CDE* and *K*) only at the second stage where the court conducts the 'ultimate balancing test'.[56] *Beoku-Betts*, then, is even further removed from the circumstances of the MPI cases than *In re Guardian*, because it does not require the court to determine a procedural matter to which third parties' Article 8 rights are relevant. It simply involves judicially reviewing the Home Secretary's failure to abide by her own statutory obligations. In relying upon this authority, Ward LJ seemingly

[54]Lord Brown sets out the history of this line of cases in *Beoku-Betts* (n 51) at [24]–[40].
[55]It might be objected at this point that I am conceptualising Article 8 rights too narrowly; that as an interest in 'family life' the children of the claimant are part and parcel of his Article 8 interests (as Baroness Hale's observation in *Beoku-Betts* suggests). I attend to this possibility in the section entitled 'The "inseparability" theory', below.
[56]*Re S* (n 21) [17].

fails to appreciate the distinction between the vertical and the horizontal types of case in which human rights are in issue.

Ward LJ also presents a subtly different, secondary line of justification for his decision to consider the interests of third parties. This is the argument that the court must consider 'the best interests of the child', and as such it calls to mind that well established principle of family law.[57] He cites *Neulinger v Switzerland*,[58] which is an ECtHR decision on deportation from the 1970s, from which he takes the broad observation that the ECHR cannot be interpreted as if in a legal vacuum; it warrants understanding as part of a wider set of supra-national human rights treaties including the International Convention on the Rights of the Child.[59] In particular, he quotes the court stating

> there is currently a broad consensus – including in international law – in support of the idea that in all decisions concerning children, their best interests must be paramount.[60]

He further cites the House of Lords' decision in *ZH (Tanzania) v Secretary of State for the Home Department*.[61] In that case, the Supreme Court held that the adverse effect upon the child of a non-citizen parent against whom deportation proceedings were being brought, when that child would inevitably have to leave with the parent if she were deported, must be taken into account. Ward LJ states that the 'universal' principle that the court should act in the child's best interests 'cannot be ignored' in such a matter as the instant case.[62] He takes inspiration from Lord Kerr, who, in *ZH*, stated that

> in reaching decisions that will affect a child, a primacy of importance must be accorded to his or her best interests. This is not … a factor of limitless importance in the sense that it will prevail over all considerations. It is a factor, however, that must rank higher than any other. It is not merely one consideration that weighs in the balance alongside other competing factors. Where the best interests of the child clearly favour a certain course, that course should be followed, unless countervailing reasons of considerable force displace them.[63]

[57]One issue relating to this 'best interests of the child' approach which remains unresolved is one we encountered earlier, namely how it is that the court came to determine that the children's interests were even relevant. However, we need not repeat our analysis of that issue here.

[58](2010) 28 EHRC 706 ('*Neulinger*').

[59]Ward LJ ([18]) refers to the second principle of the United Nations Declaration of the Rights of the Child 1959, Article 3(1) of the Convention of the Rights of the Child 1989 (UNCRC) and Article 24 of the European Union's Charter of Fundamental Rights.

[60]*Neulinger* (n 58) [135].

[61][2011] UKSC 4, [2011] 2 AC 166 ('*ZH*').

[62]*K* (n 9) [19].

[63]*ZH* (n 61) [46].

However, Ward LJ is not prepared simply to adopt this guidance without qualifying it. for

> the interests of children do not automatically take precedence over the Convention rights of others … The force of the public interest will be highly material, and the interests of affected children cannot be treated as a trump card.[64]

The principle that the courts must accord great weight to the best interests of the child, where it appears in English law, is generally a statutory duty.[65] In such instances, it is an absolute requirement. When family law cases involving children are dealt with under the common law, as the court exercises its wardship jurisdiction, the requirement is not absolute but clearly weighty. But what marks these family cases out from the scenario facing the court in *K* is the evidential basis upon which the court makes its decision. In applications for care orders, for instance, the court will act on what it considers to be the child's best interests after having received evidence on that very issue. In *K*, there is no sign that the Court of Appeal considered any *evidence* as to the potential bullying of the children. It seems clear enough (even though the decision is not reported) that the High Court which considered the application and gave an *ex tempore* judgment initially refusing the claimant injunctive relief did not consider any such evidence either, since Ward LJ finds it difficult to determine whether Collins J even took into account the children's interests.[66]

It is quite clear that Ward LJ perceives the risk of bullying to be a genuine one. However, it is surely arguable that making a finding of the risk of harm to the interests of children based on no evidence, and according that risk sufficient weight to override Article 10, of itself constitutes a disproportionate interference with the defendant's Article 10 rights. It goes against the grain of s 12(4) HRA, which requires the courts to pay particular attention to the importance of freedom of expression 'where the proceedings relate to material which the respondent claims … to be journalistic'. Of course, requiring a solid evidential basis for taking these interests into account raises the expensive spectre of extended litigation on these issues, which may not be desirable.[67] Nevertheless, imposing

[64]*K* (n 9) [19].

[65]For example, under s 1 Children Act 1989.

[66]*K* (n 9) [14]: 'It is not at all clear to what extent if at all, Collins J. had regard to the Article 8 rights of anyone bar the appellant.'

[67]*AAA* was a claim for misuse of private information brought by a young child (as the primary claimant, not a third party). The High Court noted that the authorities cited in *K* required weight to be attached to the best interests of the child. However, 'the case was not conducted as a "best interests of the child" hearing' ([114]) and the court received no detailed evidence on the child's best interests. Nevertheless, the judge's explicit indication that 'I attach considerable weight to the claimant's interests' was deemed sufficient by the Court of Appeal ([2013] EWCA Civ 554 [18]) to discharge the 'best interests' obligation.

injunctions partly on the basis of concerns that have no evidential grounding is not an adequate solution.

Notably, whilst the case of *CDE* was an authority on point which was available to the Court of Appeal in *K*, the court did not refer to it. It was not cited in argument and we are left to presume that it did not come to the judges' attention. Thus the Court of Appeal's decision in *K* stands before a doctrinal backdrop which is somewhat oblique. The deportation jurisprudence first muddies the distinction (if indeed any distinction now remains, in the light of *K*) between the courts' obligations in vertical public law cases and horizontal private law claims. Its second effect is to provide (at best) support for a broad principle that the court ought to consider the best interests of children in cases where children are involved, but these are not to be regarded as automatically trumping competing interests. None of the cases cited provide analogies with more than a fleeting resemblance to the case at hand and indeed all of them are, due to their vertical nature, clearly distinguishable. A formalistic application of this doctrine, then, does not specify *as a matter of necessity* the approach taken in *K*.

Having demonstrated that the taking of third party interests into account was not a formal *requirement* on the courts in either *CDE* or *K*, we will next turn to a discussion of the impact of those rulings and an exploration of how they might plausibly be explained.

Discussion

We have seen that, in cases involving children, the courts have been willing to allow third party interests to influence the balance which they must strike between Articles 8 and 10 ECHR. The stretching of the law is particularly remarkable in *CDE* and *K*, for it pulls away from the traditional bilateral structure of private law (which dealt only with the rights of those parties involved in the proceedings) and into the realm of the sort of all-encompassing assessment of impact upon Convention rights associated with vertical, public law cases. Particularly troubling is the lack of detailed consideration or explanation by the judges of this effect of their rulings. Indeed, there is no indication in either case that the judges even appreciated the tension between their approach and the traditional bilateralism of private law to which the judgments give rise.

Notwithstanding the lack of a clear or deeply entrenched formal basis for the recognition of the relevance of third party interests in cases such as *CDE* and *K*, their appearance in both pleadings and judgments has quickly become accepted practice. In *Rocknroll v NGN Ltd*,[68] Briggs J was prepared to accord significant weight to the interests of the claimant's stepchildren, which

---

This approach avoids the need for extended evidence by treating the judge's assessment of the balance to be struck between arts 8 and 10 as akin to an exercise of discretion.

[68] [2013] EWHC 24 (Ch) [unreported].

gave support to the claimant's application to enjoin the intended publication of naked photographs depicting him. The judge made clear that the potentially 'grave risk' of the children 'being subjected to teasing or ridicule at school' which might be 'seriously damaging' to their relationship with the claimant would, if all other matters had been equally balanced, have been 'sufficient to tip it in the claimant's favour'.[69] Clearly, then, unless the courts make a U-turn, third party interests are going to remain a core feature of privacy litigation in the years ahead.

There are two ways in which the accommodation of third party interests in this manner might plausibly be explained. Both of these, however, cast serious doubt upon the success of the *Wainwright* ruling's attempts to ensure the maintenance of legal certainty in later cases. We will now consider each of these alternatives in turn.

The 'incremental accommodation' theory

It need not follow from the analysis offered above that the courts are formally *precluded* from translating the obligation to accommodate the interests of all those persons whose Convention rights are engaged (present in vertical cases) to horizontal cases. Nor need it follow that the courts *ought* not to engage in such translation. Indeed, it is not the aim of this essay to provide an answer to the large normative issue of whether such translation is desirable. Rather the essay's primary concern is with the developmental dynamic present in this area. For what we have identified is a *development* of the law and not the mere application of established doctrine. We have, moreover, seen that such a move is neither obviously well-established nor conceptually straightforward. Yet the accommodation of third party interests might be defensible as an incremental extension of the MPI tort's scope, aimed at securing the Convention rights of members of the claimant's family who would be adversely affected by publication of the relevant private information. However, doing so is more problematic than the courts appear to have realised, and raises several issues.

First, it must be asked whether the extension of the balancing test to accommodate third party interests can properly be characterised as an 'incremental' step. Second, the tension between the courts' obligations under the HRA must be explored. On the one hand, the courts are required to act compatibly with the Convention rights of those affected and, on the other, to do so through the mechanism of the (traditionally bilateral) private law structure. Third, the fact that judges such as Eady J have clearly thought this development to be 'well established' challenges the notion that the courts are consciously engaging in incremental extension; this will need to be addressed.

---

[69] *ibid* [37]–[39].

Incrementalism is not a term with a universally agreed meaning.[70] Indeed, it is often used rather casually, as shorthand for the manner in which the common law develops as a body of what Llewellyn termed 'slow-growing wisdom'.[71] In domestic cases involving ECHR rights, however, incrementalism takes place within a field demarcated by the indirect horizontal effect of the Human Rights Act. One of the side-effects of this indirect horizontality is that it creates an adjudicative space within which tensions may arise between different aspects of the court's obligations.[72] On the one hand, the court is required, as a public body under s 6 of the HRA, not to act incompatibly with Convention rights. As such, it must plug domestic gaps in protection for Convention rights by elaborating the common law in a way that is Convention-compatible.[73] Yet because the obligation is to develop the common law (and not to give effect to a direct, statutory cause of action), there remain limits on how far the court is obliged to go in pursuit of Convention-compatibility. Phillipson and Williams argue that the court is limited by an existing common law constraint to extend the law on a merely incremental basis. They do not exhaustively define 'incremental' in their piece, but the authors have in mind 'a piecemeal and principled [mode of development] that takes due account of pre-existing legal frameworks established by Parliament and previous judicial decisions'.[74] They approve of an argument made by Aileen Kavanagh that, acting incrementally, the courts are limited to engage only

> in partial and piecemeal reform … by extending existing doctrines, adjusting them to changing circumstances or introducing small alterations to avoid an injustice in their application.[75]

---

[70]As a method for judicial development of the common law, 'incrementalism' entered into the popular legal lexicon in Brennan J's judgment in the Australian High Court negligence case of *Sutherland Shire Council v Heyman* (1985) 157 CLR 424 in which he stated: 'It is preferable … that the law should develop novel categories of negligence incrementally and by analogy with existing categories, rather than by massive extension of a prima facie duty of care … ' (481). This approach to developing the law pertaining to duties of care in negligence, whilst ultimately rejected in Australia, was endorsed in England by the House of Lords in *Caparo v Dickman* [1990] 2 AC 605.

[71]Karl N Llewellyn, *The Bramble Bush: The Classic Lectures on the Law and Law School* (OUP, 2008), 41

[72]On the concept of adjudicative space, see Richard Mullender, 'Judging and Jurisprudence in the USA' (2012) 75(5) *Modern Law Review* 914, 921–23.

[73]See generally Young, 'Mapping Horizontal Effect' (n 31).

[74]Gavin Phillipson and Alexander Williams, 'Horizontal Effect and the Constitutional Constraint' (2011) 74(6) *Modern Law Review* 878, 887.

[75]Aileen Kavanagh, 'The Elusive Divide between Interpretation and Legislation under the Human Rights Act 1998' (2004) 24(2) *Oxford Journal of Legal Studies* 259, 272, cited in Phillipson and Williams (n 74) 904.

Given the apparent centrality of 'incrementalism' to indirect horizontal effect, Dolding and Mullender's more detailed work on the concept is illuminating.[76] In their view, the term broadly refers to

> a form of adjudication involving the articulation of liability rules which are, at once, new (and, hence, can properly be regarded as the fruit of judicial law-making) and yet are conditioned by pre-existing law.[77]

Dolding and Mullender present two modes of incrementalism which they term 'narrow' and 'wide'. Both, they argue, can be shown to have been utilised in English tort law in the twentieth century.[78] Narrow incrementalism 'reduces receptivity to strongly novel claims'.[79] If, in a novel case, there is a lack of existing case law indicating a rule capable of extension to embrace the novel fact pattern, narrow incrementalism denies any opportunity for extending the law. Thus it tends to result in the courts 'refus[ing] … to contemplate' elaborating the law in novel situations; in a novel tort case, liability will only be imposed if a sufficiently 'tight' analogy can be drawn with an existing case.

By contrast, the wide incremental approach gives the courts considerably greater latitude in instances where existing doctrine is constraining. For a court operating in the wide incremental mode is less doctrine-bound than one operating in the narrow mode.[80] Rather than focusing on establishing 'tight analogies' between existing precedent and the instant case, a court engaged in the practice of wide incrementalism focuses on the underlying principles and purposes of the body of law being mobilised.[81] Thus, for instance, wide incrementalism might lead to the creation of a new category of tort (to plug a gap in, for example, rights protection) in order to give effect to that body of law's overarching, informing, 'protective' purpose.[82]

Despite not exhaustively defining incrementalism, the impression one gets from Phillipson and Williams' endorsement of Kavanagh's characterisation of it as involving 'partial and piecemeal reform' suggests they see incrementalism in a manner consistent with the narrow mode. However, there is nothing in their argument that rules out the wide form of incrementalism; all their argument requires is that the courts do not exceed the limits of incrementalism howsoever it is defined in the law. Both the narrow and wide forms are evident in recent law (as Dolding and Mullender demonstrate) and thus both have clearly been seen as acceptable

[76]Lesley Dolding and Richard Mullender, 'Tort Law, Incrementalism, and the House of Lords' (1996) 47(1) *Northern Ireland Legal Quarterly* 12.
[77]*ibid* 13.
[78]*ibid.*
[79]Richard Mullender, 'English Negligence Law as a Human Practice' (2009) 21(3) *Law & Literature* 321, 326.
[80]Dolding and Mullender (n 76) 16.
[81]*ibid* 16.
[82]*ibid* 14.

forms of judicial activity by the courts.[83] Moreover, as Phillipson and Williams ultimately concede, the proper limits of incrementalism – and thus of judicial activism – are and must be set by the courts themselves.[84] This is surely correct; the normative field within which judging takes place is one of 'interpretative possibility' and, if judging is understood as an interpretative practice, it falls to the judges to interpret the limits of incrementalism.[85]

The effect of the third party cases is not as far-reaching as the establishment of a novel tort. However, given that third party interests had previously been shown to be relevant to rights-balancing only in vertical and procedurally horizontal cases, their introduction in remedial horizontal cases cannot be said to be the result of *tight* analogising. A more significant move has taken place. The developmental mode that underpins the recognition of third party interests as relevant in MPI thus sits between the narrow and wide extremes Dolding and Mullender identify (although probably a little closer to the 'wide' end of the scale). It is, however, impeccably 'incremental'.

Seen in the light of the foregoing, the real problem with the third party interests cases upon which we have dwelt is that the courts have consistently failed to identify what they have been doing as *development* of the law. Instead we have been presented with numerous assertions to the effect that recognising third party interests as relevant is 'well established', which it clearly is not (or, at least, *was* not prior to these cases). The obfuscation is unnecessary. The courts are well within their constitutional limits developing the law in this fashion. For tort has a protective purpose and, moreover, the courts are able to point to relevant (though not directly related) higher-order public law values (in the form of the values underpinning Article 8) that provide normative support for development in a rights-protecting direction.[86]

A better way to deal with these cases would have been to acknowledge the novelty of the issue raised and explain, in the language of indirect horizontality, why recognising third party interests as relevant is appropriate. In doing so, the courts could have acknowledged the tension between the traditionally bilateral structure of the type of claim (a tort claim) that is the vehicle through which privacy violations find redress, and the courts' statutory obligation to develop the common law in a way that secures Convention rights. The courts could then have explored the limits of incrementalism and determined that the level of violence done to the traditional structure of the tort claim is less significant than the gap in protection for the Article 8 rights of the children.[87] They could thus

[83]Dolding and Mullender (n 76) 15–17.
[84]Phillipson and Williams (n 74) 906–907.
[85]Mullender, 'Judging' (n 72) 921.
[86]On tort's protective purpose, see Dolding and Mullender (n 76) 13–14.
[87]Lord Bingham cautioned against doing 'impermissible violence' to 'the principles upon which [an existing] cause of action is founded' in the name of pursuing protection for privacy in response to criticism of the Court of Appeal's decision in *Kaye v Robertson*

have concluded that bringing these interests into focus is permissible. Moreover, since they come into play only at the balancing stage, when the named claimant has already established that he himself has a reasonable expectation of privacy, the alteration to the structure of the claim is relatively minor (although, of course, it has significant consequences for the parties, and particularly for the defendant).

If the incremental accommodation model is correct, then one further matter ought to be raised. What we have unearthed is a consequence of indirect horizontality that none of the voluminous literature on horizontal effect, which sprang up in the aftermath of the HRA's passing, considered. The consequence is that the Act may embolden the courts, in their pursuit of Convention-compatible development of the common law, to rework the *very structure* of the traditional private law claim. The incremental accommodation model shows this to be a defensible development, and it may be one that, in *practice*, makes only a relatively modest difference to the lives of litigants and their families. But at a *conceptual* level, it is deeply significant. Although the horizontality literature generally skirts over, around and otherwise avoids the question of *precisely* how far the courts can or must go in their development of the common law under the auspices of the HRA, the mantra that private law would be the mechanism through which Convention rights would find expression quickly took hold in the mid-2000s. What was not considered was whether the very bilateral structure of private law might itself be altered.

For if it can be so altered there is no reason to suppose this need be limited to claims in the relatively niche tort of MPI. The HRA's horizontality obligations under s 6 are of general effect. Third party children's Convention rights might be engaged in a range of other instances. For example, in the case of *Dobson v Thames Water* (a case in the tort of private nuisance), the Court of Appeal rejected an argument that the child of two claimants ought also to have been awarded his own, separate damages to protect his Article 8 interests.[88] The rationale for the rejection was the oft-cited rule that, in order to bring a claim in private nuisance, the claimant must have a proprietary interest in the property that is subject to the nuisance.[89] However, this rule simply reflects and maintains the traditional bilateral structure of nuisance claims. Under the incremental accommodation model,

(1991) FSR 62 (for which he was one of the judges). In that case, neither the plaintiff's counsel nor the court considered the law of confidence sufficiently malleable to accommodate *Kaye*'s claim: 'the complaint in this case was not that information obtained or imparted in confidence was about to be misused, but that Mr Kaye's privacy had been the subject of a monstrous invasion but for which the [information] would never have been obtained at all.' See Thomas Bingham, 'Should There Be a Law to Protect Rights of Personal Privacy?' [1996] 5 *European Human Rights Law Review* 450, 457.

[88] *Dobson* (n 10).

[89] This long-standing rule was reiterated by the House of Lords in *Hunter v Canary Wharf Ltd* [1997] AC 655; [1997] 2 WLR 684.

the interests of others living at the claimants' property ought to be taken into account at some stage, even if they do not have a separate claim. In private nuisance, this accommodation could take place during the 'reasonable use' element of the tort, when the court considers the reasonableness of the defendant's conduct in creating the nuisance (i.e. after the establishment of a *prima facie* case, like the balancing test in MPI). The point is this: if third party interests are in play in MPI owing to the courts' HRA obligations, there is no reason why they ought not also to be in play in other areas of private law when Convention rights are at stake. This observation is clearly in need of more analysis and discussion than can be provided in this essay (which, in any event, is concerned only with MPI), but it is flagged up here in the hopes of sparking such discussion and, at the very least, highlighting the existence of the issue.

The 'inseparability' theory

An alternative to the incremental accommodation approach may be termed the 'inseparability' theory. This theory would see the accommodation of the interests of claimants' children in a rather different light. Instead of separating the children's interests from those of the parent, we might see the courts as having gleaned from Article 8 a broader right to 'family life', and made that central to MPI claims. According to this, the children's right is inseparable from that of the parent. This is a concept more familiar to family lawyers than tort lawyers. It relates to something more than merely an individual's privacy: a broader right to respect for the integrity of the family unit. It is, of course, a right far more wide-ranging and further-reaching than the limited right to control of personal information secured through MPI as traditionally conceived (as a tort guarding against the disclosure of private facts).[90]

What this theory proposes is that the collective interest in family integrity, in which each family member has a stake, is the main interest in play in the cases upon which we have dwelt. If this is correct, then the children would not properly be seen as third parties at all; rather they are further members of a class whose collective interest in family life is threatened. According to this theory, the parent bringing the action is the *sole* primary party in name only; he is the token claimant representing the collective family interest.

There is evidence that the courts are prepared to conceive of Article 8 as bestowing this sort of broader interest. In *Beoku-Betts*, Baroness Hale seemed to have this sort of interest in mind; it will be recalled that she saw the 'right to respect for family life of one [as] necessarily encompass[ing] the right to respect for the family life of others … with whom that family life is enjoyed'.[91] The theory might also explain the refusal, in *Dobson*, to grant the

---

[90]Patrick O'Callaghan, *Refining Privacy in Tort Law* (Springer, 2013) 154–55.
[91]*Beoku-Betts* (n 51) [4].

claimants' son damages for nuisance in his own right; interference with the parents' rights (for which damages were awarded) could be seen as inseparable from interference with the son's.[92] Such a move would embrace the ECtHR's insistence that Article 8 guarantees a broad right to 'physical and psychological integrity'.[93]

As a solution to the third party interests question, however, this theory is problematic. For if this broad aspect of Article 8 is the central right in play, the nomenclature 'misuse of private information' becomes rather misleading. The claimant's claim is not simply that his private information has been misused, but that the defendant has caused harm to the integrity of his family unit. What the courts would have in substance recognised is a broad tort of disrupting family integrity. It would 'convert the tort of MPI into a tort which affects the private life of the claimant'.[94] The recognition of such a broad right as underpinning this sort of claim in tort is likely to encounter strong resistance. For, as Kay puts it, there are 'few grievances that cannot be accommodated to a claim of interference with this kind of interest'.[95] He cautions that

> [s]hould [such a broad interest] govern private relations we could, effectively, have a situation where the Convention obliges every person to respect every other person's 'physical and psychological integrity' – except when, all things considered, it is better not to do so.[96]

Moreover, if the inseparability theory provides the correct answer, then there must have been been a significant amount of judicial sleight of hand in recent years, much of which seems to have gone unnoticed. For if the MPI tort has been converted into a tort of wrongful interference with the integrity of the family unit without anyone other than a handful of judges and practitioners who regularly deal with cases of this sort noticing, that alone is a testament to how unforeseeable such a development was.

This theory, then, is more radical than the incremental accommodation model. Indeed, it is so radical that it would fit with an understanding of the HRA's horizontal effect that Phillipson and Williams labelled the 'radical distortion' model.[97]

---

[92] *Dobson* (n 10).

[93] *Von Hannover v Germany (No 1)* (2004) 40 EHRR 1 [50].

[94] *O v A* (n 37) [43].

[95] Richard S Kay, 'The European Convention on Human Rights and the Control of Private Law' [2005] 5 *European Human Rights Law Review* 466, 477.

[96] *ibid* 477.

[97] Phillipson and Williams (n 74) 884–85. The model they label 'radical distortion' appears in it's Alison Young's taxonomy of 'strong indirect horizontal effect' models, where it is simply labelled 'model (E)'. See , 'Horizontality and the Human Rights Act 1998' in K Ziegler (ed), *Human Rights and Private Law: Privacy as Autonomy* (Hart, 2007), 35–51; 'Mapping Horizontal Effect' (n 31) 45–47. Whilst Young attributed this model to the work of Murray Hunt ('The "Horizontal Effect" of the Human Rights Act' [1998] *Public*

That model, which they reject outright as an implausible reading of the HRA's effect, would *require* the courts 'to distort existing causes of action in order to bring them into line with the Convention'.[98] As they rightly argue, the model is incoherent; despite its ostensible formal constraints, it is virtually unconstrained in substance:

> in imposing an absolute obligation to render existing causes of action Convention-compatible, [the radical distortion model] seems to require the courts simply to over-write existing actions with new Convention-based content.[99]

In other words, it is one thing to incrementally alter the structure of a tort claim in order to accommodate Convention rights that would otherwise be overlooked, as in the incremental accommodation model. It is quite another to suggest that the HRA *requires* the courts to recognise a broad-brush Article 8 tort. Indeed, fears of such a 'blockbuster'[100] tort were, in part, what seemed to move the House of Lords in *Wainwright* to reject a general privacy tort so emphatically.

There is one further problematic aspect to this theory. Whilst it endeavours to explain away the practical effect that this line of cases has upon the claimant (that the parent's claim is bolstered by the rights of the children) it serves only to highlight the disparity with the reverse position. For if the theory is correct, and the children's right is inseparable from the parent's right, it ought to be possible for the children to be the named claimants and draw upon the adverse effect upon the parent to bolster *their* claim for injunctive relief. But the courts have clearly rejected the notion that the children may bring a claim in such circumstances. The Court of Appeal's ruling in *O v A* emphatically rejected (albeit providing only limited detail on the reasons for that rejection)[101] the argument that an MPI claim could be brought by any person other than the subject of the

Law 423), Phillipson and Williams (n 74, 884) doubt whether this model best reflects what Hunt had in mind.

[98] Phillipson and Williams (n 74) 884.

[99] *ibid* 885.

[100] *Wainwright* (n 5). See also NA Moreham, 'Privacy in the Common Law: A Doctrinal and Theoretical Analysis' (2005) 121 *Law Quarterly Review* 628, 654; Gavin Phillipson, 'Privacy' in Hoffman (n 31), 163, 136–164.

[101] In *O v A* (n 37), the appellant (claimant), who was the child of the respondent, presented an argument that his claim in MPI should be allowed along the lines of the inseparability theory ([40]–[42]). The Court of Appeal rejected this ([45]), preferring the respondent's submission that 'in *K v News Group [Newspapers Ltd]* the children could not have made their complaint separately and that there is no case in which third parties have been able to bring an action which does not relate to them or in respect of information which they do not own' ([43]). Moreover, the Court implicitly endorsed the respondent's caution that '[t]he appellant is trying to convert the tort of MPI into a tort which affects the private life of the claimant' ([43]), since if the law went 'that far … the result would be that a person could sue whenever his family life was affected even if the information does not belong to him' ([45]).

information himself. That case, which is the most recent authority on this point,[102] thus sits squarely at odds with the inseparability theory.

As such, whilst some might take the references to Baroness Hale's characterisation of the Article 8 rights of the family as a collective interest from *Beoku-Betts* as indicative of the inseparability theory's presence in this area, the model is too incoherent plausibly to explain the emergence of this line of cases (or, indeed, to inform its future development). Moreover, it is likely to generate considerable resistance once its implications are fully appreciated.

Conclusions

The methodology adopted in both *CDE* and *K* calls into question anew the way in which horizontal rights-protection operates in England. Under any form of indirect horizontal effect (a notion around which there is broad consensus), human rights claims are dealt with through the common law, using (and if need be, incrementally developing) existing private law actions. This may even result on occasion, as with misuse of private information in *Campbell*, in the emergence of an apparently novel tort. But since the medium through which such claims are to be disposed of remains, resolutely, domestic *private* law, it seems extraordinary (at first glance) to see these very specific third party interests featuring at all in these cases. For private law claims (in, *inter alia*, tort, equity and contract) are normally by their very nature bilateral. A claimant is not traditionally able to bolster his claim by seeking to draw the court's attention to other, unrepresented parties who might be adversely affected should he lose. Keeping the child's claim separate from the parent's preserves the traditionally clear, bilateral nature of private law litigation.

As we saw in *Dobson*, the courts have taken a different stance in the tort of private nuisance, despite being under the same HRA obligations. It thus appears that the development of misuse of private information in such a way as to take into account third party interests creates an imbalance between privacy law and other causes of action in which Convention rights are at stake. The imbalance is methodological, in that the courts have adapted their method to embrace a broad-ranging balancing act only in these informational privacy cases, preferring to keep other torts strictly bilateral. There are always reasons to suspect that such methodological imbalances within the law are undesirable, not least because insofar as they result from judicial elaboration of the law, they are both retrospective (upon the instant case) and difficult accurately to foresee. Moreover, since the doctrinal underpinning for this development is both weak and not fully agreed-upon by the courts, there is a sense that it may lack a clear basis in legal principle.

[102] The Supreme Court, when it gave judgment in *Rhodes v OPO* [2015] UKSC 32 (the appeal from *O v A*) mentioned but did not comment upon the correctness of the Court of Appeal's treatment of the MPI claim, which was not an issue in the appeal to the SC.

The lack of clarity as to the normative basis for taking into account third party interests exacerbates the issue. These problems raise significant rule of law concerns and, most importantly for the argument made in this essay, they undermine the attempt to engender certainty in privacy law's future development from the restrictive *Wainwright* ruling.

There is, of course, a sense in which the conclusions reached by Eady J in *CDE* and Ward LJ in *K* are commendable. Their willingness to take seriously the interests of children affected by the violation of their parents' privacy is morally appealing. But the methodologies leading to these conclusions raise considerable problems of coherence (not least with each other) which require much more work to sort out than appears to have been appreciated. Given that the decisions cannot reasonably be said to apply existing doctrine formalistically, they do not represent the kind of predictable, narrowly incremental elaborations of the law that Lord Hoffmann seemingly (perhaps naïvely) envisaged would follow *Wainwright*.

As such, larger questions must be raised about the legacy of *Wainwright*. For what we have uncovered in this essay is evidence that, in one aspect of misuse of private information jurisprudence, the law has been significantly stretched in order to accommodate third party interests which ordinarily would play no role in private law methodology. There are other aspects of this body of case law which provide further evidence of this judicial tinkering, such as the timid emergence of a doctrine of 'false privacy',[103] and what some commentators have suggested may be in substance (if not form) the recognition of a right in one's own image.[104] It may well thus be the case that judges have in fact responded to the apparent limiting effect of *Wainwright* and *Campbell* by fashioning ways of broadening privacy protection (particularly for children) on a rather *ad hoc* basis whilst obscuring their moves by engaging in a process of ostensibly formal, *ex post facto* rationalisation of their decisions. And whilst the noble aim motivating this is no bad thing in itself, it demonstrably leaves the law in this field in a state of considerable uncertainty.

Acknowledgements

Versions of this essay were presented as papers at the Society of Legal Scholars' Annual Conference 2014 (Jurisprudence Section) and at The Campbell Legacy, Newcastle University, in April 2015. I am grateful to the participants in those sessions for their comments and criticisms. I am also grateful to Daithí Mac Síthigh, Rebecca Moosavian, Richard Mullender, Gavin Phillipson, Paul Wragg and one anonymous reviewer for their helpful comments on earlier drafts. Any remaining errors are, of course, mine and mine alone.

---

[103] *McKennitt v Ash* [2006] EWCA Civ 1714, [2007] 3 WLR 194 [86] (Longmore LJ); *Terry v Persons Unknown* [2010] EWHC 119 (QB), [2010] EMLR 16 [96].

[104] See Hugh Tomlinson QC, 'Paul Weller, Article 8 and the recognition of 'image rights'', available at http://inforrm.wordpress.com/2014/04/30/weller-article-8-and-the-recognition-of-image-rights-hugh-tomlinson-qc/ (accessed 12/8/15)

Disclosure statement

No potential conflict of interest was reported by the author.

Update (January 2017)

Since this essay was first published, the Supreme Court has heard and handed down its decision in the case of *PJS v News Group Newspapers Ltd* [2016] UKSC 26, [2016] AC 1081. The Court reinstated the High Court's decision to impose interim injunctive relief to prohibit the defendant from publishing details of a now infamous "three way" sexual liaison involving a well-known public figure. In a continuation of the third party interests doctrine, the Court gave particular prominence to the potential for harm to befall the claimant's children if further publication occurred (notwithstanding that which had already appeared on the internet). Unfortunately, the decision does nothing to clarify the formal basis of the third party interests doctrine. Whilst Lady Hale, who dwells on the doctrine more overtly than the other justices, makes clear her view that it is right and proper for the courts to consider the interests of the claimant's children (at [72]-[73]), she does not give any indication of which of the competing lines of authority (if either) she sees as supporting this conclusion. Neither does she give a clear elucidation of a principled basis for it. The other judgments rendered in the case are of no more assistance on this point. Thus whilst the Supreme Court has thrown its weight behind the third party interests doctrine – and, as a result, we can be sure that it is here to stay – at a formal level the unsatisfactory state of affairs remains. Given the rarity of privacy cases appearing before our highest court, this must go down as a missed opportunity to bring much needed clarity to the doctrine.

The harms of privacy

Eric Descheemaeker

This paper aims to identify and order the harms or losses which the law might compensate (or more widely redress) in actions for breach of privacy. Part I identifies three such detriments, to which all the others are reducible: pecuniary loss, mental distress and breach of privacy per se. Part II seeks to explain why they cannot all coexist at the same time. This is because they are based on two incompatible ways of understanding the relationship between wrong and harm, which ought not to be conflated: one that regards the loss as the detrimental consequences of the wrong (on respectively the claimant's 'pocket' and his emotional tranquillity); the other that treats the harm as the wrong itself, i.e. the invasion to – or loss of – the claimant's privacy. Part III examines some of the consequences the choice we make between them has on key issues within the law of privacy.

Introduction

This article has two aims, one narrow and relatively simple; the other wider and more ambitious. The narrow aim is to identify the various types of harm that the claimant can – at least potentially – seek redress for in an action for breach of privacy.[1] This simply entails looking at the decisions that were handed down

[1]This article is not interested in non-monetary remedies, like injunctions. Within damages (money awards) it also ignores exemplary damages, to which courts have all but closed the door in privacy actions (*Mosley v News Group Newspapers Ltd* [2008] EWHC 1777 (QB), [2008] EMLR 20 [210]), and restitutionary (disgorgement) damages, which it has been argued should be allowed: Normann Witzleb, 'Justifying Gain-based Remedies for Invasions of Privacy' (2009) 29 *Oxford Journal of Legal Studies* 325. Aggravated damages are regarded as a species of compensatory damages which do not raise separate issues. The focus of this paper is decidedly on *compensatory* damages. Adifficulty, however, is that how far a money award can be described as compensatory for loss depends on how broadly the notion of loss is construed. When loss is defined in a narrower way, this will open up a gap which some have tried to fill by resorting to the concept of vindicatory damages (see below, Part III.4).On the basis of the more extensive understanding that this paper defends, however, there is as will be seen no need for this separate response. Nonetheless, the word 'redress' is used as an umbrella term for both compensation and

on that basis and examining what courts have said, tidying up the language to avoid unnecessary duplicates. What will be argued is that they are of three sorts: pecuniary loss, mental distress and loss of privacy considered in itself. The broader ambition is to rationalise the way the law thinks about such harms, losses or injuries. This is much more difficult because it requires understanding the underpinning structures of tort law on which these various heads of damages are – implicitly – predicated. Here, the argument will be that the sorts of harm courts have claimed to compensate expose the wrong[2] of breach of privacy as the main battlefield between two models of tort law, which carry two ways of understanding the relationship between wrong and loss: a dominant one, described as 'bipolar', which contrasts the wrong with the loss or losses that flow from it; and another – 'unipolar' – model which conflates the wrong and the loss, i.e. identifies the loss with the violation of the protected right. Distress and pecuniary loss, it will be argued, are tied to the former model, whereas loss of privacy is wedded to the latter; the important point being that we ought not to combine them because they answer to two conflicting rationalities.

This broader point will require an analysis of tort law, the significance of which is in no way restricted to actions for breach of privacy.[3] But privacy[4] actions are of particular interest in this respect because they constitute possibly the clearest battlefield between the two models; and the recent case of *Gulati v MGN*,[5] now the leading judgment concerning quantum of damages in English privacy law (on which this article focuses), shows them coming to a head in an especially clear way. As will be explored in the final part, the choice between the two models has a number of implications for the shape of this fledging area of the law, in particular the (highly disputed) question of whether juridical persons have a right to privacy and the possibility of 'vindicating' that right, which itself relates to the understanding we have of loss (in the sense of the detriments the law seeks to compensate) in the context of these actions.

---

vindication so as not to beg the question that the non-punitive and non-restitutionary damages in privacy actions are necessarily compensatory.

[2]The word is used here in the sense of civil wrong. Whether it is a tort *stricto sensu* has been disputed but now seems to have been settled authoritatively (and, to my mind, correctly) in the affirmative: see *Google Inc v Vidal-Hall* [2015] EWCA Civ 311, [2015] CP Rep 28 [43]: 'if one puts aside the circumstances of its "birth", there is nothing in the nature of the claim itself to suggest that the more natural classification of it as a tort is wrong.'

[3]In an English context 'breach of privacy' means misuse of private information, English law only recognising at this stage the violation of one particular type of privacy, namely, informational privacy. Insofar as the arguments developed in this article are not tied to that species of invasions, it is however better to use the broader label.

[4]'Privacy' is used here, and frequently through this article, as shorthand for 'breach of privacy': an incorrect but useful and now well-established shortcut.

[5]*Gulati v MGN Ltd* [2015] EWHC 1482 (Ch) unreported.

I. Three heads of detriment

1. *A note on terminology*

We begin in this section by examining the various detriments that the claimant in a privacy action might have suffered and seek compensation (or more generally, redress) for. 'Detriment' is a convenient word to start with because it is not a term of art and usefully conveys the idea of worse-offness at its broadest; but it is not proposed to press it into service in any particular technical sense because, in an already crowded toolbox, it is in all but the most unusual circumstances ill-advised to introduce yet further competitors: what the law needs is for the meaning of key words to be stabilised (so that, in turn, concepts can be articulated with precision), not for writers to add to the confusion by putting forward additional terms.

The difficulty is that, naturally, none of the possible candidates – 'loss', 'harm', 'injury', 'damage' and possibly others (e.g. 'prejudice') – have a stable meaning. 'Damage' has too much of an overtone of the sort of physical corruption we contemplate when we speak of 'damage to property' to be useful. 'Injury' is unsuitable in the present context for the very same reason that ordinarily makes it a convenient label for scholars, namely, its constant oscillation – and refusal to choose – between the wrong and the consequences of the wrong. There remain 'loss' and 'harm'. It seems fair to say both that 'harm' is the less cogently defined of the two (because it is the less technical one, 'loss' being the main term of art that lawyers have pressed into service) and also that it is wider, in the sense that there are many situations where it is easy to imagine lawyers being happy to use it but not to speak of 'loss', whereas the opposite would not appear to be true. Situations of detriments referred to as 'abstract', 'legal' or 'normative' losses spring to mind, such as loss of autonomy, of use or of privacy considered in themselves: while (as the very labels suggest) *some* would be happy for the word 'loss' to be used – if perhaps always with a qualifier – equally it is clear that many would take argument with such a 'strained and artificial'[6] use of the term. To avoid using question-begging terminology when examining issues which, as will be seen, largely hinge on how broadly the notion of 'loss' is construed, the word 'harm' is being preferred in this paper, at least as a starting point. It will be used interchangeably with 'loss' in its broadest sense: that of any detriment, i.e. any actualisation of real-life events which make the claimant worse off than he would have been without the conduct complained of.

Against this background, an examination of the cases shows that there are three, and only three, types of harms that the law of privacy concerns itself with.[7] They are: (1) pecuniary loss, (2) mental distress and (3) the loss of privacy itself. The only complication is that the terminology used is unstable;

[6]A phrase used by Lord Nicholls in *Attorney General v Blake* [2001] 1 AC 268, 279.

[7]Naturally this does not mean that they will all be present in each case: indeed, if the argument in this paper is correct, they should never all co-exist.

but it should not be difficult to accept that they are distinct clusters exhausting the field and also that no further meaningful distinction can be made within these clusters.

2. *Pecuniary loss*

There is no particular significance attached to the above order; it is simply one of convenience. Pecuniary loss comes first because it is the most obvious type of loss generally: as has been rightly remarked, it lies at the heart of the concept of loss[8] – to the point where, still today, the idea that loss that is not directly valuable in money is not 'real' or 'proper' loss never lies deep below the surface of the law. On the other hand, no-one would want to deny that such injuries to the pocket are loss (naturally there might be disputes as to whether they are *wrongful* losses, but this is an entirely distinct question).

It is therefore striking that, in the context of privacy claims, pecuniary loss – i.e. economic loss, whether direct or consequential – tends to be noticeably absent. It is rarely even pleaded, and it is questionable whether it has in fact ever been redressed using this cause of action. While proving negatives is always difficult, it is remarkable that the leading authority in the English-speaking world, *Tugendhat and Christie's The Law of Privacy and the Media*, only references one privacy case under that heading – the *Douglas v Hello!* saga, where damages were awarded for 'the expected revenue which would have come from the editions carrying the authorized wedding exclusives as they were originally planned by the publisher'[9] – even though this case was *not* in fact an instance of economic loss consequential on breach of privacy.

The plaintiff couple in that case, Michael Douglas and Catherine Zeta-Jones, sued 'Hello!' for publishing unauthorised photographs of their wedding in New York: a clear breach of their privacy which, given their celebrity status, also caused economic loss to a third party, 'OK!', who had secured the exclusive right to publish a selection of approved photographs. As a result they sold fewer copies of their magazine than they would otherwise had, some of the public's appetite for the event having already been satisfied by their competitor. 'OK!' consequently sued for damages alongside the celebrity couple. But in no sense was their economic loss, for which damages were ultimately awarded (the House of Lords reversing the decision of the Court of Appeal, which had itself overruled the trial judge) consequential upon a breach of privacy. For one thing, of course, any privacy right would have been the Douglases', not the magazine's.

---

[8]Andrew Tettenborn, 'What is a Loss?' in Jason Neyers, Erika Chamberlain and Stephen Pitel (eds), *Emerging Issues in Tort Law* (Hart, 2007) 441–466, 443.

[9]Mark Warby, Nicole Moreham and Iain Christie (eds), *Tugendhat and Christie's The Law of Privacy and the Media* (OUP, 2nd edn 2011) s13.95. I am grateful to Dr Moreham for having allowed me advance access to the relevant sections of the as yet unpublished third edition, which remain unchanged.

Besides, and more fundamentally, the fact that the published photographs concerned a private event was a mere happenstance; what mattered to the claimant magazine was that it was confidential information. That point was put with utmost clarity by Lord Hoffmann in the House of Lords, speaking for the majority on that point:

> It is … necessary to avoid being distracted by the concepts of privacy and personal information … [T]his appeal is not concerned with the protection of privacy. Whatever may have been the position of the Douglases … 'OK!'s' claim is to protect commercially confidential information and nothing more. So your Lordships need not be concerned with Convention rights. 'OK!' has no claim to privacy under article 8 nor can it make a claim which is parasitic upon the Douglases' right to privacy. The fact that the information happens to have been about the personal life of the Douglases is irrelevant. It could have been information about anything that a newspaper was willing to pay for.[10]

If the economic loss was actionable, therefore, it was not *qua* consequential upon a breach of privacy but rather because it flowed from another wrong: either breach of confidence (the solution adopted by the House of Lords) or one of the twin economic torts of inducing breach of contract and causing loss by unlawful means (which were discussed but rejected by the Court). In other words, the same set of facts – the taking and publishing of the photographs – gave rise to more than one cause of action; and while the economic loss arose from the same facts as those which made out the action for breach of privacy, and subsequently to it, it was not in any sense consequential upon that wrong. *Post hoc sed non propter hoc.*

Nonetheless, it is very difficult to deny that economic loss could potentially arise in a privacy case – which would however seem to be necessarily consequential rather than direct – and that, if it did, it should and would be recoverable on the usual conditions. If nothing else, this could be because the privacy-infringing information is also defamatory of the claimant:[11] defamatory statements do by nature have a tendency to cause economic losses, since they are liable to cause others to think less well of the claimant, and oftentimes these third parties will respond by modifying their behaviour in such a way that his pocket will suffer. This would amount to economic loss consequential upon the breach of privacy.[12]

---

[10] *Douglas v Hello! Ltd (No 3)* [2007] UKHL 21, [2008] 1 AC 1 [118] (conjoined appeal with *OBG Ltd v Allan* and *Mainstream Properties Ltd v Young*).

[11] If it is both, suing in privacy would allow, for instance, to bypass the defence of truth.

[12] Still, such a scenario would in a very real sense be a quasi-defamation action, i.e. it would be an action clothed in the appearances of a misuse of private information claim, but where the gist of the plaintiff's grievance would be that it reflected detrimentally on him. Outside of these cases, i.e. in 'pure privacy' cases, it is actually difficult to imagine how economic loss could truly be said to be consequential on the informational misuse (as opposed to

3. *Mental distress*

The second type of harm that can be identified in breach of privacy actions is mental distress in the broadest sense of unpleasant emotions. It does not pose significant analytical difficulties: as long as one accepts that mental distress can at least potentially occur in privacy cases (which is self-evident) and that this detriment counts as a harm (which would also be fairly obvious on the basis of the definition sketched out above), then it is aptly described as one of the 'harms of privacy'. Indeed privacy cases are dotted with references to such harms, from 'distress'[13] to 'hurt' or 'injured' 'feeling[s]',[14] to 'pain',[15] 'embarrassment'[16] or 'humiliation'.[17] (The more interesting question in that context really is whether there is, or could be, *any* successful action in privacy in the absence of such harm, a point that is returned to below).

The only slightly difficult issue is that of labels. As can be seen, a variety of terms have been used by courts to describe what Peter Handford calls 'unpleasant emotions'.[18] Without going as far as suggesting that they are all interchangeable, which is clearly not the case, it is equally clear that courts do not have a particular taxonomy of such emotions in mind when they use the above terms, whether in isolation or in combination. Rather, congruent with ordinary language, they are pressed into service in an unsystematic way to approximate the underlying (and always complex) spectrum of human emotions at play. It does not seem that any injustice is being done to them if we say that all of the above labels boil down to an idea of emotional disturbance or upset. In turn, the term 'mental distress', which is both broad and commonly used, seems as good a term as any to operate as an umbrella category encompassing them all. ('Mental harm', 'loss of happiness', 'sentimental harm' or 'emotional harm' would also be suitable labels, the main point being one of consistency.) The interest that is being considered here, through its various disruptions, is that in emotional tranquillity or wellbeing. Accordingly the focus is on the internal consequences of the wrong suffered on the mind on the claimant.

4. *Loss of privacy*

The third type of harm that one encounters in privacy cases would be, perhaps tautologically, the injury to the claimant's privacy itself: his 'loss of privacy' to use a

---

arising sequentially from the same set of facts). This cannot be pursued here but the point is worth noting.

[13]E.g. *Gulati* (n 5) [168]; *Mosley* (n 1) [216], [224]; *Campbell v MGN Ltd* [2004] UKHL 22, [2004] 2 AC 457 [33], [34].

[14]E.g. *Gulati* (n 5) [169]; *Mosley* (n 1) [216].

[15]E.g. *Campbell* (n 13) [33].

[16]E.g. *Mosley* (n 1) [235]; *Weller v Associated Newspapers Ltd* [2014] EWHC 1163 (QB), [2014] EMLR 24 [196]; *Campbell* (n 13) [75].

[17]E.g. *Campbell* (n 13) [75].

[18]Peter Handford, Nicholas Mullany and Philip Mitchell (eds), *Mullany and Handford's Tort Liability for Psychiatric Damage* (Lawbook Co, 2nd edn 2006) 56–7.

phrase that is in common usage, even though many would probably want to deny that, in and by itself, it is in fact a loss (although it most certainly is a harm in the above sense of detriment). The best two judicial illustrations of loss of privacy being a compensable harm are probably to be found under the pen of Mann J in *Gulati*, when he wrote that damages in a privacy action 'should compensate not merely for distress … but … also … for the loss of privacy … as such',[19] and that of Dingemans J in *Weller*, who considered that 'damages for misuse of private information should compensate the [c]laimants for the misuse of their private information',[20] in other words, for the loss of (or injury to) their privacy itself.

Again, there are terminological difficulties. In particular, the right or interest of the claimant's whose violation is characterised as the harm can be phrased in different ways and, besides loss of privacy, courts have also spoken of 'loss of autonomy'.[21] 'Autonomy' (literally, the state of being a law unto oneself) is a complex and multifaceted concept but, in the present context, it seems clear that it is not meant to describe a different injury from the injury to privacy. Either the two words are used as synonyms, as in *Gulati*[22] or – a doctrinally more suitable interpretation to my mind – autonomy is to be regarded as a higher-level interest, of which privacy would constitute one species among potentially many others.[23] On both readings, the injury to privacy constitutes ipso facto the injury to autonomy and the two need not be distinguished (indeed they should not, lest the same injury be counted twice).

What matters for the present purpose is to identify this head of detriment as separate from the previous one. This should not be controversial, for loss of privacy or autonomy is not – certainly not directly – a form of emotional disturbance. It is defined abstractly in terms of the loss of the 'good' represented by the protected interest, here privacy, not concretely in terms of the emotional disruption suffered by the claimant. While some difficulty in the relationship between the two might be immediately perceptible (and will be returned to in part II), this has to be our starting point: the two notions are clearly distinct in their self-understanding.

5. *'Loss of dignity'?*

It was argued at the outset that there were three types of relevant harms in privacy actions. The reason why a fourth heading on 'loss of dignity', a label that appeared

[19] *Gulati* (n 5) [168].
[20] *Weller* (n 16) [192].
[21] *Gulati* (n 5) [108], [111], [168], building on *Campbell* (n 13) [50] and *Mosley* (n 1) [7].
[22] This is transparent from the language used in the judgment, e.g. [168]: 'the loss of privacy or autonomy as such.'
[23] This would seem to be the approach in *Mosley*: 'The law now affords protection to information in respect of which there is a reasonable expectation of privacy … That is because the law is concerned to prevent the violation of a citizen's autonomy … ' [7]. The view that autonomy is an overarching principle underpinning most, if not all, other rights is a fairly common one, see e.g. Robert Stevens, *Torts and Rights* (OUP, 2007) 339.

in particular in *Mosley*[24] and in *Gulati*,[25] is nonetheless included here is that, whilst it does not in fact amount to a separate type of loss or detriment, this is not immediately apparent and therefore deserves separate treatment.

Analytically, there are three ways loss of dignity as harm can be analysed none of which makes it a distinct species. The first possibility is that it should be interpreted as being the loss of privacy, as already encountered, reframed at a higher level of generality (similarly to 'loss of autonomy'). On that reading, privacy would be one dignitary interest among others; and saying that the claimant suffered a loss of his privacy and a loss of his dignity would be describing the same harm in two different ways, using either a specific or a more general term (like describing someone as 'a Yorkshireman' then 'an Englishman'). The second possibility is that it would describe a concrete harm: 'loss of dignity' as 'indignity' in the non-legal sense of humiliation. Literally, to be humiliated is to be brought down to the ground (*humus*), that is to say, losing one's status as an upright human being. On that alternative reading, loss of dignity would now count as a type of mental distress, as defined above. Finally, the third possibility is that it would be a combination of these two.

All three understandings can be seen to surface in the case law. Dangerous though it might be to read too closely judgments which did not mean to consider the question in any great detail, it would seem that *Mosley* leans towards the second interpretation[26] and *Gulati* stands somewhere between the second and the third,[27] whereas Lord Hoffmann in *Campbell* appears to have had the first meaning in mind when he held that 'private information [is] something worth protecting as an aspect of human autonomy and dignity'.[28] Whichever is correct, what matters for the present purpose is that, one way or another, loss of dignity is reducible to other types of harm. It is neither necessary nor desirable to carve out a further category to accommodate it.

6. *Relationship*

The above survey identified, behind the various labels that courts (and scholars) might use, three – and only three – types of harm that can be redressed, at least in

---

[24] *Mosley* (n 1) [216], [224].

[25] *Gulati* (n 5) [141] (also, in combination with the words 'damage' or 'affront' rather than 'loss', [108] and [168]). At [108], 'dignity' is implicitly equated with 'standing'.

[26] This is implied in Eady J's words, where three notions are reduced to two and then one, as if the various phrases were interchangeable: 'damages for such an infringement may include *distress, hurt feelings and loss of dignity.* The scale of the *distress and indignity* in this case is difficult to comprehend. It is probably unprecedented. Apart from *distress*, there is another factor which probably has to be taken into account ... ': *Mosley* (n 1) [216] emphasis added.

[27] *Gulati* (n 5) [168]: 'I have already found that the damages should compensate not merely for distress (still using that word as a shorthand, as described above), but should also compensate (if appropriate) for the loss of privacy or autonomy as such arising out the infringement by hacking (or other mechanism) as such. (This may include, if appropriate, a sum to compensate for *damage to dignity* or standing, *so far as that* is meaningful in this context and *is not already within the distress element.*)' (emphasis added).

[28] *Campbell* (n 13) [50].

principle, in privacy actions: pecuniary loss, mental distress and loss of privacy. If we used a common dichotomy we would classify the first one as 'pecuniary loss' and the other two as 'non-pecuniary losses'.[29] But, besides being uninformative in that the second class is defined in a purely residual way, this would also suggest that these heads of detriment operate on the same level and can all be compensated if and when they arise: neither of which, as will be seen, is (or at least should be) true. Instead the distinction should be between, on the one hand, two concrete harms – the injury to the claimant's wallet (pecuniary loss) and the injury to his emotional well-being (distress) – and, on the other hand, an abstract harm: the loss of privacy per se, i.e. considered in and by itself. How the relationship between these three heads of detriment should be understood in a principled way is a difficult question that will form the basis of the next part. By way of preliminary, this final section simply examines the way courts have in fact articulated them, implicitly or explicitly. Pecuniary loss having, it seems, never been successfully claimed in a privacy action, this means looking at how the other two heads, distress and breach of privacy, are treated by courts.

Cases can be put on a spectrum in this respect. At one end would stand those judgments that were dealt with using the exclusive language of distress, i.e. with no suggestion being made that (absent economic loss) any other injury has been suffered by the claimant. *Campbell* is a case in point.[30] At the other end of the spectrum one would place the action of the Weller twins, whose case was adjudicated without any reference to actual or potential emotional consequences that the taking and publishing of photographs of them might have caused, and who recovered substantial damages on the sole ground that their privacy had been invaded. In the middle are those judgments where not only both considerations (distress and breach of privacy) were present as part of the factual and legal background to the verdict, but damages were explicitly granted to redress both (whether 'both' means two separate injuries or one injury with two heads, which is immaterial for the present purpose). The case of the oldest Weller child, who was recognised to also have suffered 'real embarrassment'[31] (besides the misuse of her own private information), and that of Max Mosley, are good examples. In the latter case it was held that, as well as compensating for the emotional consequences of the injury, damages should also 'mark' the infringement of the right to privacy,[32] whatever exactly that might have meant.[33]

[29]As e.g. in *Tugendhat and Christie* (n 9) ch 13D.

[30]*Campbell* (n 13) e.g. [33], [34], [75], [81], [98], [124], [130], [158], [168] [169]; cf in the Court of Appeal ([2002] EWCA Civ 1373; [2003] QB 633) [55] and in the High Court ([2002] EWHC 499; [2002] EMLR 30) [1]–[2] ('Miss Naomi Campbell ... seeks damages for breach of confidentiality ... She claims that ... she suffered distress, embarrassment and anxiety') [141].

[31]*Weller* (n 16) [196].

[32]*Mosley* (n 1) [216].

[33]On which see below, Part III.4.

What a survey of relevant cases shows is that whether what we have here is one head of damages known under two names, or two separate heads which are always remedied, or two separate heads which may or may not be both redressed – whether or not through compensation – depending on the circumstances of the case, has to put it mildly no clear judicial answer. Perhaps the best illustration of the muddle, and constant to-ing and fro-ing, that courts have walked themselves into is provided by the key paragraph pertaining to quantum of damages in privacy actions in *Gulati* which, although a first instance judgment, is the leading case on the question to date. What made the case especially difficult (and interesting for the present purpose) was that the celebrity claimants whose phone had been hacked by *News of the World* remained unaware of it until the affair blew up and hence suffered no distress while the wrongs were being committed. Mann J, considering the basis on which the award of damages should be made, opined:

> the damages should compensate not merely for distress ... but should also compensate (if appropriate) for the loss of privacy or autonomy as such arising out of the infringement ... (This may include, if appropriate, a sum to compensate for damage to dignity or standing, so far as that is meaningful in this context and is not already within the distress element.)[34]

From this paragraph it would appear that we need to compensate distress but also loss of privacy per se *if appropriate* (what does that mean?); and that damages for loss of privacy *may* (not 'must'), *if appropriate* (ditto), include damages for loss of dignity, *provided* this has not already been compensated for under the first head (when would that be the case?). One could be forgiven for not understanding what the logic of the law is on these points, or doubting that there in fact such a logic that can be understood.

II. Two analytical frameworks

What the second part of this article seeks to argue is that the principal reason why the law struggles to understand the way these various harms, losses or detriments relate to one another is that it has been meandering, in the context of breach of privacy, between two analytical models of the law of torts which entail two very different understandings of the relationship between, on the one hand, the wrong that triggers a cause of action and, on the other hand, the harms or losses which damages seek to redress. (The existence of these two models and the competition between them are, as mentioned, not restricted to the law of privacy; but this tort does constitute the clearest battlefield between the two models and hence the best context in which to introduce and analyse the conflict.) Because the law is only dimly aware of the existence of these two opposing models and the way they

[34] *Gulati* (n 5) [168].

clash, it has found itself unable to understand – and therefore to resolve – its own difficulties in terms of identifying and quantifying harms in privacy cases.

1. *The 'bipolar' model: wrong and ensuing loss(es)*

On the arch-dominant model on which English tort law[35] operates, the wrong will be clearly contrasted with the losses[36] that ensue. The wrong is the actualisation of real-life events which give the claimant a tortious cause of action: in modern scholarship, this is typically described as a violation of – or injury to, encroachment upon – a right or, conversely, the breach of a duty owed to the claimant. The losses, on the other hand, are detriments which flow from the wrong and are therefore, by construction, distinct from it. The point might sound too obvious to be worth labouring, but it needs to be highlighted in anticipation of what follows: there is on the one hand the violation of a right and on the other hand the detriments that ensue. It is these detriments that money awards granted to the successful plaintiff seek to compensate. While the wrong naturally needs to be there, because it is what makes the ensuing losses wrongful (hence liable to be remedied), it is in itself transparent. The law does not seek to redress the wrong but to blot out, as far as money can do, its consequences.

In turn, these losses are typically thought of as being of two sorts: pecuniary and non-pecuniary, depending on whether they are directly valuable in money or, to put the same point in ordinary language, whether they leave the claimant 'out of pocket' or not. This is not controversial. Slightly more contentious, but important, is the idea that all non-pecuniary loss boils down, in the final analysis, to mental distress in the broad sense of the term (i.e. a disruption of the claimant's emotional well-being, irrespective of the specific label used by courts). The point was recognised in particular by Andrew Burrows, who argues that 'ultimately all non-pecuniary loss is concerned with the claimant's distress or loss of happiness'.[37] It is also implicit in the categorisation of non-pecuniary losses adopted by the leading English authority on the topic, *McGregor on Damages*, where the authors distinguish between four types of non-pecuniary losses, which can all be seen as forms of emotional disturbance: (1) 'physical inconvenience and discomfort'; (2) 'pain and suffering and loss of amenities'; (3) 'mental distress' and (4) 'social discredit'.[38] Accordingly we have on the one hand damage to the

---

[35]Though not only English law: the rest of the common-law does not appear to be any different; indeed it dominates the civilian tradition as well.

[36]Because, as will be seen, this model is wedded to a narrower, and uncontroversial, definition of loss, it is entirely appropriate to use the word – preferably to 'harm' – in this context.

[37]Andrew Burrows, *Remedies for Torts and Breach of Contract* (OUP, 3rd edn 2004), 31.

[38]Harvey McGregor et al (eds), *McGregor on Damages* (Sweet & Maxwell, 19th edn 2014) s5–003. 'Amenities' means 'pleasures'. By construction, we are not concerned here with

claimant's wallet (his 'having') and on the other hand damage to his emotional tranquillity (his 'being').[39]

There is no need here to trace the genealogy of this model in any detail, but it can already be seen to operate in the Roman action on the *lex Aquilia* (the ancestor of the general principles of liability for harm caused by fault in modern civilian legal systems, which has also had a not inconsiderable influence on the English tort of negligence). The action, which visited certain types of damage to property, distinguished sharply between the tangible injury (*corrumpere*) caused to the thing (*res*) and the financial detriment that flowed from it (the *damnum*). The wrong was the causation of physical damage but the loss redressed by the law was the *damnum*, with this important consequence that if no loss ensued, no money award would be granted – a famous example being that of a castrated slave boy, whose value actually went up when he (in law, a *res*) was damaged.[40]

2. *The 'unipolar' model: wrong as loss*

While the above framework undoubtedly dominates the law, there exists another model of tort lurking in the background, clearly a minority position but making increasingly significant inroads into the modern law.[41] On that model, the wrong and the loss – to use a terminology sometimes resorted to in that context, the *iniuria* and the *damnum* – collapse onto another, to the effect that the loss becomes the violation of the right. The detriment that the claimant has now suffered is that he has been wronged. Rights – typically thought of in that

---

any pecuniary consequences of these disturbances, which are being dealt with as part of pecuniary loss.

[39]Naturally both need not be present each time, either because they did not occur on the facts of the case or because the law does not recognise that one type of loss is recoverable when it flows from a given wrong or injury.

[40]D.9.2.27.28 (Ulpian, 18 *Edict*): 'Further, if someone castrates your slave-boy and thus increases his value, Vivianus writes that the *lex Aquilia* should not apply, but that you should instead bring the action for insult or sue under the edict of the aediles for four times his value' (trans Watson Digest).

[41]This is not the place to speculate at length over the reasons. Two obvious factors that would have played a role are, on the one hand, the universally observable tendency of the law to redress more harms as it develops, especially harms of a non-tangible nature (which might not be readily accommodated under the requirement of loss in the usual sense of the term) and, on the other hand, the rise and rise of the language of rights in the common-law tradition over the last 20 years – in particular following the publication of Ernest Weinrib's *The Idea of Private Law* (Harvard University Press) in 1995 and, in the UK, the passing of the Human Rights Act in 1998. While the wedge drawn by people like Robert Stevens between rights-based and loss-based theories of tort is to my mind a false dichotomy, it is nonetheless easy to see how the terminology of rights leads directly to an idea of compensation, or redress, for the violation of the right itself, hence the use of such language as 'substitutive' or 'vindicatory' damages.

context as a list of protected interests, i.e. of 'goods' to which humans aspire, such as 'liberty, physical integrity, land, possessions, reputation, wealth, privacy [and] dignity'[42] – form a sphere of protection around the plaintiff: as he gets physically injured, defamed or imprisoned, as his wealth is depleted, his chattels damaged or his privacy violated, he suffers a diminution of these 'good things'. His interests have been invaded and that *is* the detriment, harm or loss that he has suffered. There is, on this model, not two levels of enquiry but one. The harm that the law redresses is not the noxious consequences of the wrong, it is the wrong (right-injury) itself.

Like the first one, this 'unipolar' model has an old pedigree. It can be traced back to the high scholastics, who understood harm as the taking away of what belongs to a man his 'goods', whether the good – in modern parlance the protected right or interest – be in his chattels, his person, his dignity or the relationship he has with another person.[43] Grotius' definition of *damnum* – loss – in his *Law of War and Peace* (1625) captures the gist of that alternative model most concisely: he suffers a *damnum*, *quis minus habet suo*, i.e. 'who has less than what is his', that is to say, in this context, 'less than his right'.[44] The right that has been violated, encroached upon, abstracted, *diminished*, must be restored either in nature (hence such ideas as restoration of honour through forced apologies) or by equivalent.

Before we can return to the way these two models are going to play out in the context of breach of privacy, we need to explain how they relate to one another and also why they ought not to be combined. The latter point, in particular, is crucial to the argument developed in this paper.

3. *Connecting the two models*

These two models described as respectively bipolar and unipolar, because the former relies on two separate elements – the wrong (*iniuria*) and the loss (*damnum*) – whereas the latter conflates them, aim to explain the totality of the law of torts. They are two analytical frameworks aspiring to making sense of it as a whole. To use a simple analogy, they are like the imperial and the metric systems, which are both capable of accounting for any measurement in the physical world but operate on two parallel planes. These ought not to make contact lest units from the one are added to units from the other, resulting in nonsense.

When it comes to length, the conversion mechanism is simple: given e.g. any distance expressed in miles, dividing it by 1.609,344 will give us the equivalent in

[42]This is Tony Weir's list: 'There are several good things in life, such as liberty, physical integrity, land, possessions, reputation, wealth, privacy, dignity, perhaps even life itself. Lawyers call these goods "interests"': Tony Weir, A Casebook on Tort (Sweet and Maxwell, 10th edn 2004) 6.

[43]James Gordley, *The Jurists* (OUP, 2013) 86.

[44]Hugo Grotius, *De Iure Belli ac Pacis* (Blaeu, 1646) 2.17.2.

kilometres. The process is more complicated when it comes to the bipolar and unipolar models of tort, but a similar exercise of 'conversion' must be carried out to understand how each makes sense of the other.

(a) Conversion from the unipolar to the bipolar model is straightforward enough. The bipolar model accepts the existence of the wrong as a necessary requirement but, as was said, does not regard it as a compensable injury itself. It looks to the consequences of the wrong, not to the wrong itself, which is simply a peg that allows the subsequent losses to be wrongful and hence actionable. The underlying logic is that, once the (concrete) consequences of the wrong have been redressed, as far as money allows, then the wrong itself has been blotted out in the eyes of the law and no further remedy does, indeed should, avail.

One logical consequence of this analysis is that, if losses of the relevant type (pecuniary loss or mental distress) are absent in the instance case, in that the wrong does not cause any such detriment,[45] no compensatory damages will be granted. On this model either no action will lie at all, or a different remedy will avail (for instance nominal damages, which mean to recognise the existence of the wrong but deny, by definition, that any loss was caused).[46] Indeed, one strong incentive to switch over to the alternative model would be the refusal to accept that logical consequence, i.e. the desire to grant substantial damages in situations where no loss in the above sense is present.[47]

(b) How to translate the bipolar model into the unipolar one is rather more complex, but it needs to be sketched out if we are to understand its logic (which, it must be emphasised, is dictated by the need to make sense of the law as it currently stands: it is an exercise in interpretation, not in devising an alternative system from first principles). The first step is to distinguish, among all the consequences of the right-invasion, those which are described by the law as 'consequential' from those which are not. Consequential loss – almost always pecuniary, though it could in principle be of any sort – is loss that is one step removed from the wrong. This can be contrasted with 'direct' loss that flows immediately from it. Where the line is drawn is a complex question which has no authoritative answer, but it needs to be looked into in the present context. In most instances it will be clear-cut: for instance if you smash my car and as a result I have to spend £2000 in repairs, that sum counts as direct loss: the need for repair is, of course, a consequence of the wrong, but it is not consequential loss in the technical, and narrower, sense of the term. On the other hand if,

---

[45]A complication is that the law can analyse or value these harms differently. For instance, distress could be understood as the particular claimant's actual distress or the distress that would be experienced by an ordinary claimant placed in the same circumstances.

[46]Conversely, of course, on the unipolar model any infringement of a right will warrant substantial compensatory damages for the harm represented by the wrong itself, irrespective of any (concrete) consequences.

[47]Below, Part III.4.

being a cab driver, I lose a further £5000 in earnings while my car is immobilised, that additional loss counts as consequential loss.

If we leave aside for now those further losses, the way the unipolar model would re-interpret the consequentialist thinking of the dominant bipolar model would be by treating the direct 'flowing' loss as the *flipside* of the right-violation itself. In other words, by directly compensating for the diminution of the right, that is to say, by putting a monetary value on the amount by which it was reduced, the law indirectly compensates for these direct losses, both to the wallet and to feelings, whenever they are in fact present. Once the right has been compensated for, the direct consequences of its infringement are regarded as made up for and the claimant cannot additionally recover for them, which would amount to double recovery.[48] In the above example, the law would likely value the right-diminution at £2000 (or a little more to take into account the associated distress, provided its availability is recognised in that context, which is not entirely clear as the law stands).

There remains non-direct, i.e. consequential, loss, for instance the £5000 in the above scenario. Here, we know that as a matter of law these are recoverable according to general principles, in particular in terms of causation and remoteness, and so they can be claimed on that basis. However, on the logic of the unipolar model, the result is crying out for an explanation. If a loss is the violation of a right, the fact that further consequential loss suffered by the claimant is recoverable would seem to signify that it amounts to a *separate* wrong (i.e. the violation of another right). This cannot be explored further in the present context but it is interesting to note that this line of reasoning underpinned an important defamation judgment handed down by the Supreme Court of Appeal of South Africa in 2011. In that case, *Media 24*,[49] a taxi company sued a media defendant over defamatory incriminations they had published concerning the immoral and illegal behaviour of the claimant, seeking 'general damages' for the injury to its reputation and 'special damages' for the further economic loss (loss of profits) they had allegedly suffered as a result.

The Court held that they could recover in defamation (*actio iniuriarum* in a South African context) for their loss of reputation but, if they wanted to recover for the economic loss, they had to sue using a different cause of action (injurious

[48]Aggravated damages complicate the picture but can be easily reconciled with that model on the understanding that the extra money award compensates for the additional distress caused by the defendant's conduct, itself the flipside of the violation of another right of the claimant's, which Birks called the right to a 'proper share of respect' and is violated when the defendant behaves towards the claimant in a hubristic way, denying him that right and causing him to feel humiliated: Peter Birks, 'Harassment and Hubris: The Right to an Equality of Respect' (1997) 32 *Irish Jurist* (new series) 1, 14.
[49]*Media 24 v SA Taxi Securitisation* (437/2010) [2011] ZASCA 117; 2011 (5) SA 329 (SCA); cf Eric Descheemaeker, 'Three Keys to Defamation: *Media 24* in a Comparative Perspective' (2013) 130 South African Law Journal 435, 439ff.

falsehood which, in South African law, is regarded as part of the *actio legis Aquiliae*: a rough equivalent of the tort of negligence in England). Accordingly, in order to succeed, the claimant would need to establish the wrongful character of the economic loss according to the separate – and much more restrictive – rules of Aquilian liability/negligence. Although that point was hardly noted by the Court, the implication of this reasoning is that the economic loss is no longer to be regarded as consequential. It is now *pure* loss, corresponding to the violation by the defendant of the claimant's interest in his wealth. Indeed, on the logic of the unipolar model, there is no such thing as consequential loss; each loss corresponds to a different injury, hence a different wrong, hence the violation of a different right.

4. *Mixing and matching*

From both systems' ability – and, logically, their claim – to be an interpretative framework for all wrongs, it follows that (1) they ought not to be combined and (2) it would, at best, be an unnecessary complication for the law to switch back and forth between them. This is the key point that needs to be accepted before we return to the application of these two models in the context of privacy claims.

On a principled level, adding, or moving between, secondary detriments recognised by the bipolar model (i.e. pecuniary loss and mental distress) and direct detriments on the unipolar one (any diminution of a right, for instance the loss of privacy) amounts to amalgamating objects which are ontologically different: events and their consequences, concrete losses and abstract losses. It is like adding apples and oranges or, to follow the previous metaphor, miles and kilometres. The flipside of this argument is that, practically, redressing both would amount to double recovery, that is to say, to counting the same injury twice: the first time as the diminution of a right, the second as the ensuing loss. Naturally there are all manner of complications to the argument, in particular because it depends on how right-diminutions are valued, and also on how systematically or not the law moves from one level of analysis to the other; but the gist of the argument, as the law currently operates, is straightforward enough and should not be difficult to accept. It can be illustrated with two examples, one from the 'having' side of the law (patrimonial loss) and the other from its 'being' side (mental distress).

On the having side, it is self-evident that, in the above example of the smashed car, if I recover £2000 for the diminution of my property right, I cannot recover £2000 again for the cost of repair: it would be redressing the same injury twice.[50] This is easy to see because, when it comes to pecuniary

[50] Cf Stevens (n 23) 59ff, in the context of the discussion of what he calls 'substitutive damages', a theory which – despite marked differences – has strong overtones of the unipolar model.

losses, they are directly valuable in money. On the other hand, in respect of non-pecuniary losses, which by definition are not directly so valuable, any award is bound to be arbitrary. This does not mean that they cannot be compensatory in a true sense of the term, nor that they are necessarily unfair or inconsistent, but it does make it very hard to prove that double recovery is at work. One good example to illustrate the issue can however be derived from the judicial *Guidelines for the Assessment of General Damages* – i.e. damages for non-pecuniary harm or loss – *in Personal Injury Cases*. To take one example at random, they tell us that 'complete loss of smell and taste' should lead to an award 'in the region of £28,750'.[51] We know that the £28,750 are compensatory and we know that they do not compensate for any pecuniary loss, which is assessed separately; but what are they meant to compensate for? The dominant answer seems to be for mental distress (called 'pain, suffering and loss of amenities', or PSLA, in the context of personal injuries).[52] This is consistent with the bipolar model: it is the emotional consequences of the wrong which are redressed. An alternative analysis, however, would be to regard them as compensating for the physical injury itself (as indeed suggested by the phrasing of the *Guidelines*): having lost his sense of taste and smell, the claimant now has less of his physical integrity than he once did. His right has been diminished and the award values this loss; by compensating for the wrong itself, the law ipso facto compensates for its emotional consequences. The important point, which this example should make reasonably easy to accept because the amount the claimant will receive has been stabilised, is that it cannot be both/and. If the claimant recovers £28,750 for his distress, he cannot get more (leaving aside, again, the complication of aggravated damages) for the very fact that he was injured – and vice-versa.[53]

5. *Application to breach of privacy*

We are now, finally, in a position to return to the particular cause of action under examination. As was said in the first part, there are three types of harm that are potentially redressable in privacy actions: pecuniary loss, mental distress and breach of privacy – all the other labels being reducible to one of these. To use

[51]Judicial College, *Guidelines for the Assessment of General Damages in Personal Injury Cases* (OUP, 12th edn 2013) 20.

[52]E.g. Judicial College, Guidelines (n 51) ix. This is an excellent example of presumed (indeed, deemed) distress.

[53]The alternative analysis does not appear to be followed in a pure way by any author, but a combination of both ways of thinking is not uncommon. For instance, *Charlesworth & Percy on Negligence* speaks of compensation for 'the injury itself', coming *in addition to* pain and suffering and loss of amenities as part of 'non-pecuniary loss' (CT Walton et al (eds), *Charlesworth & Percy on Negligence* (Sweet & Maxwell, 13th edn 2014) ss 5-93–5-94 ('the injury by itself properly attracts an award of damages')). On the purely bipolar model, on the other hand, the physical injury is in itself transparent; what matters is its consequences.

an imperfect but helpful Latin terminology, we can call the first *damnum*, the second *solatium* (though *solatium* designates, in the later civilian tradition, the award granted 'in solace for' the suffering rather than the suffering per se) and the last *iniuria* (in the sense of the wrong itself).

If the argument that was developed in this part is correct the law can either, following the bipolar model, compensate for *damnum* and *solatium* – the *iniuria* being the peg, in itself transparent, on which the losses hang – *or* it can, flipping over to the unipolar model, compensate for the *iniuria* and thereby, indirectly, compensate for all direct *damnum* and *solatium*.[54] In that context the *iniuria* means the breach of privacy, which itself is the flipside of the loss of privacy. It is important to emphasise that loss of privacy is not a loss (or harm) that flows, like distress or pecuniary loss, from the breach of the claimant's privacy: rather it *is* the breach itself – the diminution of the claimant's privacy – looked at from a different angle. It is analytically there by virtue of the wrong of breach of privacy having been committed: saying that one has lost some of one's privacy is the same thing as saying that one's privacy has been encroached upon.

The key to the present argument is, as mentioned, that these are – or ought to be – alternatives. Because the two levels of analysis (the wrong and its consequences) both seek indirectly to redress the other one, all three types of harm should not be compensated at the same time. If damages for *damnum* and *solatium* are granted, the claimant will have received full redress for the wrong he suffered (the above example of physical injury being directly transferrable to breach of privacy). Conversely, if the law grants substantial compensatory damages for the loss of privacy then, on the logic of this alternative model, it must be regarded as *having already compensated* for all direct losses, both pecuniary and emotional – there only remaining consequential (i.e. further) loss, in the unusual cases where such loss does in fact occur.

Response to an objection

One difficulty with this argument, and possibly the main reason why it might struggle to be accepted, especially by people who are solely interested in privacy (and perhaps closely related actions such as defamation, but are not tort lawyers generally) is that it would be entirely possible, in principle, to do things differently. The law *could* decide, in any successful action, to grant *x* by way of compensation for the breach itself – by reference not to its consequences but,

[54]There would remain, as explained, non-direct (consequential) loss, but given that this is virtually bound to be economic loss – though one could, for instance, imagine a situation where the claimant became sick as a result of the breach of his privacy – and that, as explained, genuinely consequential economic loss is a rare (if at all existing) scenario in privacy cases, these losses can for all intents and purposes be ignored in the present discussion.

perhaps, to its intrinsic gravity – and also *y* for the distress – assessed more or less objectively by reference to what an ordinary claimant would have felt like – in addition to *z* for any pecuniary loss if and when it arises. It would be possible to give one award for the breach per se and another award for its consequences, pecuniary or emotional. This would indeed appear to be the basis on which two Weller children got substantial damages for the wrong suffered, despite their complete unawareness that their privacy had been breached, while the eldest child got more because she *also* suffered distress.[55]

This would be far from absurd on a principled level, but it would run against hundreds of years of legal development. The rest of the law of tort does not grant, nor has it ever granted, damages for the abstract wrong and additionally damages for its concrete consequences. As was seen, the dominant model by far is to grant damages for the latter and consider that these indirectly blot out the wrong itself. Indeed, combining compensation for the wrong and for its consequences would not even be compatible with the rest of the law of privacy. For, on that logic, *all* claimants should get an award for the loss of their privacy, independently of – and on top of – any redress for distress, given that they have by definition suffered it. But even a cursory glance at the case law shows that this is not the case.[56] Regardless of its intrinsic merits (or lack thereof), the 'both/and' approach is incompatible with the existing law as it has developed over hundreds of years. The law of privacy should not tolerate the coexistence of incompatible models within its own midst, nor should it be allowed to harbour logics which throw the rest of the law into disarray.

III. Four consequences

Two important questions have been left almost entirely unaddressed so far: first, which model should the law of privacy adopt; second, what difference does it make which one we opt for? The first question would necessitate a separate treatment examining the entirety of tort law and accordingly will not be explored further in the present context, except insofar as it obliquely relates to the second. In this part, we look at four issues of privacy law which are dependent

[55] *Weller* (n 16) [196]–[197].

[56] There is one further difficulty which cuts across the previous ones. It is that the law could consider 'emotional well-being' as a separate protected interest standing level with the others. In that case, the same set of facts causing a breach of privacy and distress to the claimant would amount to the diminution of *two rights* hence two wrongs: the wrong of breach of privacy and the wrong of unlawfully causing distress (in which case, any damage for distress should be cut off from the law of privacy, or indeed any other cause of action, so as to avoid double-counting). Again it is conceivable but it is simply not the way the law works, save perhaps in exceptional, and therefore anomalous, circumstances. Happiness is not regarded as a protected interest in itself (which is why distress does not amount to sufficient damage for the purpose of the tort of negligence); rather it is parasitic on all other protected interests.

on the choice made between the two models. On all four it will be argued that the unipolar model achieves results that are more satisfactory, which gives us at least some reasons to favour it. Yet the starting point has to be that, in most circumstances, the two models would reach the same results, because they are two ways of approaching the same injuries from different perspectives – both trying to do indirectly what the other does directly, namely, redress wrongs and compensate ensuing concrete losses. It is only in circumstances where a clear discrepancy arises between the wrong and the losses that flow from it that they will come to a head. However, if we accept that the law of privacy ought not to follow a micro-rationality of its own, apart from the mainstream of tort, the theoretical significance of choices that need to be made in our particular context is considerable, committing the law of civil wrongs as a whole (if not beyond).

1. *The privacy of juridical persons*

The first issue on which the choice between the bipolar and unipolar model would have a clear bearing is the question whether juridical (or 'juristic', 'legal', 'artificial') persons have a right to privacy, a question which continues to vex the law in a number of jurisdictions. While the link between the two is not mechanical, it is nonetheless very strong.

If we accept that non-physical persons are by construction incapable of experiencing emotions, it immediately becomes, given the centrality of damages for mental distress on the bipolar model, very difficult to understand how companies, associations, partnerships and the like might enjoy a right to privacy. The argument against it would be that natural persons are granted such a right because they (ordinarily) suffer distress when their privacy is violated; because juridical persons are not susceptible to upset, it is at best not apposite – and at worst nonsensical – to grant them a right to privacy. This is indeed the basis on which a number of authorities have explicitly denied the existence of privacy rights for non-natural persons.[57]

Admittedly the conclusion does not follow as a matter of analytical necessity. There are at least two ways the above argument could be circumvented, even while

[57]See, in England, *R v Broadcasting Standards Commission, ex p BBC* [2001] QB 885 [48], [49]: 'I do not see how [privacy] can apply to an impersonal corporate body, which has no sensitivities to wound'; 'an artificial "person", having no sensibilities, cannot be made to suffer [emotional distress]' (Lord Mustill – note however that His Lordship was thinking of a form of territorial privacy for which there is a stronger argument to be made that it requires a *corpus* on the plaintiff's part); in Australia, *ABC v Lenah Game Meats Pty Ltd* [2001] HCA 63, 208 CLR 199, [128]: 'of necessity, this artificial legal person lacks the sensibilities ... which provide a staple value for any developing law of privacy'; cf, in an American context, Robert Sack, *Sack on Defamation: Libel, Slander and Related Problems* (PLI, 2010) 12.3.5: 'Unlike actions for defamation, suits for invasion of privacy can be brought only by individuals. Neither corporations, associations nor partnerships have "feelings" ... and they therefore may not recover damages ... for such injury.'

accepting the need for noxious consequences before an action is granted. First, by arguing that legal persons do in fact have feelings. This is not as evidently absurd as might first appear: if legal persons are held capable – through the ordinary rules of attribution – of signing a contract, willing an act, being in good or bad faith, and committing torts and crimes *personally*, it is not entirely evident why they cannot equally be attributed emotions. The second counter-argument is that, while juristic persons cannot be wounded in their feelings, they can evidently be injured in their wallet, and the right to privacy is meant to protect the latter as well as the former.[58] This is an argument that is very commonly run in the context of defamation (in which, despite some significant exceptions, the law is by and large happy to assimilate legal to natural persons).

However both counter-arguments are weak. The attribution of feelings to juridical persons would be a novel idea; adopting it solely in that context in order to recognise a right to privacy for non-natural persons would likely come across as desperate. If the idea of attributed feelings was to be pursued, this should be done in a principled and systematic way. As to the protection of economic interests, the obvious rebuttal is that, if the primary *aim* of the right (as opposed to an incidental effect) is to protect against financial losses, breach of privacy is the wrong cause of action to use; and pressing it into service for that purpose would be an abuse of the tort[59] – not to mention that, as was explained, many economic losses that we might want to describe as consequential upon breach of privacy are not in fact consequential at all.[60] This parallels the argument frequently made in the context of defamation that legal persons should sue in injurious falsehood (or negligence) if they want to protect their economic interests, not by towing them to an artificial cause of action for injury to their reputation. Therefore the bipolar model makes it, if not absolutely impossible, at least very difficult and strained to accept that a juridical person might have a right to privacy.

On the other hand, on the unipolar model, it becomes a very natural conclusion. Again, one must be careful because the link is not one of necessity, but the correlation is very strong. Once one has escaped the fetters of consequentialist thinking, the only question becomes whether juridical persons are capable of holding a right

[58]See e.g. in a New Jersey context, *NOC Inc v Schaefer* (1984) 484 A 2d 729, 731: 'While a corporation may have its reputation or business damaged as a result of intrusive activity, it is not capable of emotional suffering' (cited in *Lenah* (n 57) [127]). This is probably also what is meant by commentators who argue that privacy is, for non-natural persons, a means to an and rather than an end in itself: 'A corporation does not want privacy for its own sake. Privacy to a corporation is only an intermediate good': Anthony D'Amato, 'Comment: Professor Posner's Lecture on Privacy' (1978) 12 *Georgia Law Review* 497, 500 (also cited in *Lenah* (n 57) [127]).

[59]I have argued more fully in a different context that the 'patrimony defence' of personality rights for non-corporeal persons, i.e. the idea that they ought to be endowed with a personality *because* they can suffer in their pocket, is profoundly misguided: Descheemaeker (n 49) 445–6.

[60]Above, 3 Part I.2.

to privacy and, if so, whether it is a good idea to grant it to them. On the first limb, it is very hard to deny that they can. The ability to hold rights is typically regarded as the keystone of personhood-at-law; and (contrary for instance to *corpus*, i.e. physical integrity) there is nothing definitionally impossible with a privacy right for non-natural persons. That they also have an interest in controlling the flow of information about themselves, in the sense that it is a good to which they might aspire, is equally self-evident. Of course one could insist that privacy is properly an attribute of corporeality (or humanity), and therefore that legal persons should not be possessed with such a right, but this argument starts looking remarkably like one is not taking seriously the notion of a juristic person.[61] Following this line of thinking, legal persons would probably be denied all the rights that we typically describe as 'personality rights' (reputation, privacy, liberty, dignity, autonomy and the like) and be confined to property rights. This would fly directly in the face of what it means to be a person in the eyes of the law. Accordingly the unipolar model leads very naturally to the idea that legal persons do have a right to privacy (at least of the informational sort). At the very least it puts the onus on those who deny it to provide arguments why a person-at-law should not have a right of personality when there is no logical impossibility to it.

De lege lata, the issue has proved highly controversial and it is not difficult to attribute the unsettled character of the law to the underlying – yet unidentified – conflict between the two rationalities sketched out in the previous part, each pulling in the opposite direction to the other. South Africa has accepted that, in principle, all non-natural persons do have such a right.[62] In the United States, on the other hand, the right has for the most part been denied.[63] While not determinative, judicial pronouncements have been very largely negative in Australia[64] and in England,[65] even though it is possible that English law might turn out to be

[61]This is in fact visible in the use of inverted commas in Lord Mustill's quote above (n 57). This article is not the place to argue fully, on a normative basis, for the privacy of non-natural persons: interested readers can be referred e.g. to Alan Westin, *Privacy and Freedom* (Bodley Head 1970) 42–51.

[62]*Financial Mail (Pty) Ltd v Sage Holdings Ltd* [1993] ZASCA 3, 1993 (2) SA 451 (A) 460G–461H (Supreme Court of Appeal of South Africa, reasoning by analogy from the right to reputation which itself has been recognised as an attribute of legal persons in a South African context, albeit with very little theoretical discussion).

[63]On the basis of absence of feelings: see *Sack on Defamation* (n 57) 12.3.5; cf *United States Restatement Second, Torts*, s 652I ('an action for invasion of privacy can be maintained only by a living individual whose privacy is invaded'). There is however a (small) strand of 'dissenting' opinions: see Lee Bygrave, 'A Right To Privacy For Corporations? *Lenah* in an International Context' (2001) 8 *Privacy Law & Policy Reporter* 130, 133 n39 and references cited.

[64]*Lenah* (n 57) esp [43] (Gleeson CJ grounding privacy in 'human dignity', which 'may be incongruous when applied to a corporation') [116], [126] (legal persons lack 'sensibilities'), [132].

[65]The position is explained clearly in *Tugendhat and Christie* (n 9) ss 8.72–8.76 (including the complication brought in by *ex p BBC* (above n 57), which concerned a claim for breach

constrained by the European Convention on Human Rights to protect at least that segment of the privacy right which concerns a juridical person's right to respect for its correspondence and freedom from intrusion onto its premises ('*domicile*' in the French text, which has a wider scope than 'home' in English).[66]

2. *The privacy of non-sentient natural persons*

The very same reasoning applies to natural persons who are incapable of being distressed by the misuse of private information about them. The class may be defined more or less broadly depending on whether one insists that they should be distressed (or capable of distress) at the time when the wrong is committed or not, but at the very least it would include physical persons in a permanent coma or, as suggested in *Gulati*, claimants who died before discovering the covert invasion of privacy they had been subjected to.[67] It is likely also to include children who are too young to care, at least at the time when the action is brought on their behalf.[68] On the dominant bipolar model it is, for the same reasons as above, all but impossible to see how they could recover. On the other hand, on a unipolar model, these persons should be able to recover as a matter of principle, irrespective of any associated upset. If one believes that this is the right outcome, it becomes in turn a strong argument for the superiority of that model.

3. *The meaning of loss in privacy actions*

The third issue the choice of model has a direct bearing on is the meaning of loss in privacy actions. It should have already become apparent that many of the arguments or difficulties expounded above find their source in the fact that there

---

of a statutory duty not common-law privacy) and need not be repeated here. The main reason for Lord Mustill's reluctance in that case to recognise the privacy of non-natural persons was, again, that privacy is an 'essentially human and personal concept' [49]. In an interesting echo of Roman *iniuria*, he linked that idea to that of 'the insult done to the person as a person' which the breach of privacy represents (ibid).

[66] *Tugendhat and Christie* (n 9) ss 8.77–8.78. However, the authors are very quick to dismiss the significance of the ECtHR's case-law beyond these specific circumstances. Logically, if the Court recognises that juridical persons enjoy *any* (sub-)type of privacy interest, English law would have no choice but to accept that these can have a right to privacy – even if a different and narrower one – if it is to remain Convention-compliant (unless this is held to come within the Member States margin of appreciation).

[67] *Gulati* (n 5) [136].

[68] As in the case of the Weller twins (above) or young David Murray, the son of author Joanne Murray (better known as JK Rowling). It is however noticeable that the court in *Murray* reintroduced the idea of distress when it suggested that the reason why the parents of a young child who had not suffered distress at any point between the wrong and the judgment should be able to bring an action on his behalf was to protect his 'freedom ... to live normal lives without the constant fear of media intrusion' (*Murray v Express Newspapers plc* [2008] EWCA Civ 446, [2009] Ch 481 [50]): a form of pre-emptive protection against future distress.

exist different ways of construing compensable detriments in the context of these actions. The issue must now be examined in closer detail. However, for reasons already stated, this cannot be done without stepping back and examining the law of tort generally: whatever loss means, it should not be allowed to bear one meaning in a given context and something incompatible in a different context.

Despite the complexity of the details, it seems to me that the big picture of what tort law means by loss is in fact remarkably simple. Examining the substrata of English law (both past and present), we can discern three – and no more than three – understandings of the concept, which operate in concentric circles and can be related straightforwardly enough to the analytical models sketched out in the previous part.

The first, narrowest, circle would be loss in the Roman sense of *damnum*, that is to say, financial or pecuniary loss: loss that is directly valuable in money or, to put the same point differently, that leaves the claimant 'out of pocket'. While no-one would probably want to argue today that, as a matter of principle, loss is restricted to *damnum* to the exclusion of anything else, this idea can in fact be seen to resurface time and again in modern discussions: the law has never quite got over the idea that loss that is not to the pocket is not real or proper loss.[69] The second circle, which is clearly the dominant paradigm, is to regard a loss as a concrete detriment suffered by the claimant: in Robert Stevens' words, the situation of being 'factually worse off'.[70] This is not easy to pin down with words – in particular, it is not the same as tangible injury – but it is not difficult to grasp intuitively. On that reading, both pecuniary losses and the sort of harms that were described in part I as non-pecuniary losses (which, it was argued, boil down to mental distress) count as loss. They make the claimant worse off in a *concrete* way. But this definition falls short of including losses sometimes described as 'abstract', 'legal' or 'normative', that is to say, harms which do not leave the defendant worse off either financially or emotionally and only are losses because the law says so.[71] Loss of use, loss of autonomy, loss of liberty and the like, considered in and by themselves (i.e. independently of any noxious consequences which may or may not actualise), are examples of 'non-concrete' losses which are excluded on the intermediary – and dominant – understanding of loss. The third concentric circle, on the other hand, includes these abstract losses as well as the concrete ones. On that model, every violation (or diminution) of a right – i.e. every wrongful interference with a protected

[69]One example of this line of thinking among many others: 'Mental distress is a harm, but to say that it is a "loss" courts the danger of its being understood as a compensable pecuniary detriment; and the fact that it is not then begins to suggest that it is not the proper subject of any award at all': Birks (n 48) 30.

[70]Stevens (n 23) 59: 'although loss is not limited to financial loss, in principle it requires proof that the claimant was factually worse off as a result of the infringement of the right'; also 78: '"Loss" has been used in the sense of being factually worse off.'

[71]This is different from saying that they only are *actionable* losses because the law says so, which is of course invariably true.

interest – counts as a loss, irrespective of its financial or emotional consequences on the claimant. To follow Tony Weir's above taxonomy,[72] losses consist in the diminution of – encroachments on the rights to – 'liberty, physical integrity, land, possessions, reputation, wealth, privacy, dignity' and any other 'goods' that the law might recognise and protect against at least a range of interferences.

From the above characterisation, it can easily be seen that the two analytical frameworks outlined earlier to understand the relationship between wrong and loss are tied to two different understandings of 'loss' which correspond to two different constructions of what compensable detriments in privacy actions are. The bipolar model, which counts as losses *damnum* and loss of happiness, is predicated on the intermediary definition of loss as being factually worse-off: the two are the flipside one of the other and it is therefore entirely unsurprising that they should have risen to prominence together. On that reading, the losses privacy concerns itself with are, *like any other cause of action*, financial loss and mental distress. The unipolar model, on the other hand, is wedded to the widest definition of loss as being a 'right-diminution': as was explained, it conflates the loss with the wrong, that is to say, with the encroachment upon the right – in our context, the right to privacy. On that conceptualisation, the loss or harm suffered by the claimant in a privacy action is loss of privacy and, consequential losses apart, *nothing but it* – ordinary distress and direct pecuniary loss being subsumed underneath.

The two models being grounded in two conflicting logics, the choice made on one level pre-empts the choice made on the other: what one cannot have is a unipolar model with the intermediate meaning of loss (which would be a contradiction in terms) or the bipolar model with the widest understanding of loss (which would amount to treating the same loss – here loss of privacy – both as the wrong itself and a consequence of the wrong: a contradiction in terms).

4. *Vindicating the right to privacy*

The final point to be examined concerns the relationship between compensatory and so-called 'vindicatory' money awards in the law of privacy. The argument flows logically from the previous section and, again, the law of privacy must be examined here in the broader context of tort law.

As can easily be seen, on the narrower of the two main understandings of loss sketched out above (i.e. the middle one, of loss as factual worse-offness), there will by construction be detriments or harms that cannot be called losses. They are those losses included in the widest definition, but excluded by the intermediary one, which we described as abstract, legal or normative losses: for example, in our instant case, the loss of privacy considered per se. If they are not losses, by definition they cannot be compensated.[73] From this a simple alternative follows,

[72]Above, n 42.

[73]I treat it as an apodictic proposition that compensation is for losses and losses only. This does not appear to be doubted by anyone.

with three branches. The law can either (1) deny redress altogether on the basis that there is no ground for the law to intervene, as the Roman *lex Aquilia* did with the castrated slave-boy;[74] (2) grant nominal damages to mark the right-infringement *sans* loss; or (3) grant substantial damages anyway. The second branch has historically been the response of the common law in situations of wrong without loss (in the factual worse-offness sense of the term). What is of interest to us in the present context is the third one. As is well known, English law has increasingly come to recognise a class of substantial damages in situations where a wrong has been suffered but, on the usual understanding of the term, no loss suffered. The term 'vindicatory damages' has now established itself to designate this sort of award. Why the law would want to recognise such an (at least apparently) novel category and how it relates to existing categories are difficult questions which have already caused a lot of ink to spill. In particular, it has been remarked that all money damages in tort have a vindicatory function, in the sense of affirming judicially the existence of the claimant's right and the need to respect it[75] – which makes it peculiar to use the term to designate a narrow, and largely residual, type of monetary awards. But this discussion belongs elsewhere.

The one point worth mentioning here is that, while the concept of vindicatory damages (in the sense of substantial damages which are meant neither to compensate the plaintiff for a loss nor make the defendant disgorge a gain or punish him for some wrongdoing) is required under the intermediary meaning of loss – itself tied to the bipolar model – so as to step into the breach opened by the exclusion of non-'lossful' detriments from the ambit of compensatory awards, it becomes redundant under the widest meaning of loss and the unipolar model that is wedded to it. For, if loss of privacy – or liberty or any other interest in the context of which the label might be used – is a proper loss, it follows that it can – indeed it should – be compensated with proper – i.e. substantial – money damages.[76] On the other hand, if courts refuse to characterise it as loss but still want to award more than nominal damages, then they need to come up with an alternative label and an alternative logic.[77]

---

[74]Above, n 40.

[75]E.g. Normann Witzleb and Robyn Carroll, 'The Role of Vindication in Tort Damages' (2009) 17 *Tort Law Review* 16, 16: 'The award of every judicial remedy, whether in the nature of declaration, coercion, compensation, restitution or punishment, can be said, in general terms, to vindicate the legal rights of the plaintiff.'

[76]Of course the amount awarded is arbitrary but that is true of all losses which do not leave the claimant out of pocket.

[77]It is tempting to go one step further and argue that the current explanation is precarious – being massively over-inclusive – precisely because it originates in an unworkable attempt to redress violations of right per se while retaining a narrower, and incompatible, understanding of loss grounded in the old bipolar model.

Within privacy, the concept of vindication-apart-from-compensation was touched upon, if with a level of ambiguity, by the High Court in *Mosley*, when Eady J opined that, when it came to assessing quantum of damages, there was

> [a]part from distress ... another factor which probably has to be taken into account ... that of vindication to mark the infringement of a right ... to mark the fact that ... a[n] individual has taken away or undermined the right of another – in this case taken away a person's dignity.[78]

However, in the wake of *Weller*[79] and *Gulati*[80] (which themselves followed on the important judgment of the Supreme Court in *Lumba*),[81] it would appear that vindicatory damages are, as a matter of principle, no longer available in breach of privacy actions. This has very significant implications for our debate. Since the view that breaches of privacy which do not cause either distress or pecuniary loss are no longer actionable, or only sound in nominal damages, would be blatantly inconsistent with these two decisions, it would seem that the only option left to us is to accept that substantial *compensatory* damages are available for loss of privacy per se. Having removed the safety valve of vindicatory damages, which allowed it to maintain ambiguity concerning what harms it actually compensates, the law would have no choice but to switch to the widest meaning of loss and therefore to the unipolar model. This seems to have been recognised by Mann J in *Gulati*, when he held that '[d]amages awarded to reflect the infringement are not vindicatory in the sense of *Lumba*. They are truly compensatory'.[82]

It is difficult not to recognise the superior logic of this alternative model, which can be broken down in four limbs: (1) loss of privacy is, in itself, a real loss; (2) it is a real loss because privacy is a real 'good'; indeed this is the reason why the law grants it protection in the first place; (3) if it is a real loss then it can be redressed with real, i.e. *substantial* (not nominal) *compensatory* (not vindicatory) damages; (4) the compensation of the loss indirectly operates, as per the usual principles, as vindication of the right infringed.[83] Yet, this pristine logic stands at odds with the

[78] *Mosley* (n 1) [216]. He however added, puzzlingly, that '[i]f other factors mean that significant damages are to be awarded, in any event, the element of vindication does not need to be reflected in an even higher award'. This seems to be a way of straddling the two models by saying that substantial-damages-as-vindication are a fall-back option to be resorted to when substantial-damages-as-compensation collapse because of the narrower meaning of loss used by courts. If this was true, however, it would destroy the meaningfulness of the concept of loss.

[79] *Weller* (n 16) [190].

[80] *Gulati* (n 5) [128].

[81] *R (Lumba) v Secretary of State for the Home Department* [2011] UKSC 12, [2012] 1 AC 245.

[82] *Gulati* (n 5), [132].

[83] '[T]he vindication is effected through compensation': Witzleb and Carroll (n 75) 22.

rest of tort law, which as was seen follows, by and large, a different model. Accepting it in the particular context of breach of privacy would therefore have a massive rippling effect on the rest of the law, it being well nigh impossible (as well as undesirable) for privacy actions to follow a separate logic of their own.

Conclusion

This article has sought to identify and order the harms or losses which the law might redress in actions for breach of privacy. This entailed straddling an uneasy divide between, on the one hand, a close examination of privacy cases and, on the other, much broader issues of private law theory. The existence of two theoretical models of tort law, coming with two different ways of understanding the relationship between wrong and harm, or loss, was identified and applied to the context of privacy actions, which constitutes perhaps the clearest battlefield between the two models. It was argued that on one model, the wrong is in itself transparent and what the law seeks to compensate are the detriments that flow from it, which are themselves either to the pocket (pecuniary loss) or to the feelings (mental distress). On the other model, the harm conflates with the wrong and it is the diminution of the right itself which is compensated, even though the noxious consequences will factor into the valuation of the injury – and, for that reason, direct losses should not be compensated as well lest double recovery should occur. Because these models are alternative, and incompatible, ways of understanding the operation of tort law, courts should neither combine them nor apply a specific logic to privacy actions. The implication is that the three heads of detriment recognised by the law in this context, and which were identified in the first part as pecuniary loss, mental distress (broadly construed) and loss of privacy, ought not to be combined. The law should aim to compensate *either* the first two *or* the last, these being two ways of approximating, from two opposite perspectives, the very same injury or injuries suffered by the claimant.

On a theoretical level, the choice we make between these two models – described as respectively 'bipolar' and 'unipolar' – has momentous consequences, in particular in terms of our understanding of the notion of loss and the role of vindicatory damages, first in the law of privacy and then, by a rippling effect, across the law of tort. The recent cases of *Weller* (2014) and *Gulati* (2015) – both of which are currently under appeal – are especially significant in this respect in that they appear to mark a clear switch away from the traditional consequentialist model of tort law and focus on the right-injury instead, thereby pressing into service the loss-as-wrong model of tort. The practical implications are also highly significant, in particular when it comes to the availability of actions for breach of privacy to juridical persons and natural persons who have not been affected emotionally by the wrong. In the background to this apparently technical debate stand fundamental, and highly value-laden, questions about the nature of personhood and what it means for a person to be the holder of rights.

Acknowledgements

A preliminary version of this paper was presented at a conference on 'The Campbell Legacy: A Decade of "Misuse of Private Information"', that was held at Newcastle Law School on 17 April 2015. Thanks are extended to Daithí Mac Síthigh for the invitation and to the participants, in particular Nicole Moreham and Hugh Tomlinson, for their helpful comments. A fuller version of the paper was also presented at the University of Otago and the Victoria University of Wellington on 16 and 21 July 2015, where again I benefited from the ensuing discussions.

Disclosure statement

No potential conflict of interest was reported by the author.

Update (January 2017)

The most significant development since this article first went to press is the appeals in *Weller v Associated Newspapers Ltd* [2015] EWCA Civ 1176, [2016] 1 WLR 1541 (judgment handed down on 20 November 2015) and *Gulati v MGN Ltd* [2015] EWCA Civ 1291, [2016] 2 WLR 1217 (17 December 2015). The approach taken by Mann J at first instance in *Gulati*, which I described as an illegitimate conflation of two models of tort damages, was regrettably endorsed by the Court of Appeal. Borrowing the language of "diminution of a right" which this article traced to Grotius, Arden LJ opined that in privacy cases "the damages are an award to compensate for the loss or diminution of a right to control formerly private information *and* for the distress that the claimants could justifiably have felt because their private information had been exploited, and are assessed by reference to that loss" (at [48], emphasis added). The second *Weller* judgment said nothing more about the issue of damages, and permission to appeal to the Supreme Court was refused in both cases on 23 March 2016. For the time being, therefore, the English law of privacy seems set to follow a logic that is incompatible with some of the most fundamental tenets of its tort law. The issue will not go away and will need to be revisited.

Index

Note: Page numbers followed by 'n' refer to notes

For Product Safety Concerns and Information please contact our EU representative GPSR@taylorandfrancis.com Taylor & Francis Verlag GmbH, Kaufingerstraße 24, 80331 München, Germany

Batch number: 10725973

Printed by Printforce, the Netherlands